Amelia Cole and the HIDDEN WAR

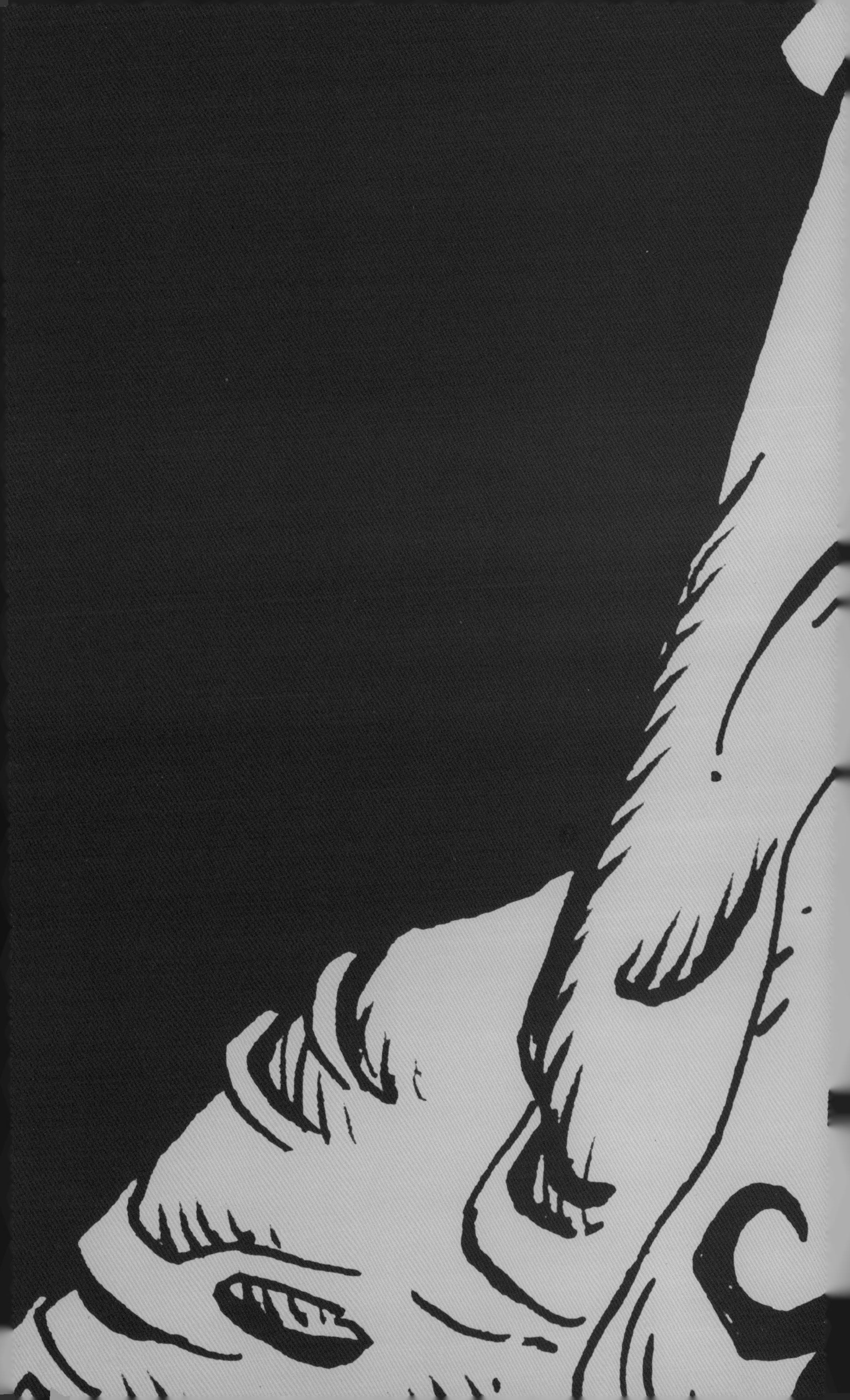

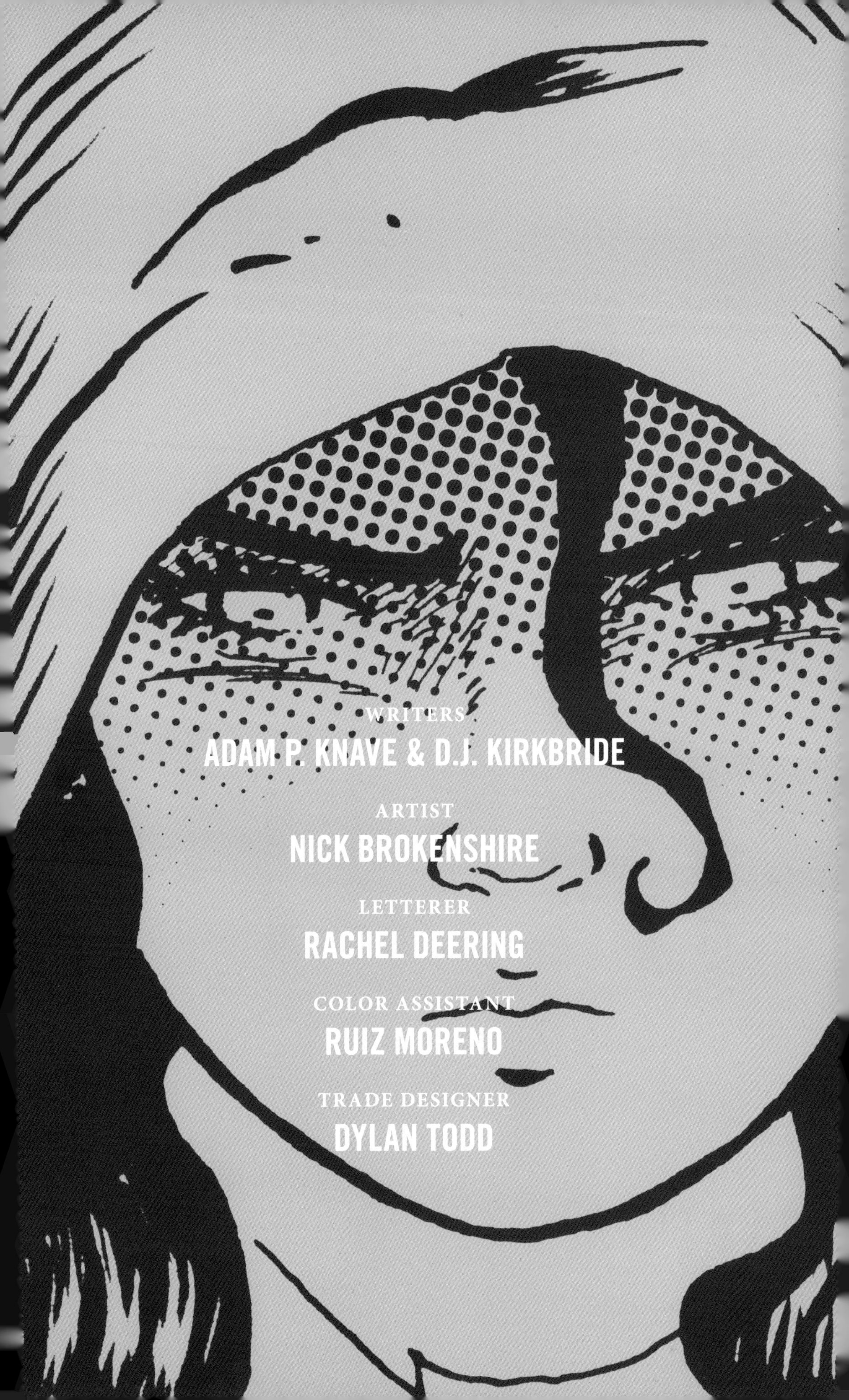

WRITERS
ADAM P. KNAVE & D.J. KIRKBRIDE

ARTIST
NICK BROKENSHIRE

LETTERER
RACHEL DEERING

COLOR ASSISTANT
RUIZ MORENO

TRADE DESIGNER
DYLAN TODD

ISBN: 978-1-61377-953-8

17 16 15 14   1 2 3 4

www.IDWPUBLISHING.com

IDW founded by Ted Adams, Alex Garner, Kris Oprisko, and Robbie Robbins

Ted Adams, CEO & Publisher
Greg Goldstein, President & COO
Robbie Robbins, EVP/Sr. Graphic Artist
Chris Ryall, Chief Creative Officer/Editor-in-Chief
Matthew Ruzicka, CPA, Chief Financial Officer
Alan Payne, VP of Sales
Dirk Wood, VP of Marketing
Lorelei Bunjes, VP of Digital Services
Jeff Webber, VP of Digital Publishing & Business Development

Facebook: **facebook.com/idwpublishing**
Twitter: **@idwpublishing**
YouTube: **youtube.com/idwpublishing**
Instagram: **instagram.com/idwpublishing**
deviantART: **idwpublishing.deviantart.com**
Pinterest: **pinterest.com/idwpublishing/idw-staff-faves**

INTRODUCTION

We pass through doors as we mature, and eventually they lock behind us; sometimes it's a welcome salvation or revelation, that latch clicking, and sometimes it's a profound loss. Sometimes it's both.

As I sit down to write this, my father is cleaning out the cabin he and my mother built when I was small. They were teachers, and we spent every summer and most weekends there throughout my childhood and teens. Now the place requires maintenance we can't keep up with; it's time to sell. As bittersweet as it's been for all of us, it's time. But when it's clean and the sale happens, I'll feel a door has closed that's been open behind me, at least a crack, my whole life— the cabin will become one of the places I can't go back to.

As he cleans, my dad has been sending me packages—books, some lovely pillowcases, a cribbage set—things he thinks I might want or need. I get sniffly pretty often, from the nostalgia and the communication these objects carry between us; but when I opened the box full of comics, I cried with a kind of raw joy. Poor battered things, creased and handled, rolled up in my back pockets or my fishing creel, many of them coverless now; they would make a proper collector weep for entirely different reasons. But I don't see damaged collectibles; I see hundreds of perfect hours rereading fantastic stories built to tease my imagination— what's behind that rock? Where did the mysterious circus lady go? How did the bandits get the amulet? Looking through them, it's like looking at maps of how I got where I am.

A year ago, when I started reading *Amelia Cole* with issue #1, I was immediately taken with Amelia's resourcefulness, with the natural earnestness of her decision-making, with her casual heroism. Finding herself cut off from both the worlds she was raised in and trapped in a third with unfamiliar laws, social stratifications and monster breeds, Amelia dusts herself off, builds herself a golum buddy and gets to work being kind, making friends, and saving lives. It's my favorite kind of heroism: the kind that takes being decent and watching out for others for granted. I was hooked well before the end of the issue.

Her first story arc, *Amelia Cole and the Unknown World*, was everything I wanted it to be: a coming-of-age adventure with magic, plenty of humor, and some really satisfyingly sinister mysterious forces at work. The tension between Amelia and Hector the Protector was fun, the magical battles were awesome, the graceful friendships between Amelia and her neighbors were endearing, and Lemmy was a hoot. Nick Brokenshire's art reminded me of when I first saw comics by Herge and Moebius, and the diversity and warmth of the storytelling made me want to hug him and writers Adam Knave and D. J. Kirkbride. I admit I was so happy to watch Amelia and this new place get to know one another, I didn't much want to look back to her home worlds or feel her loss of them; watching her move forward, vibrant and determined, was too compelling.

But in this new arc, *Amelia Cole and the Hidden War,* a couple things are happening: we're seeing the world beyond Amelia's city, and we're seeing more of who she was as a child and what she left behind. Amelia is maturing; the doors that have closed behind her and the new ones opening before her are taking on more weight. Doing the right thing, knowing what it is, is getting a little harder, and the stakes are getting higher. It's deftly done: the story is just as fun, just as adventurous as before, but enriched, as our lives are, by a growing sense of purpose and consequence.

I have typed and deleted a hundred spoilers just getting to this point; I don't want to ruin any surprises. I can assure you, though, that D. J. and Adam have packed plenty of them into the book you're now holding, and that they have more on the way. I can promise you that Nick, along with Rachel Deering and Ruiz Moreno, will delight your eyes and stir your imagination—there are lots of rocks, literal and figurative, with lots of questions behind them.

So find yourself a good reading spot—I'm feeling nostalgic about sunny creek banks under pine trees, but a bed or a seat on a commuter train work too—whatever you choose, settle down and open this door, go on through and take Amelia's hand. You'll be glad you did.

JEN VAN METER
20 November 2013

Jen Van Meter writes Hopeless Savages *and lots of other comics. She lives in Portland, Oregon, with her husband, Greg Rucka, and their two children.*

PREVIOUSLY

Amelia Cole, a young mage trapped in an *UNKNOWN WORLD*, uses her magic to help people, regardless of their ability to wield magic or not. Sadly for her, the law wasn't on her side about that. The Magistrate turned a powerful civil servant called The Protector against her, pushing his buttons to cause a huge blowout confrontation in the heart of the city. When the smoke and rubble cleared, Amelia was the victor due to sheer tenacity and refusal to give up regardless of the odds. This resulted in her being anointed the city's new Protector. Amelia's always been leery of the law … but now she *is* the law!

(This is all way cooler in the actual comic, with snazzy art and fun dialogue, as opposed to us just telling you. There's also a lot of other fun stuff, and side characters and all, so pick up a copy of *Amelia Cole And The Unknown World* if you haven't yet. It's hopefully on the shelf right next to this book or popped up on the website when you searched for it.)

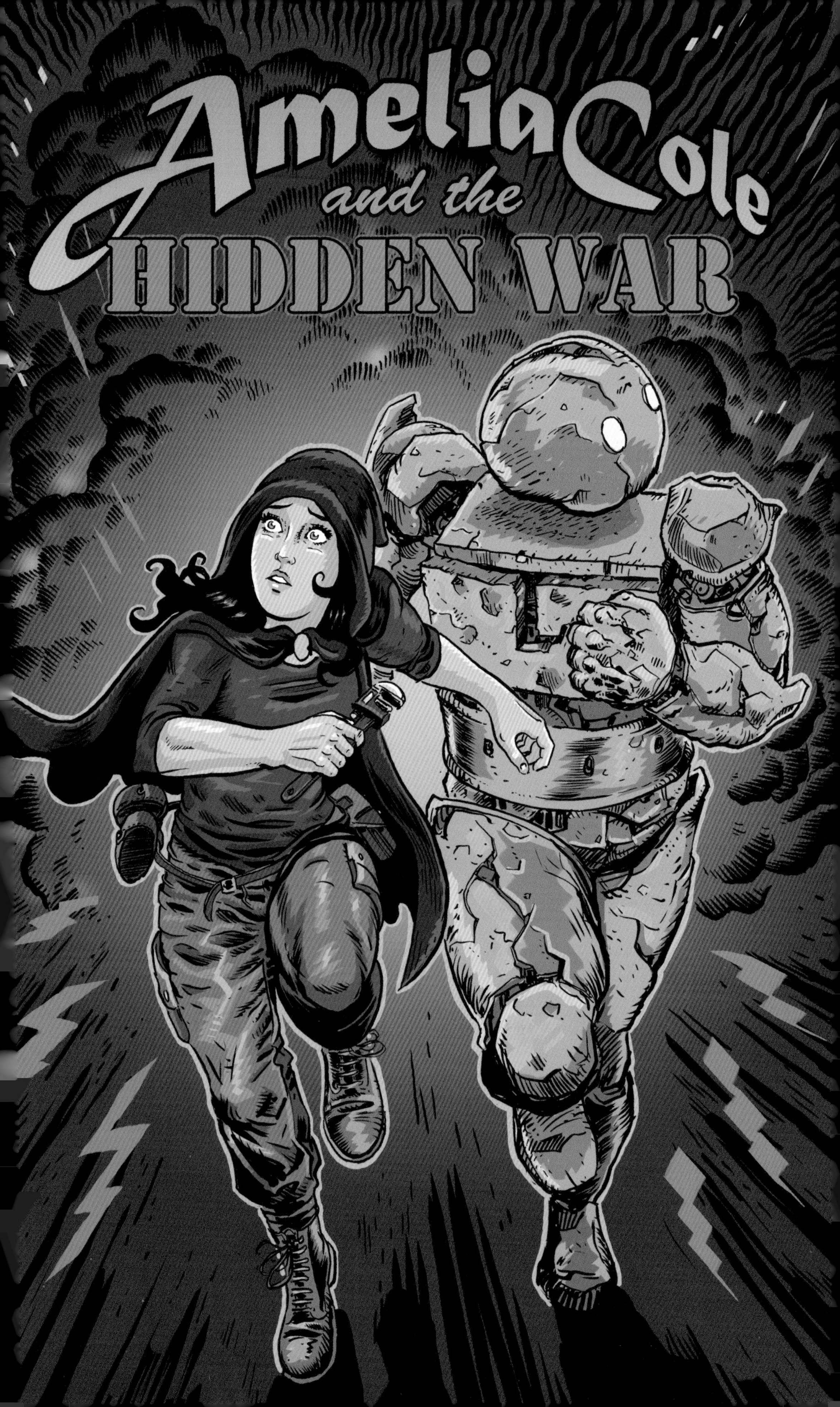
Amelia Cole
and the
HIDDEN WAR

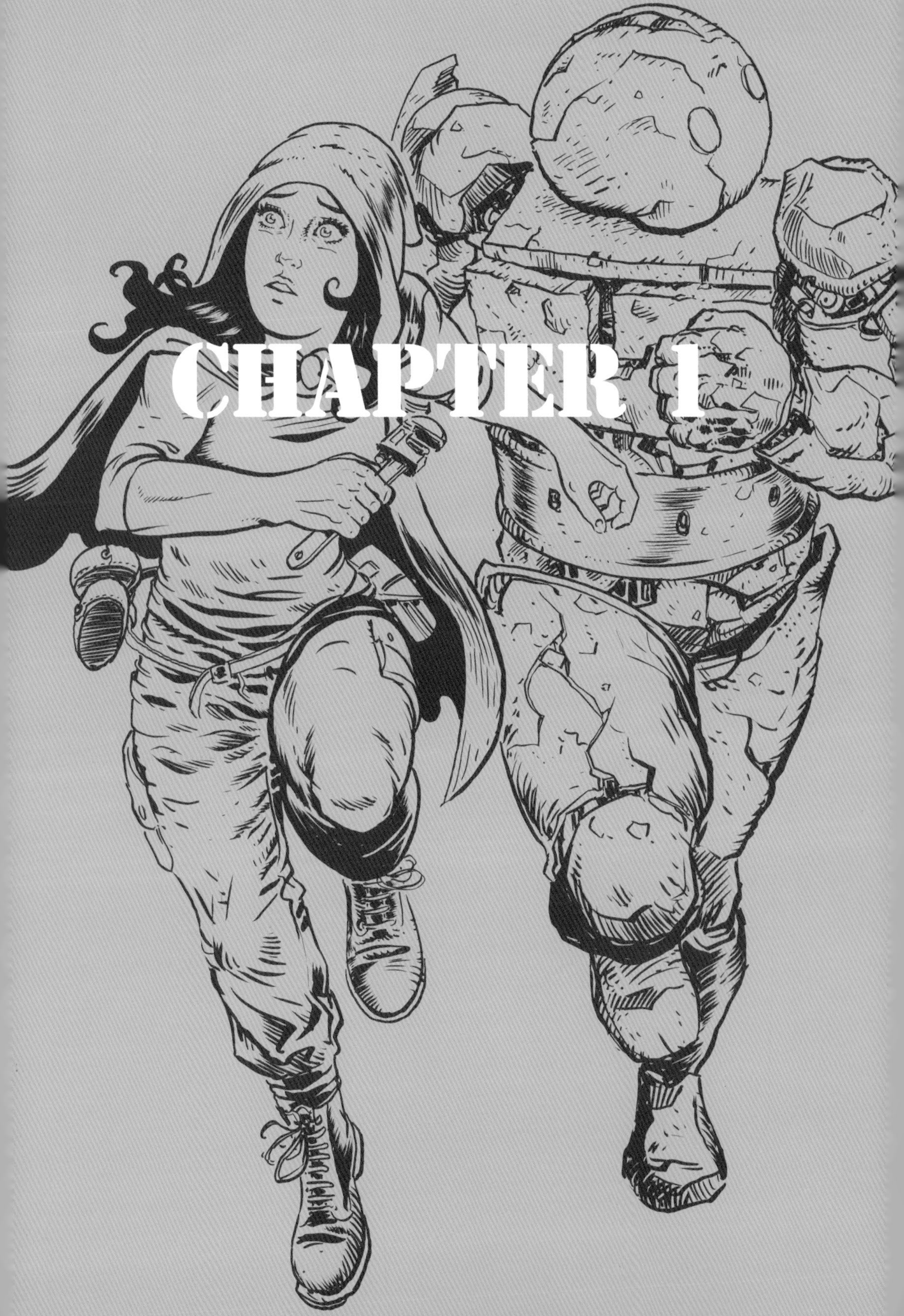
CHAPTER 1

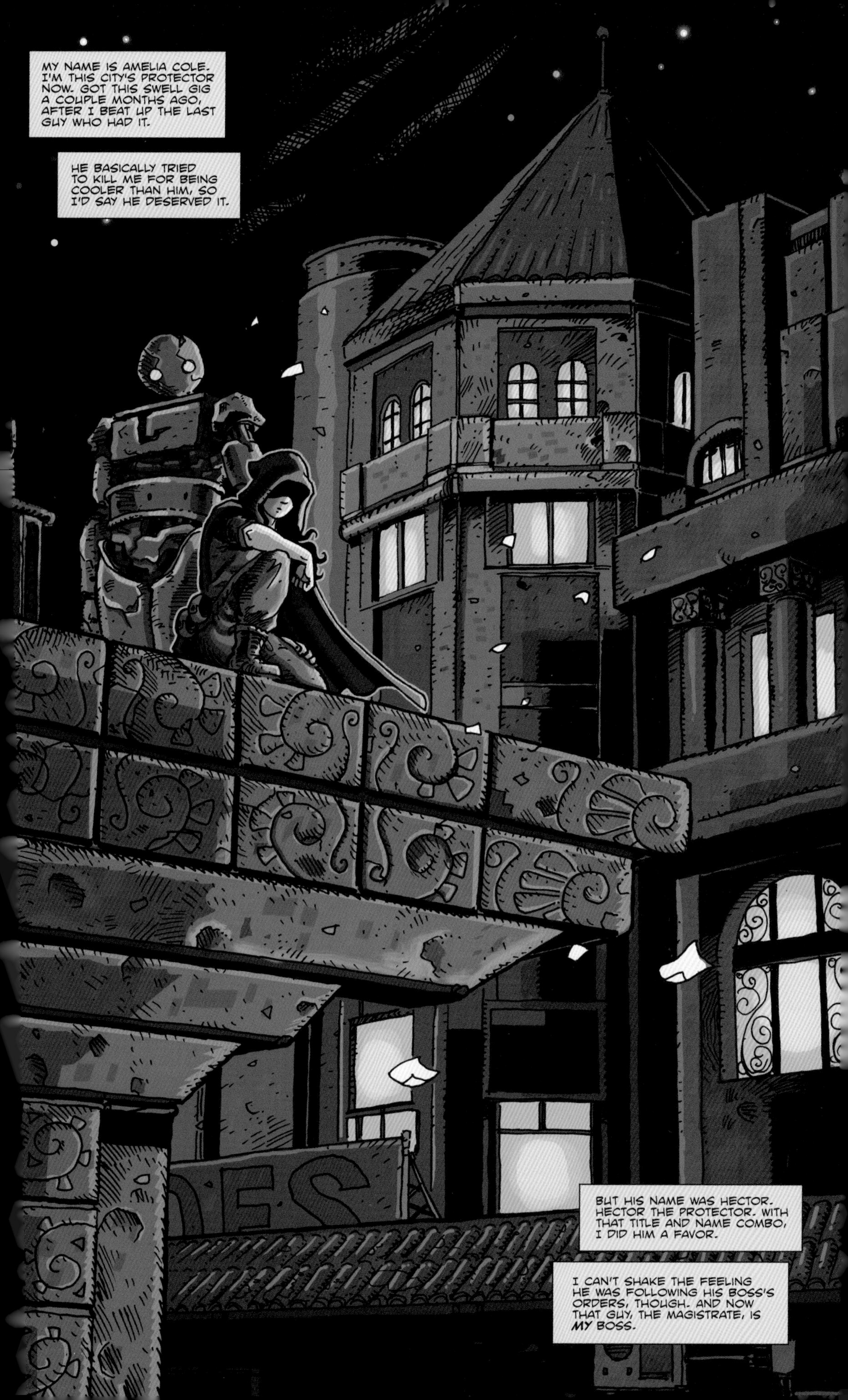
MY NAME IS AMELIA COLE. I'M THIS CITY'S PROTECTOR NOW. GOT THIS SWELL GIG A COUPLE MONTHS AGO, AFTER I BEAT UP THE LAST GUY WHO HAD IT.
HE BASICALLY TRIED TO KILL ME FOR BEING COOLER THAN HIM, SO I'D SAY HE DESERVED IT.
BUT HIS NAME WAS HECTOR. HECTOR THE PROTECTOR. WITH THAT TITLE AND NAME COMBO, I DID HIM A FAVOR.
I CAN'T SHAKE THE FEELING HE WAS FOLLOWING HIS BOSS'S ORDERS, THOUGH. AND NOW THAT GUY, THE MAGISTRATE, IS **MY** BOSS.

KEEP YOUR ENEMIES CLOSER THAN YOUR FRIENDS OR WHATEVER. ANYWAY...

...LEMMY AND I HAVE BEEN TRYING TO FIND A MUGGER FOR A FEW NIGHTS NOW. HE HITS THIS NEIGHBORHOOD A LOT BUT KEEPS GETTING AWAY.

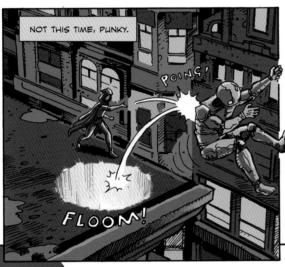

NOT THIS TIME, PUNKY.

POING!

FLOOM!

PUH-PLEASE, I'LL GIVE YOU MY WALLET -- JUST DON'T HURT ME!

NOT SURE WHICH OF US MAKES THE COOLER ENTRANCE.

LEMMY'S DEFINITELY LOUDER, THOUGH.

PO

WHUMP!!

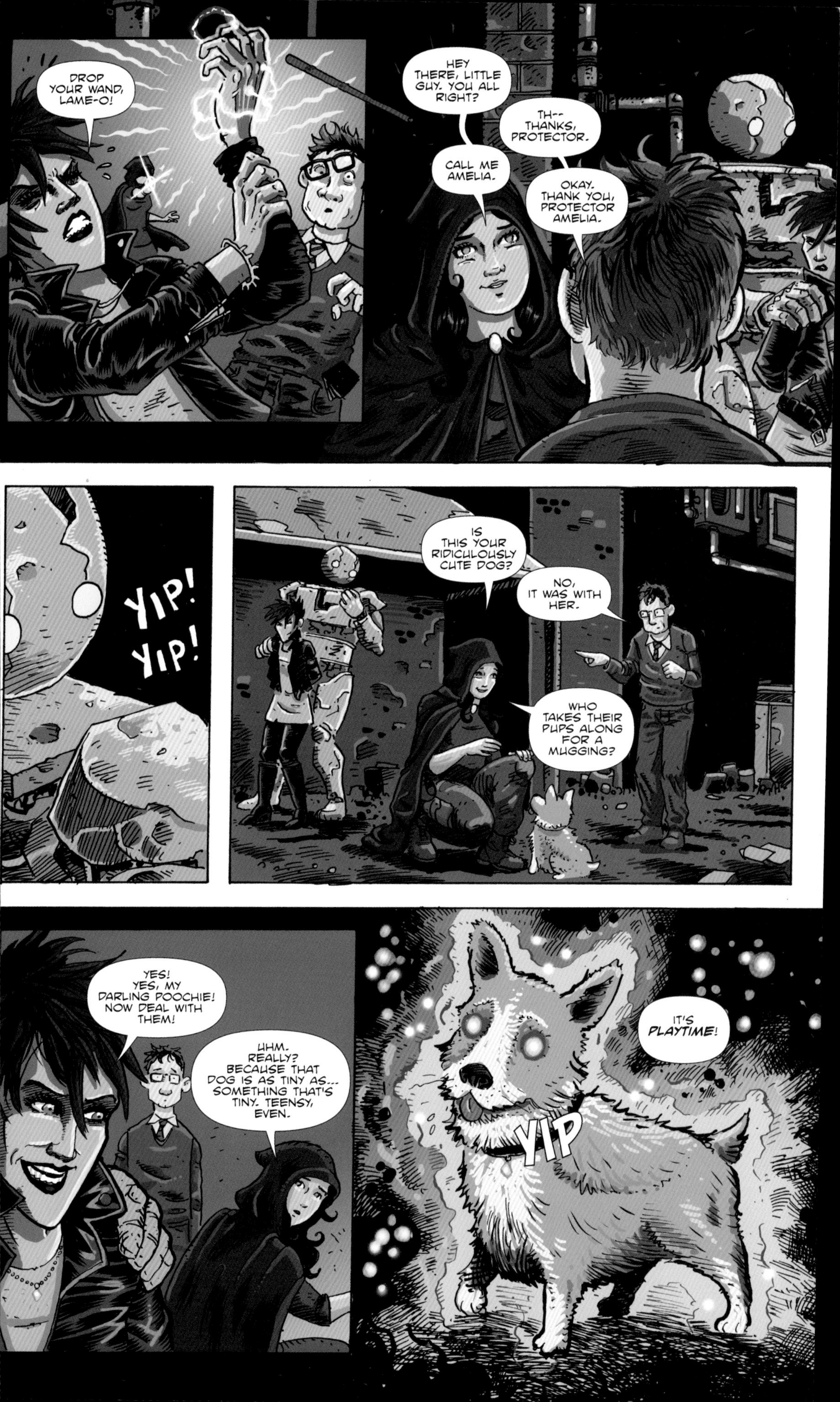
DROP YOUR WAND, LAME-O!
HEY THERE, LITTLE GUY. YOU ALL RIGHT?
TH-- THANKS, PROTECTOR.
CALL ME AMELIA.
OKAY. THANK YOU, PROTECTOR AMELIA.
YIP! YIP!
IS THIS YOUR RIDICULOUSLY CUTE DOG?
NO, IT WAS WITH HER.
WHO TAKES THEIR PUPS ALONG FOR A MUGGING?
YES! YES, MY DARLING POOCHIE! NOW DEAL WITH THEM!
UHM. REALLY? BECAUSE THAT DOG IS AS TINY AS... SOMETHING THAT'S TINY. TEENSY, EVEN.
IT'S *PLAYTIME*!
YIP

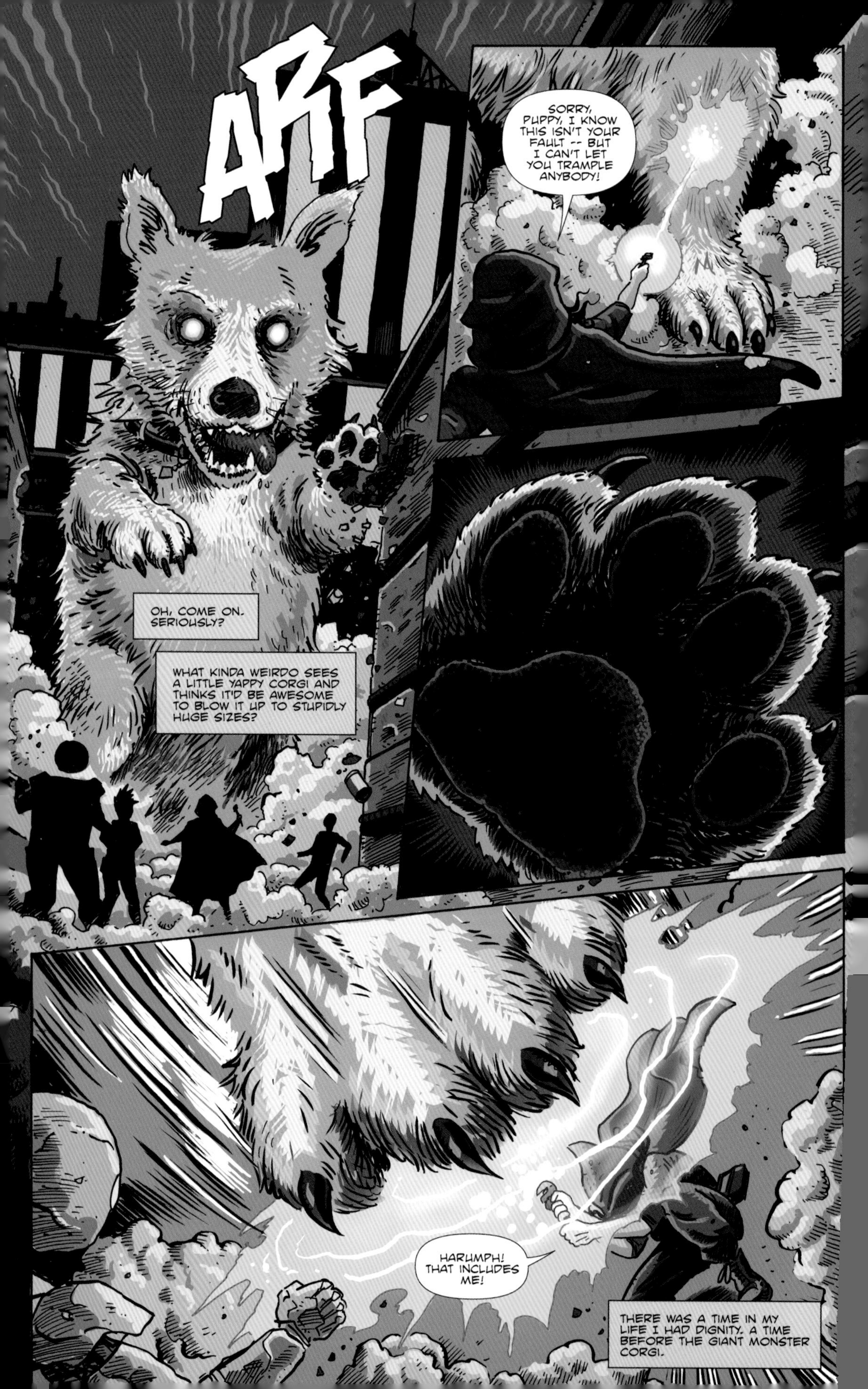
ARF
SORRY, PUPPY, I KNOW THIS ISN'T YOUR FAULT -- BUT I CAN'T LET YOU TRAMPLE ANYBODY!
OH, COME ON. SERIOUSLY?
WHAT KINDA WEIRDO SEES A LITTLE YAPPY CORGI AND THINKS IT'D BE AWESOME TO BLOW IT UP TO STUPIDLY HUGE SIZES?
HARUMPH! THAT INCLUDES ME!
THERE WAS A TIME IN MY LIFE I HAD DIGNITY. A TIME BEFORE THE GIANT MONSTER CORGI.

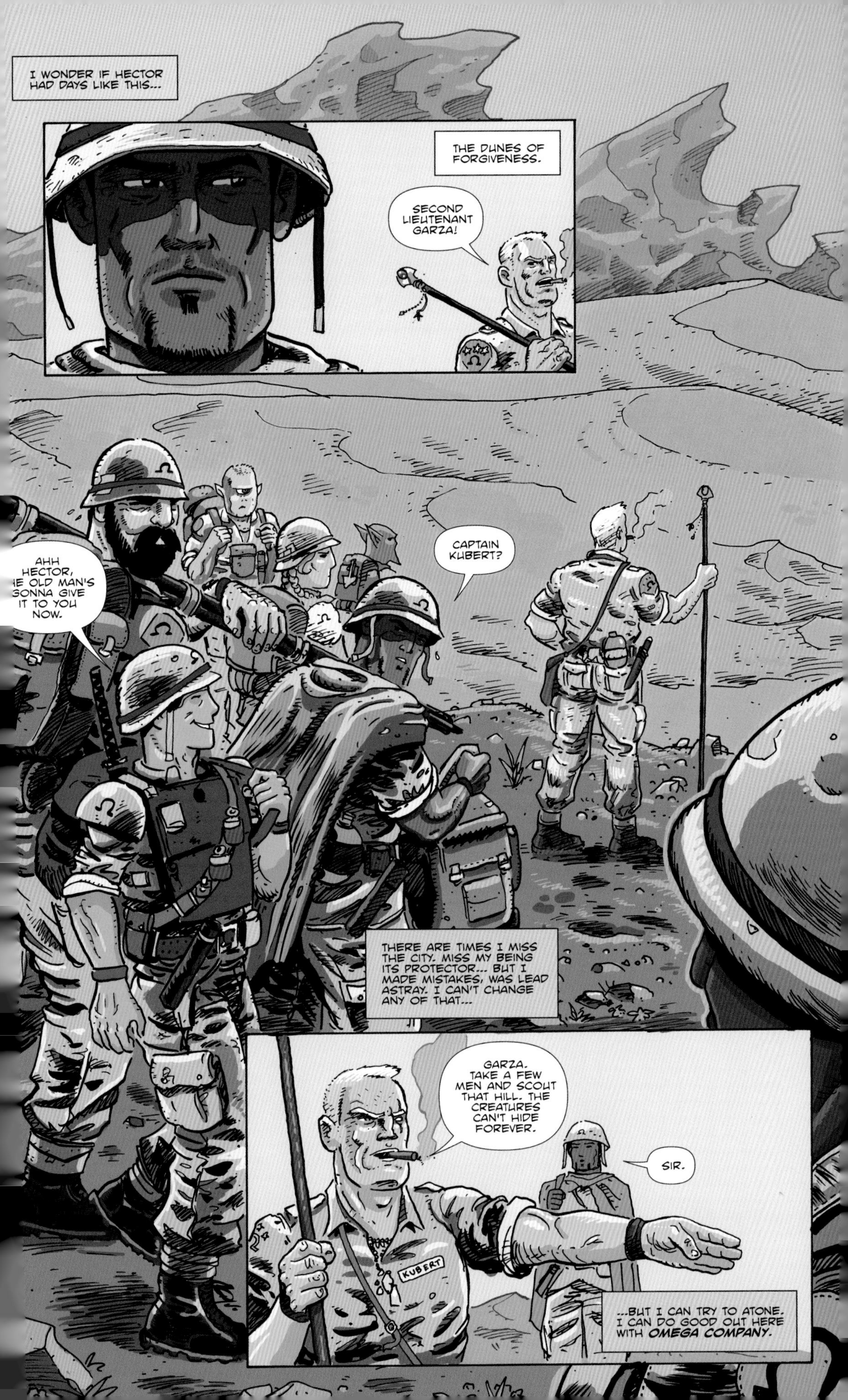
I WONDER IF HECTOR HAD DAYS LIKE THIS...
THE DUNES OF FORGIVENESS.
SECOND LIEUTENANT GARZA!
CAPTAIN KUBERT?
AHH HECTOR, HE OLD MAN'S GONNA GIVE IT TO YOU NOW.
THERE ARE TIMES I MISS THE CITY. MISS MY BEING ITS PROTECTOR... BUT I MADE MISTAKES, WAS LEAD ASTRAY. I CAN'T CHANGE ANY OF THAT...
GARZA. TAKE A FEW MEN AND SCOUT THAT HILL. THE CREATURES CAN'T HIDE FOREVER.
SIR.
KUBERT
...BUT I CAN TRY TO ATONE. I CAN DO GOOD OUT HERE WITH OMEGA COMPANY.

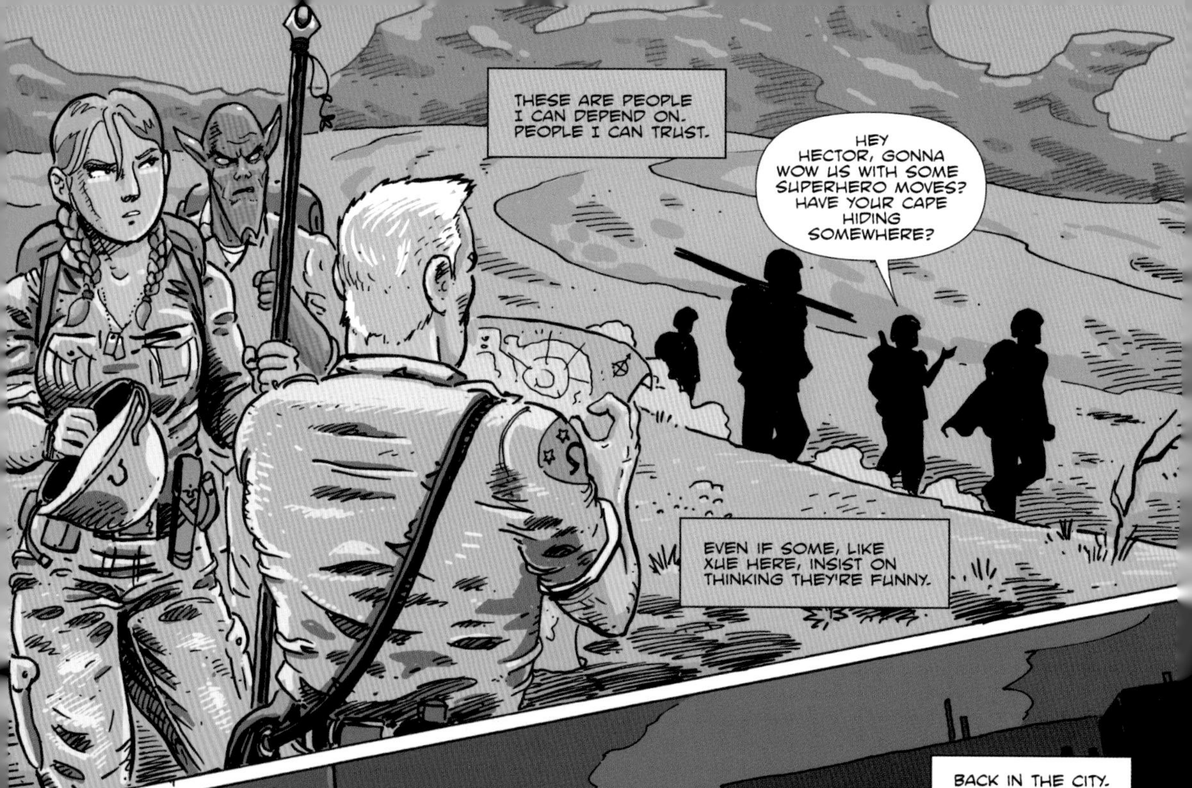
THESE ARE PEOPLE I CAN DEPEND ON. PEOPLE I CAN TRUST.
HEY HECTOR, GONNA WOW US WITH SOME SUPERHERO MOVES? HAVE YOUR CAPE HIDING SOMEWHERE?
EVEN IF SOME, LIKE XUE HERE, INSIST ON THINKING THEY'RE FUNNY.

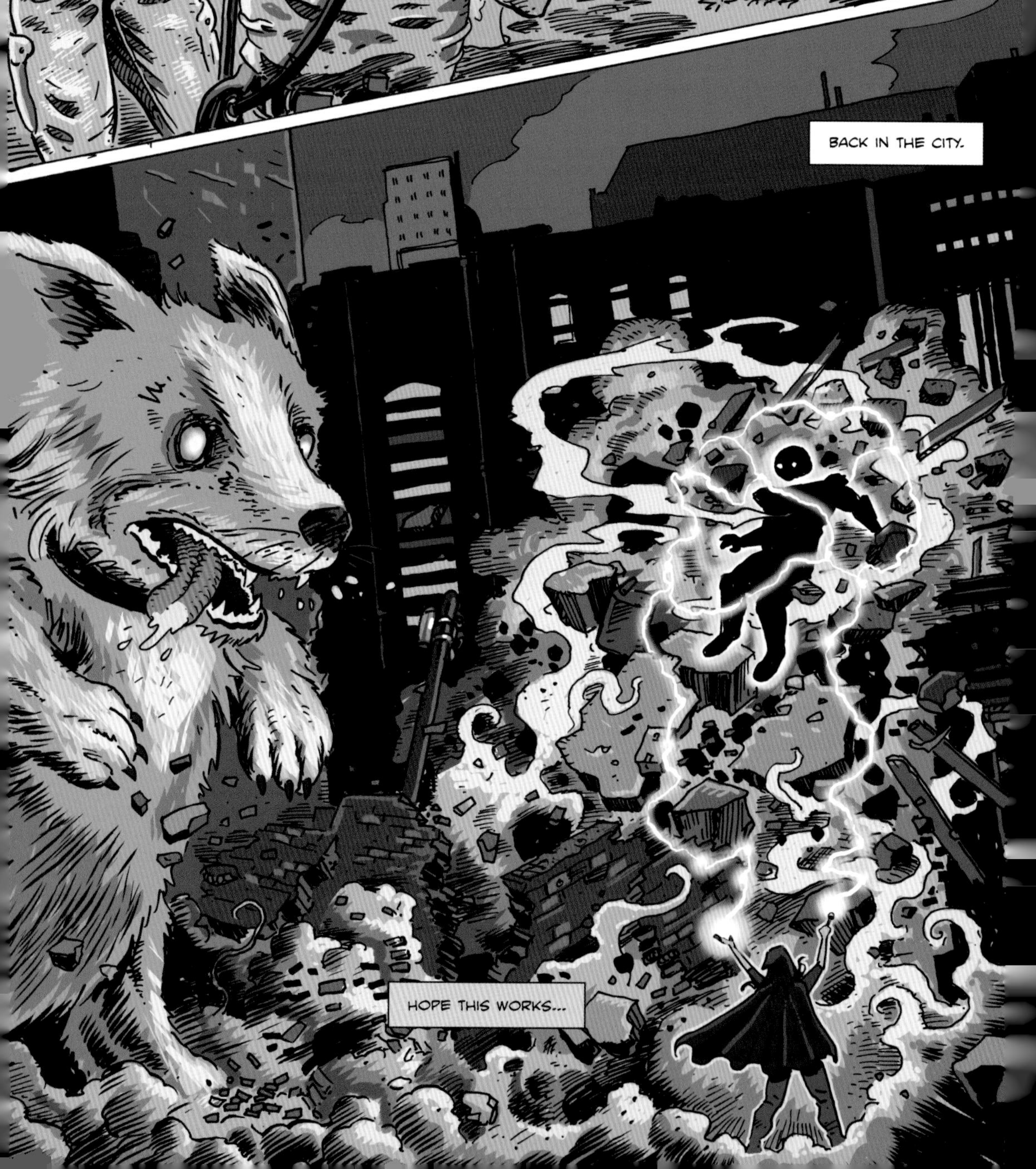
BACK IN THE CITY.
HOPE THIS WORKS...

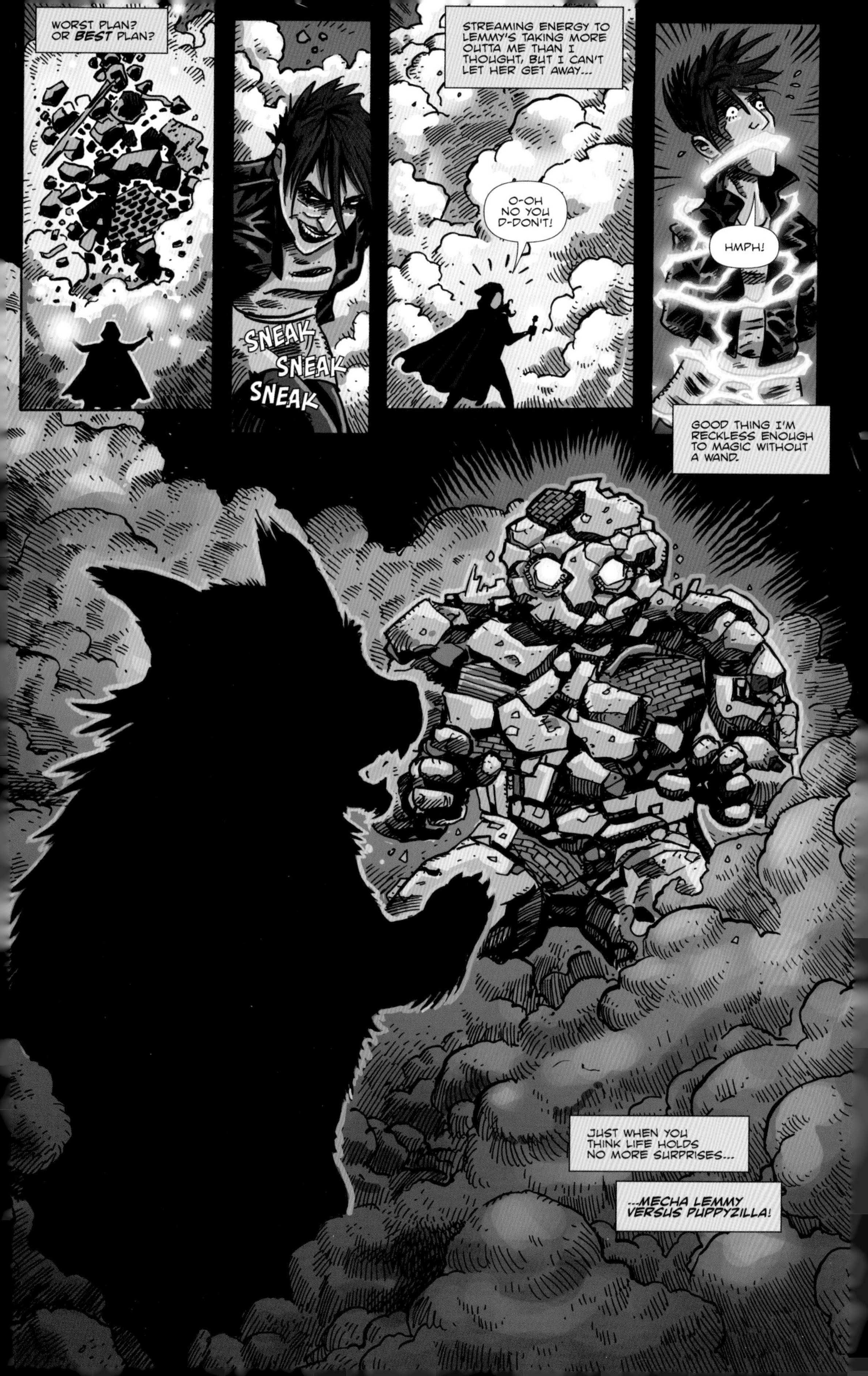
WORST PLAN? OR BEST PLAN?
SNEAK SNEAK SNEAK
STREAMING ENERGY TO LEMMY'S TAKING MORE OUTTA ME THAN I THOUGHT, BUT I CAN'T LET HER GET AWAY...
O-OH NO YOU D-DON'T!
HMPH!
GOOD THING I'M RECKLESS ENOUGH TO MAGIC WITHOUT A WAND.
JUST WHEN YOU THINK LIFE HOLDS NO MORE SURPRISES...
...MECHA LEMMY VERSUS PUPPYZILLA!

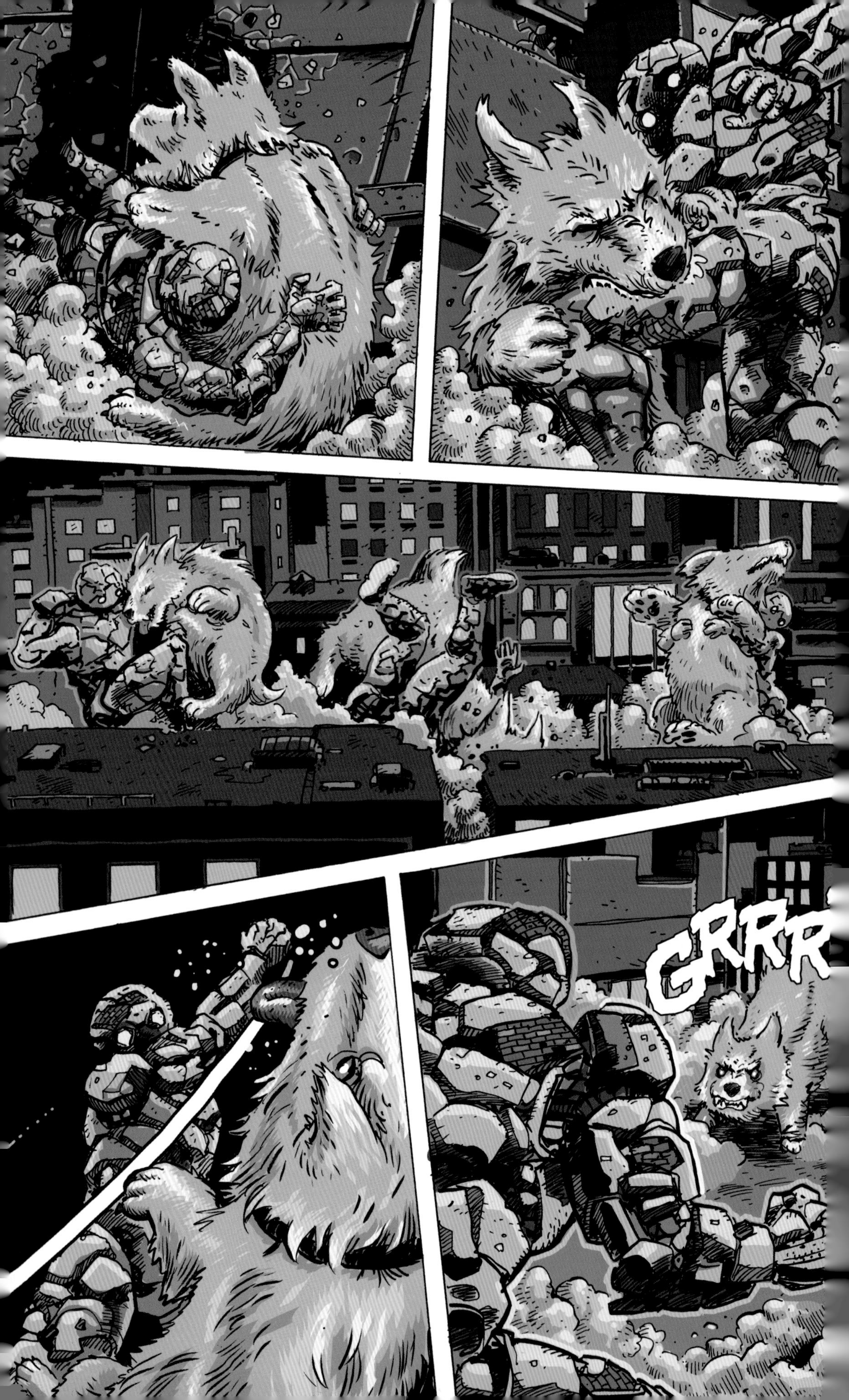
GRRR

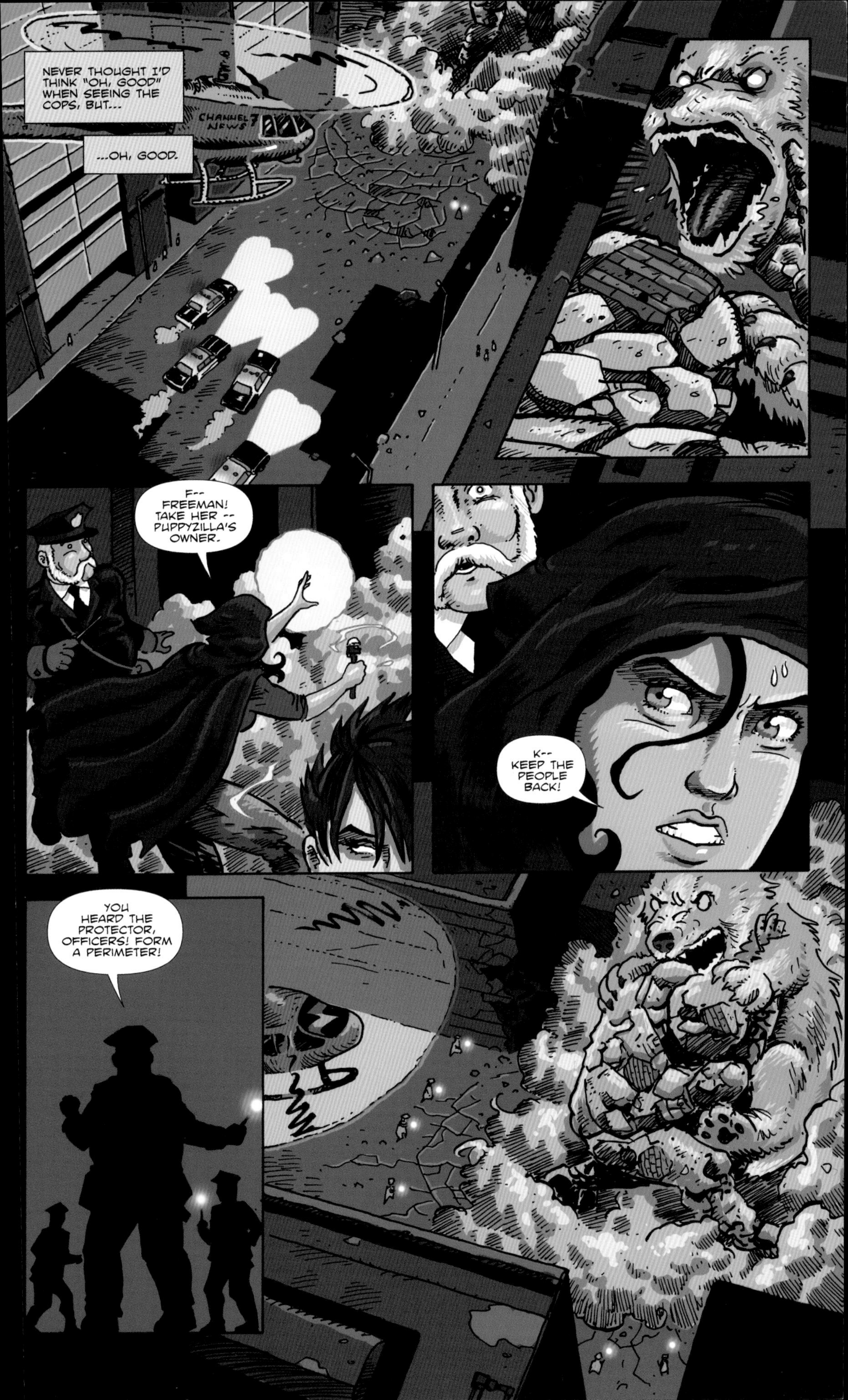
NEVER THOUGHT I'D THINK "OH, GOOD" WHEN SEEING THE COPS, BUT...
...OH, GOOD.
CHANNEL 7 NEWS
F-- FREEMAN! TAKE HER -- PUPPYZILLA'S OWNER.
K-- KEEP THE PEOPLE BACK!
YOU HEARD THE PROTECTOR, OFFICERS! FORM A PERIMETER!

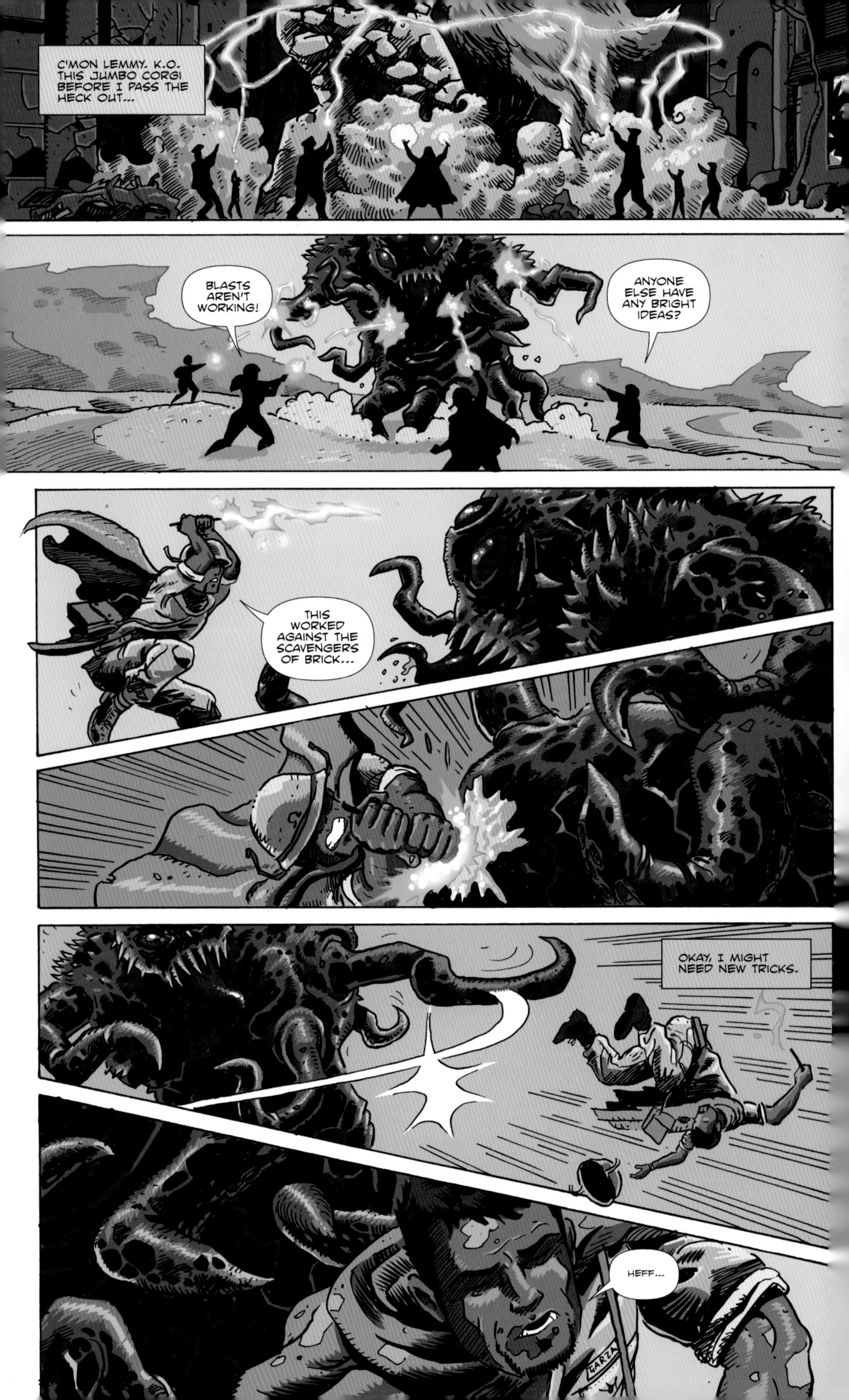
C'MON LEMMY. K.O. THIS JUMBO CORGI BEFORE I PASS THE HECK OUT...
BLASTS AREN'T WORKING!
ANYONE ELSE HAVE ANY BRIGHT IDEAS?
THIS WORKED AGAINST THE SCAVENGERS OF BRICK...
OKAY, I MIGHT NEED NEW TRICKS.
HEFF...

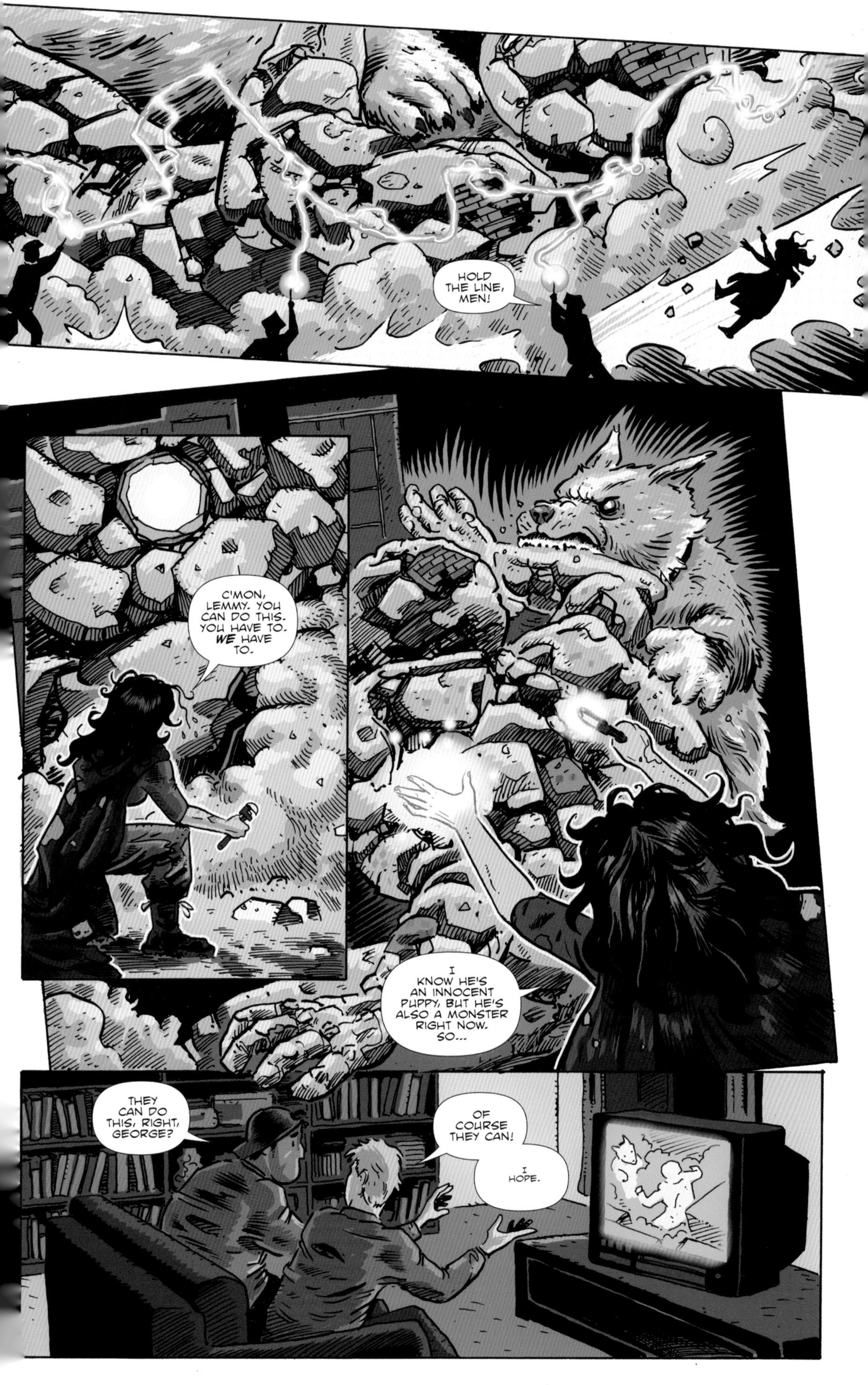
HOLD THE LINE, MEN!
C'MON, LEMMY. YOU CAN DO THIS. YOU HAVE TO. WE HAVE TO.
I KNOW HE'S AN INNOCENT PUPPY, BUT HE'S ALSO A MONSTER RIGHT NOW. SO...
THEY CAN DO THIS, RIGHT, GEORGE?
OF COURSE THEY CAN!
I HOPE.

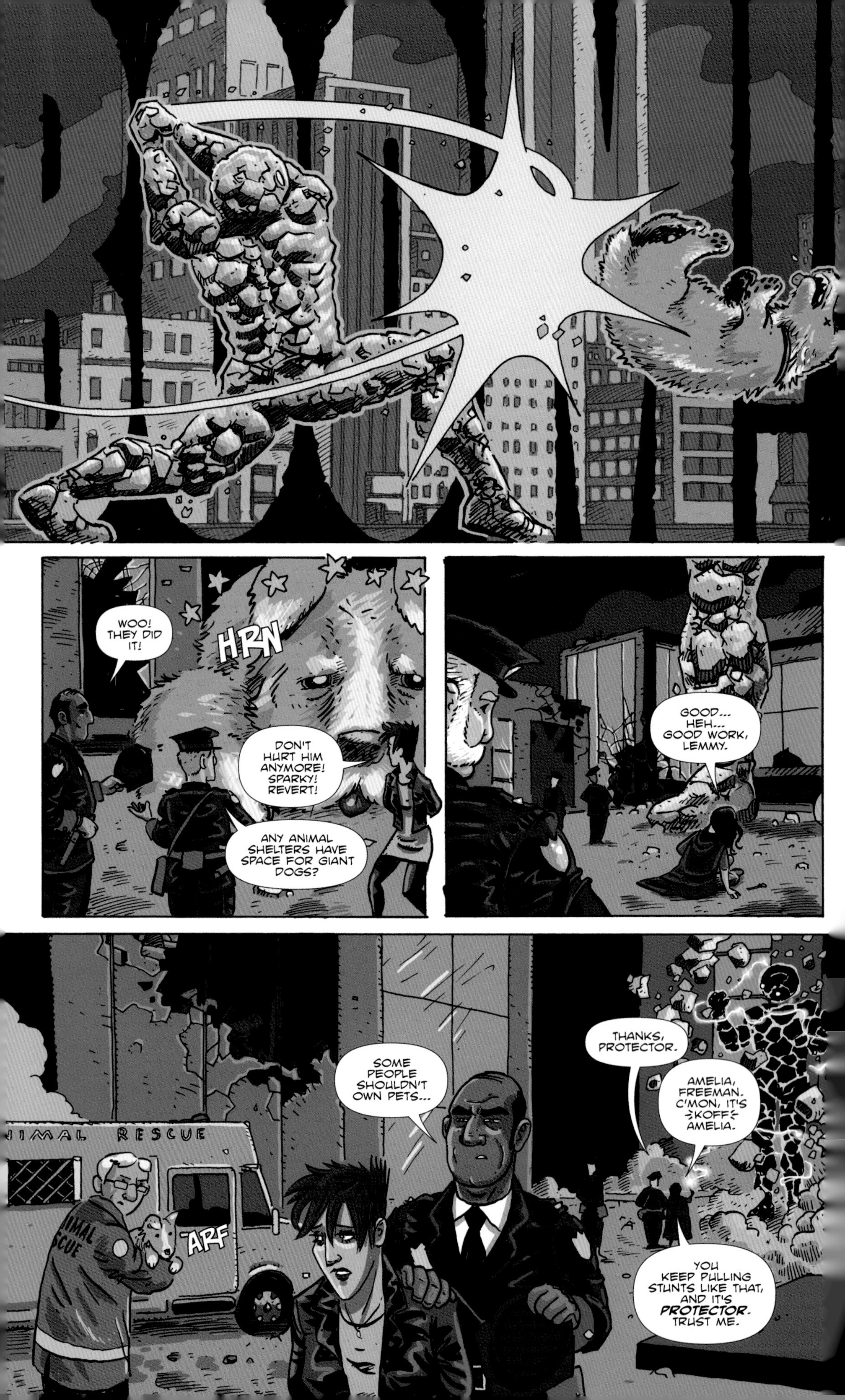
WOO! THEY DID IT!
HRN
DON'T HURT HIM ANYMORE! SPARKY! REVERT!
ANY ANIMAL SHELTERS HAVE SPACE FOR GIANT DOGS?
GOOD... HEH... GOOD WORK, LEMMY.
RESCUE
ARF
SOME PEOPLE SHOULDN'T OWN PETS...
THANKS, PROTECTOR.
AMELIA, FREEMAN. C'MON, IT'S *KOFF* AMELIA.
YOU KEEP PULLING STUNTS LIKE THAT, AND IT'S **PROTECTOR**. TRUST ME.

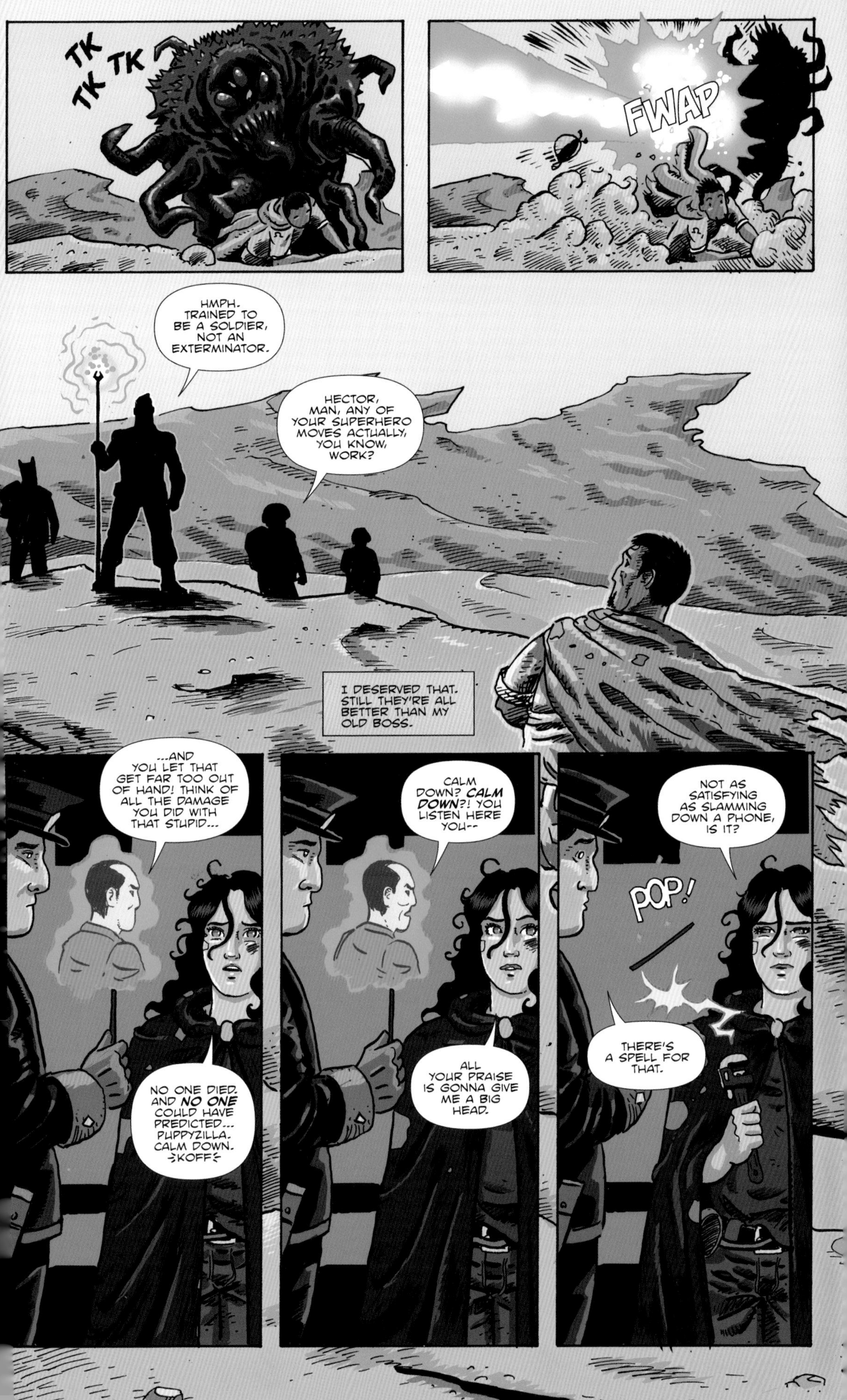
TK TK TK
FWAP
HMPH. TRAINED TO BE A SOLDIER, NOT AN EXTERMINATOR.
HECTOR, MAN, ANY OF YOUR SUPERHERO MOVES ACTUALLY, YOU KNOW, WORK?
I DESERVED THAT. STILL THEY'RE ALL BETTER THAN MY OLD BOSS.
...AND YOU LET THAT GET FAR TOO OUT OF HAND! THINK OF ALL THE DAMAGE YOU DID WITH THAT STUPID...
NO ONE DIED. AND NO ONE COULD HAVE PREDICTED... PUPPYZILLA. CALM DOWN. KOFF
CALM DOWN? CALM DOWN?! YOU LISTEN HERE YOU--
ALL YOUR PRAISE IS GONNA GIVE ME A BIG HEAD.
NOT AS SATISFYING AS SLAMMING DOWN A PHONE, IS IT?
POP!
THERE'S A SPELL FOR THAT.

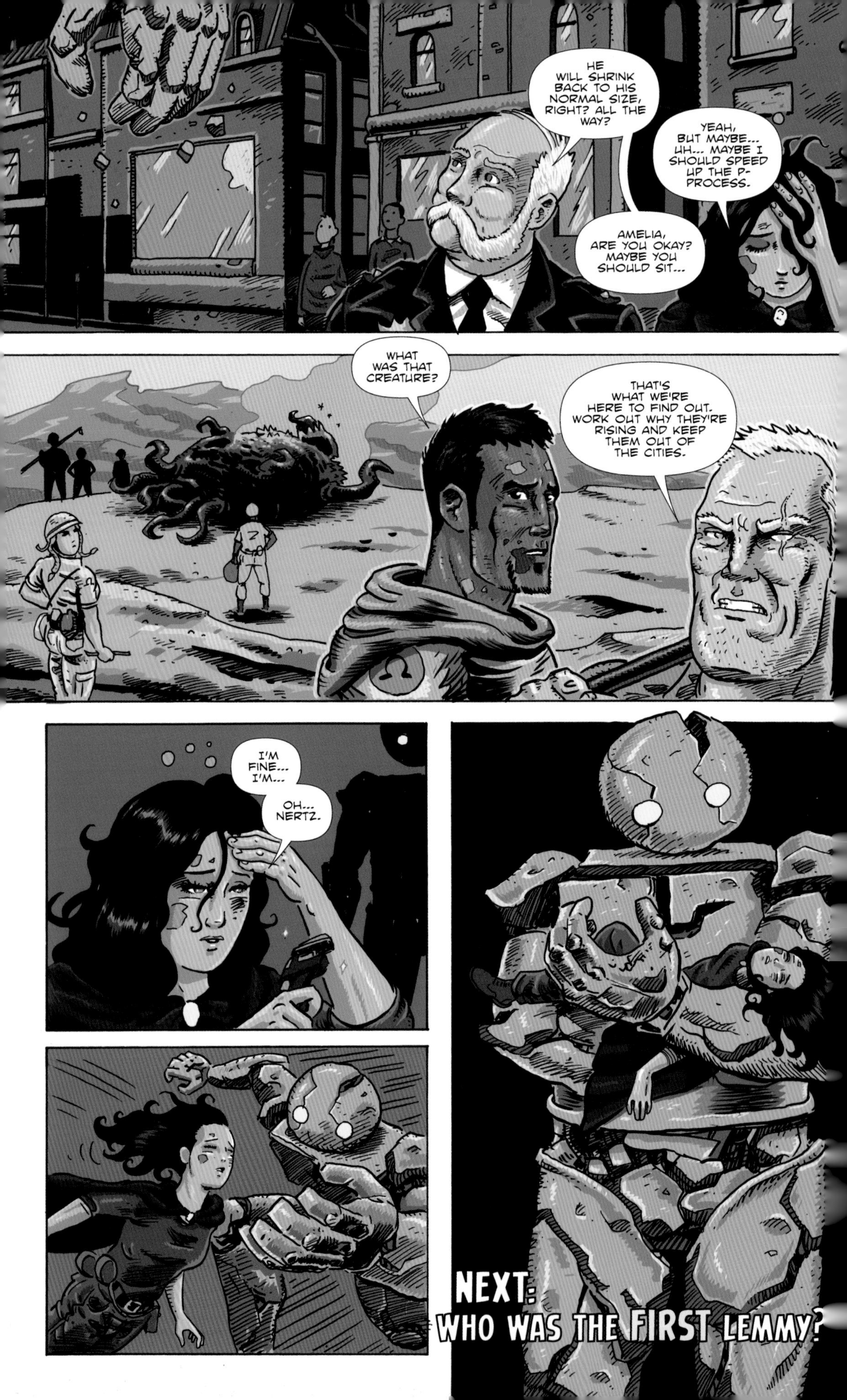
HE WILL SHRINK BACK TO HIS NORMAL SIZE, RIGHT? ALL THE WAY?
YEAH, BUT MAYBE... UH... MAYBE I SHOULD SPEED UP THE P-PROCESS.
AMELIA, ARE YOU OKAY? MAYBE YOU SHOULD SIT...
WHAT WAS THAT CREATURE?
THAT'S WHAT WE'RE HERE TO FIND OUT. WORK OUT WHY THEY'RE RISING AND KEEP THEM OUT OF THE CITIES.
I'M FINE... I'M...
OH... NERTZ.
NEXT:
WHO WAS THE FIRST LEMMY?

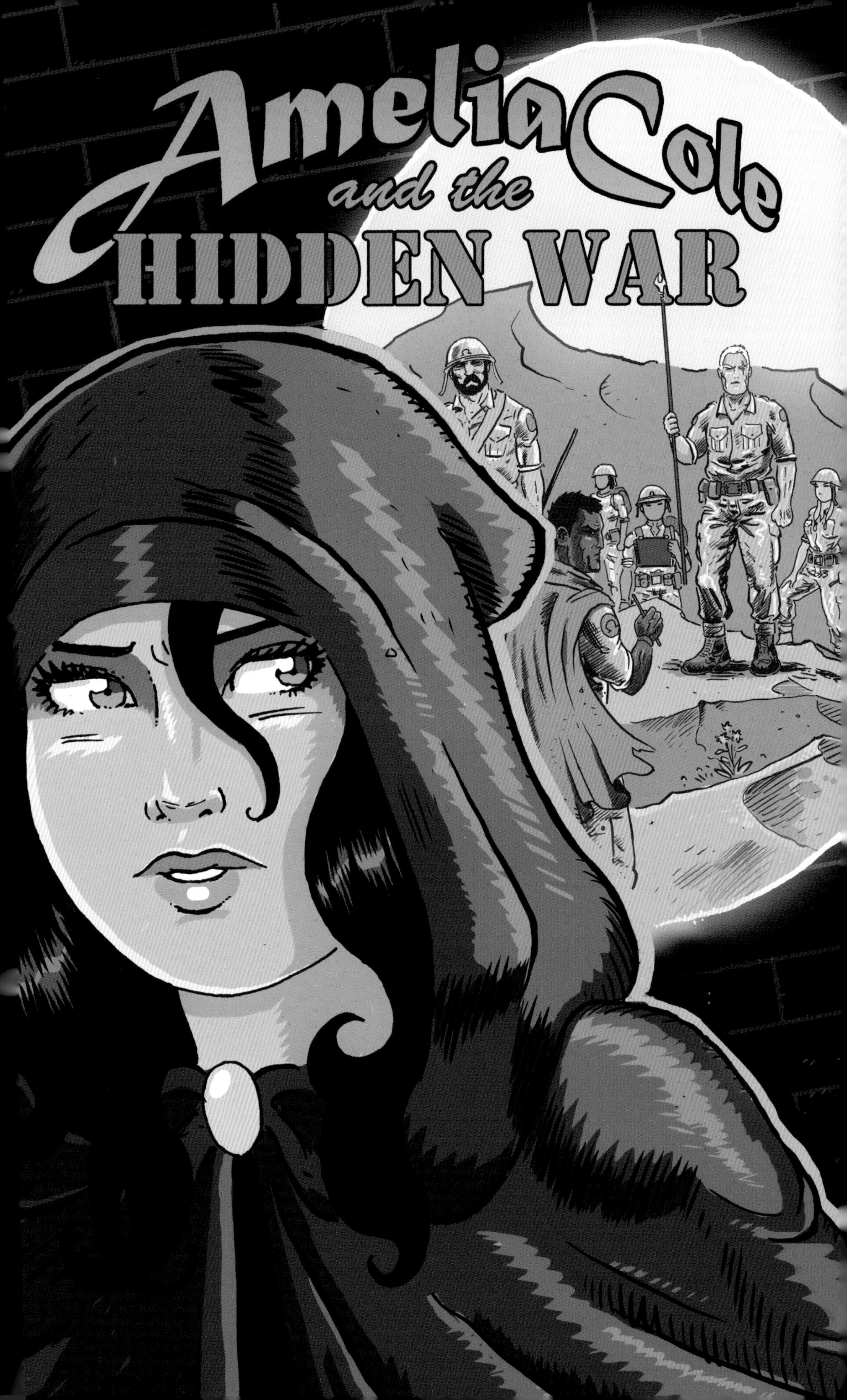
Amelia Cole
and the
HIDDEN WAR

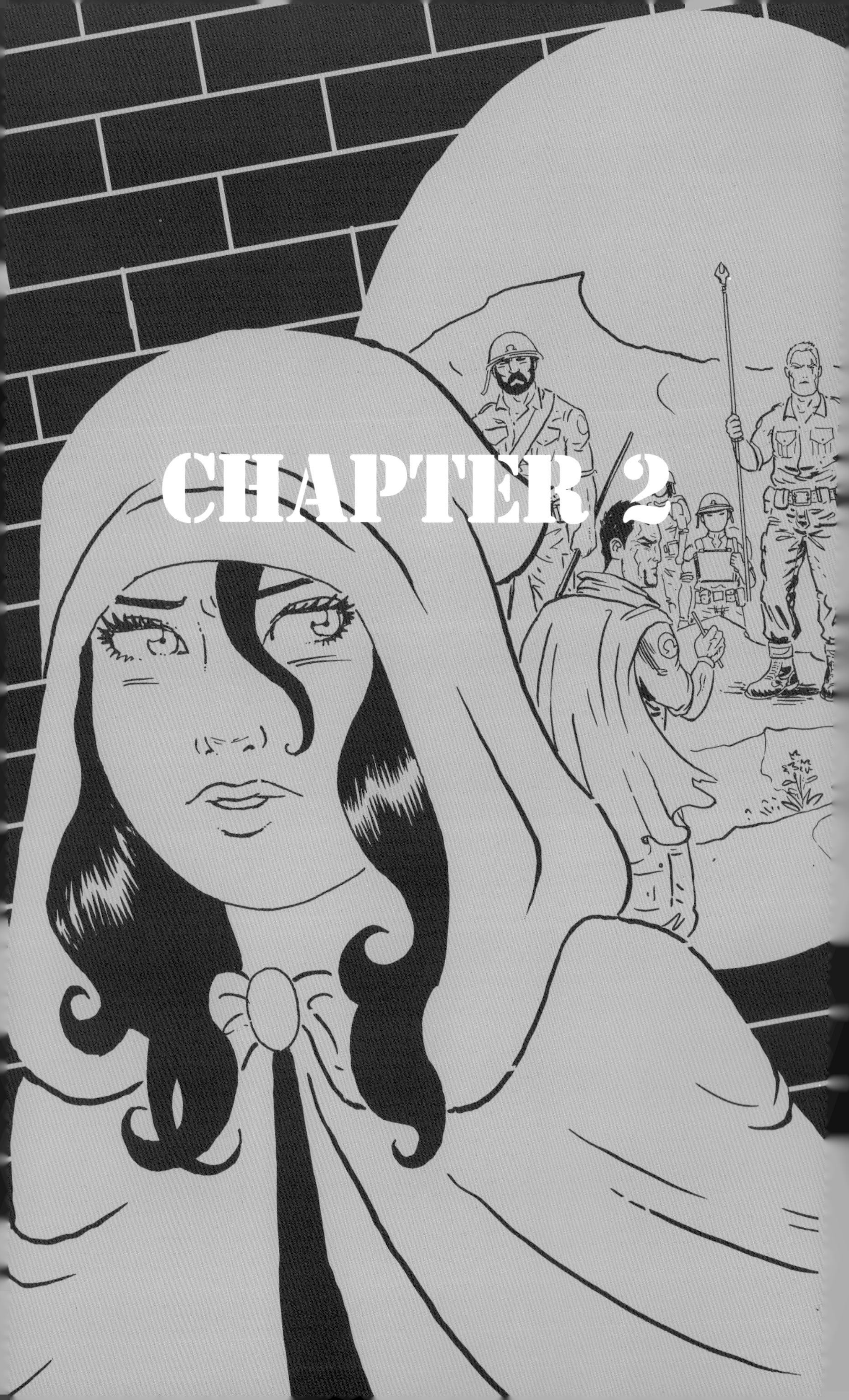
CHAPTER 2

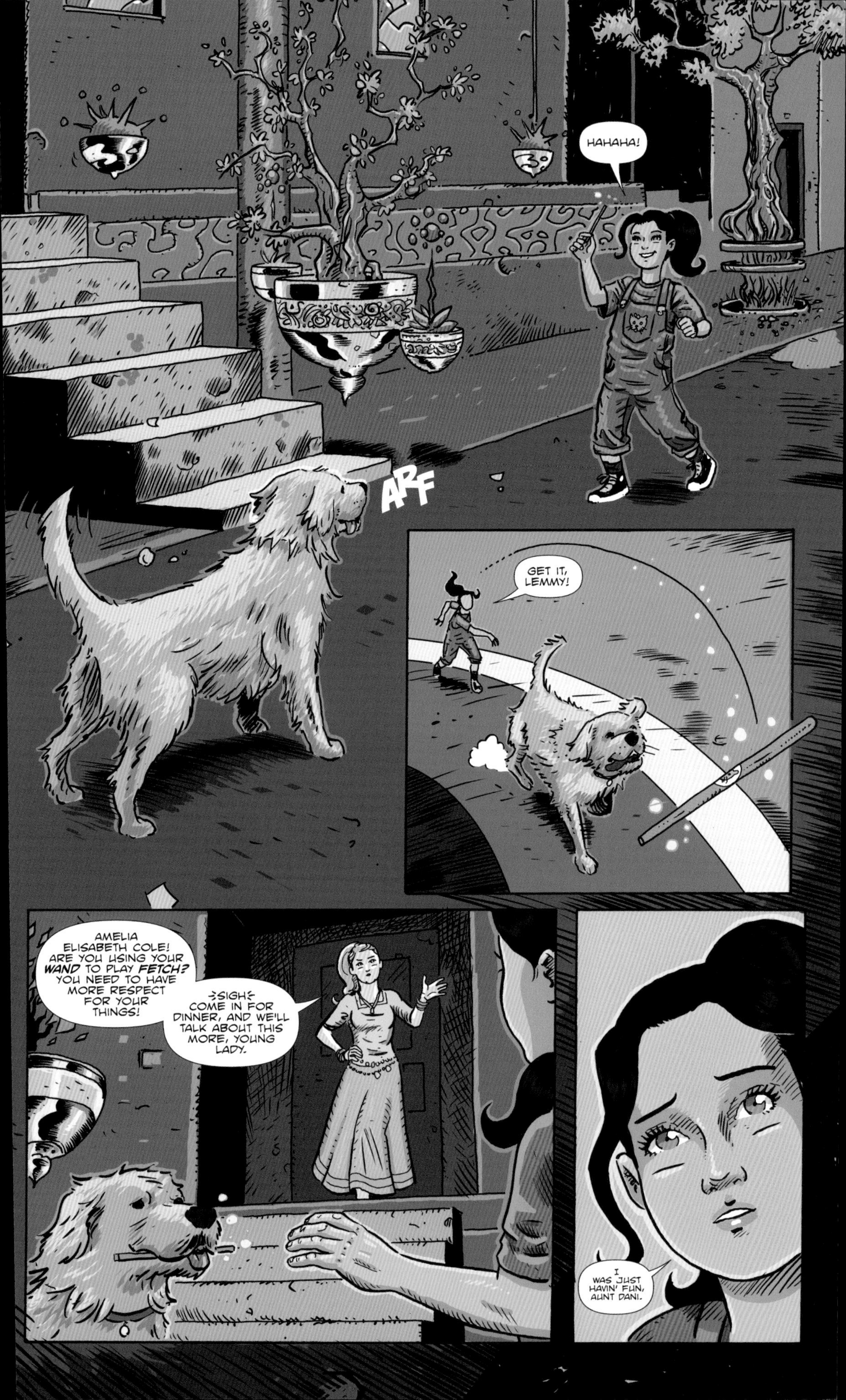
HAHAHA!
ARF
GET IT, LEMMY!
AMELIA ELISABETH COLE! ARE YOU USING YOUR WAND TO PLAY FETCH? YOU NEED TO HAVE MORE RESPECT FOR YOUR THINGS!
SIGH COME IN FOR DINNER, AND WE'LL TALK ABOUT THIS MORE, YOUNG LADY.
I WAS JUST HAVIN' FUN, AUNT DANI.

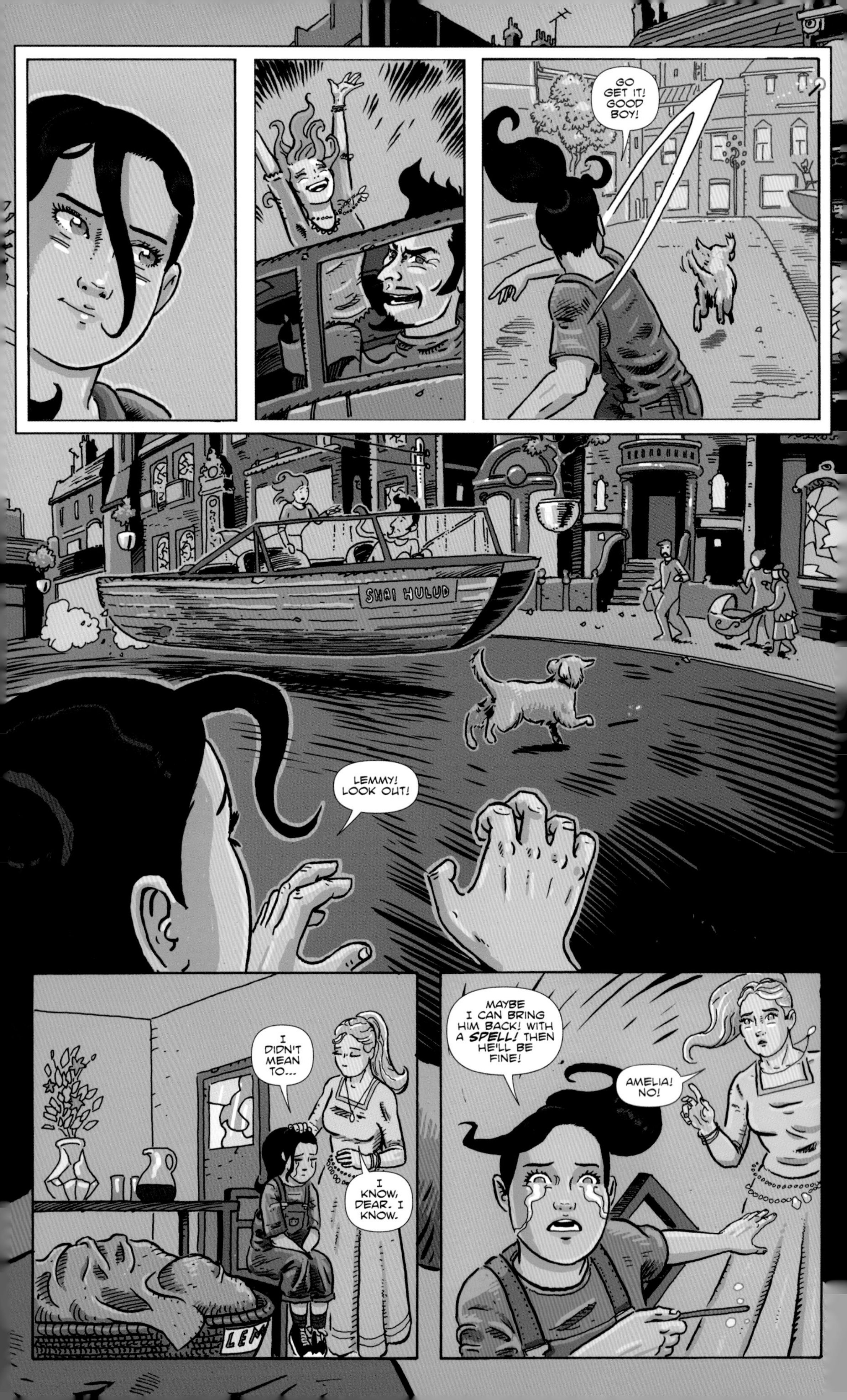
GO GET IT! GOOD BOY!
SHAI HULUD
LEMMY! LOOK OUT!
I DIDN'T MEAN TO...
I KNOW, DEAR. I KNOW.
LEM
MAYBE I CAN BRING HIM BACK! WITH A SPELL! THEN HE'LL BE FINE!
AMELIA! NO!

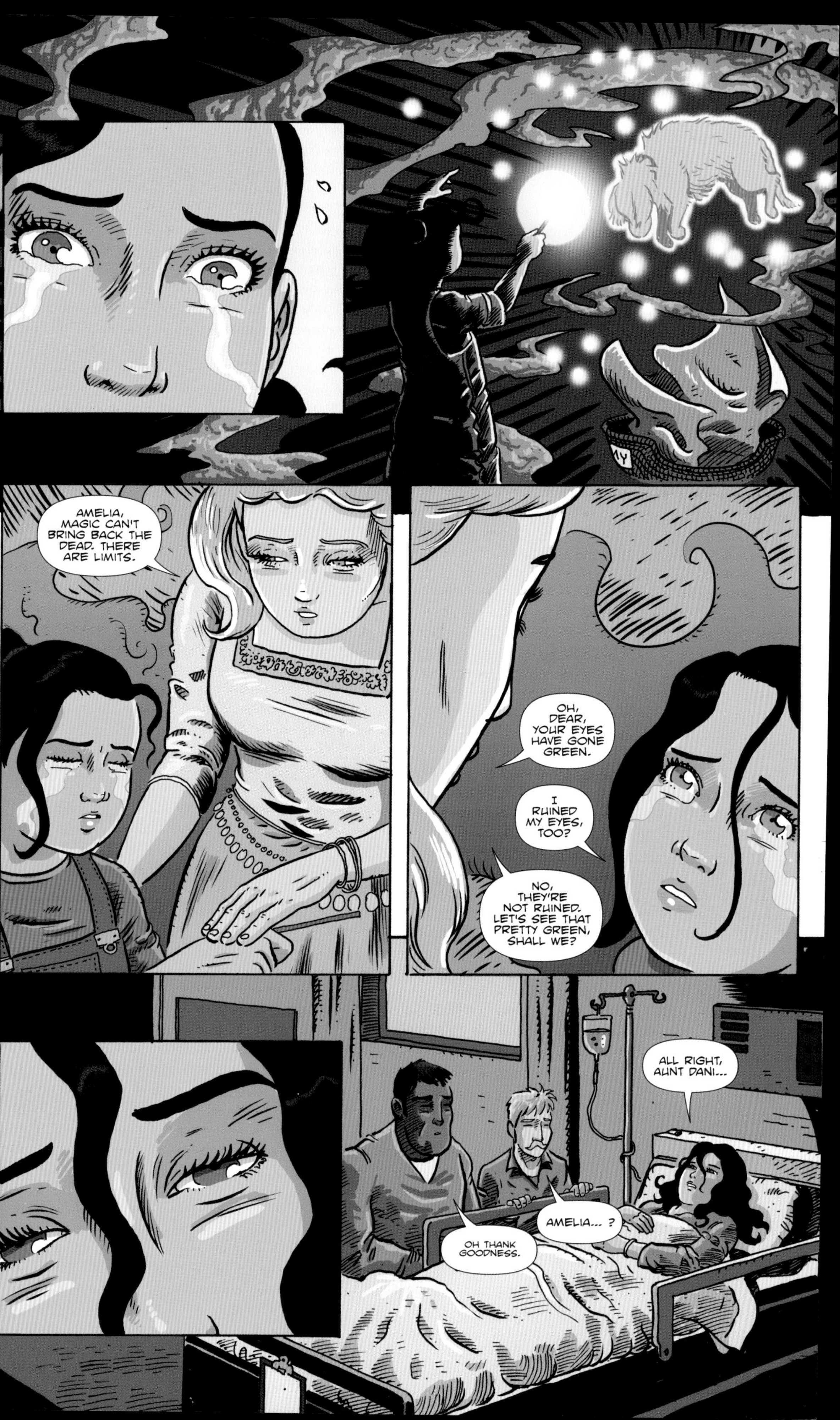
AMELIA, MAGIC CAN'T BRING BACK THE DEAD. THERE ARE LIMITS.
OH, DEAR, YOUR EYES HAVE GONE GREEN.
I RUINED MY EYES, TOO?
NO, THEY'RE NOT RUINED. LET'S SEE THAT PRETTY GREEN, SHALL WE?
ALL RIGHT, AUNT DANI...
AMELIA... ?
OH THANK GOODNESS.

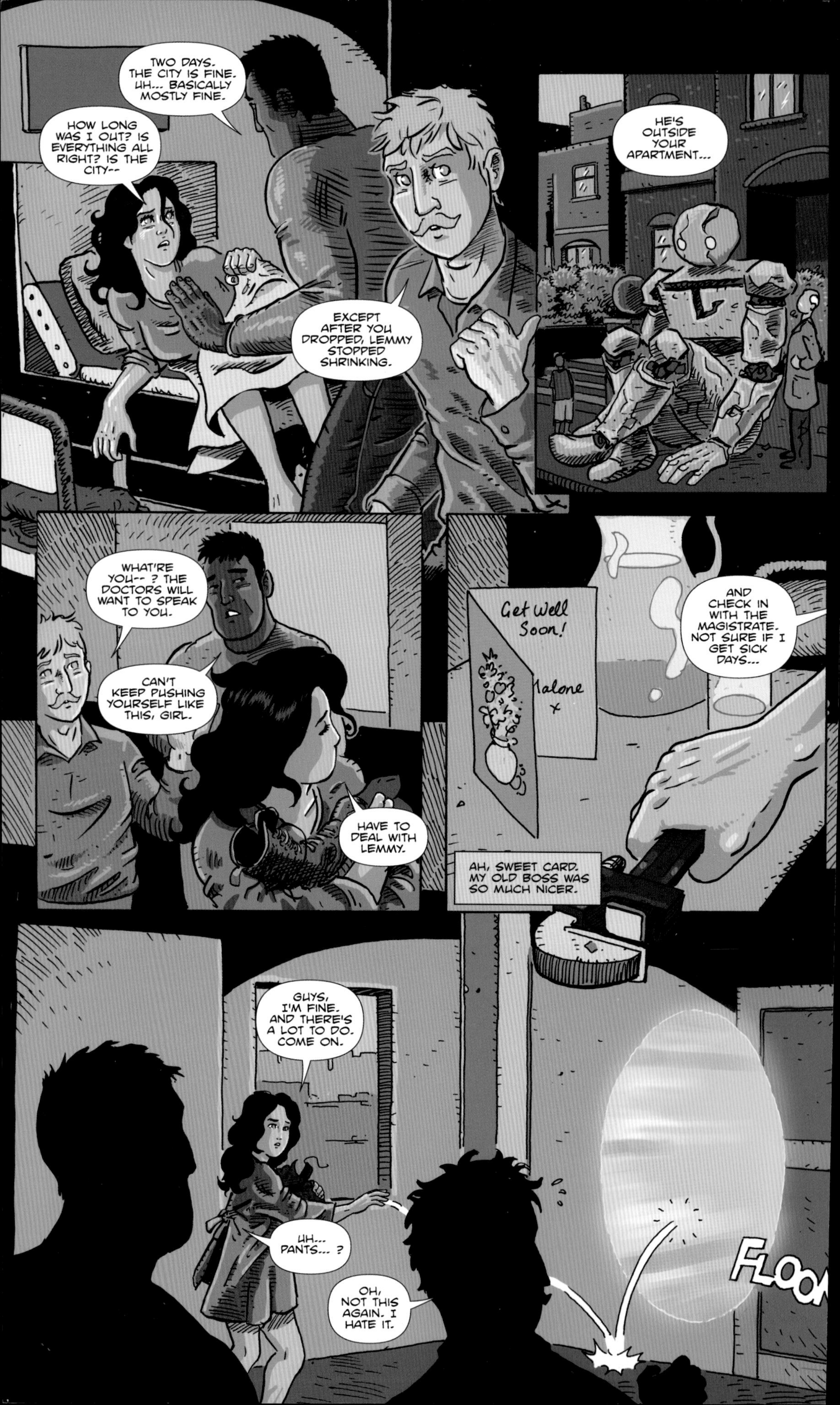
HOW LONG WAS I OUT? IS EVERYTHING ALL RIGHT? IS THE CITY--
TWO DAYS. THE CITY IS FINE. UH... BASICALLY MOSTLY FINE.
EXCEPT AFTER YOU DROPPED, LEMMY STOPPED SHRINKING.
HE'S OUTSIDE YOUR APARTMENT...
WHAT'RE YOU-- ? THE DOCTORS WILL WANT TO SPEAK TO YOU.
CAN'T KEEP PUSHING YOURSELF LIKE THIS, GIRL.
HAVE TO DEAL WITH LEMMY.
Get Well Soon!
Malone x
AND CHECK IN WITH THE MAGISTRATE. NOT SURE IF I GET SICK DAYS...
AH, SWEET CARD. MY OLD BOSS WAS SO MUCH NICER.
GUYS, I'M FINE. AND THERE'S A LOT TO DO. COME ON.
UH... PANTS... ?
OH, NOT THIS AGAIN. I HATE IT.
FLOOM

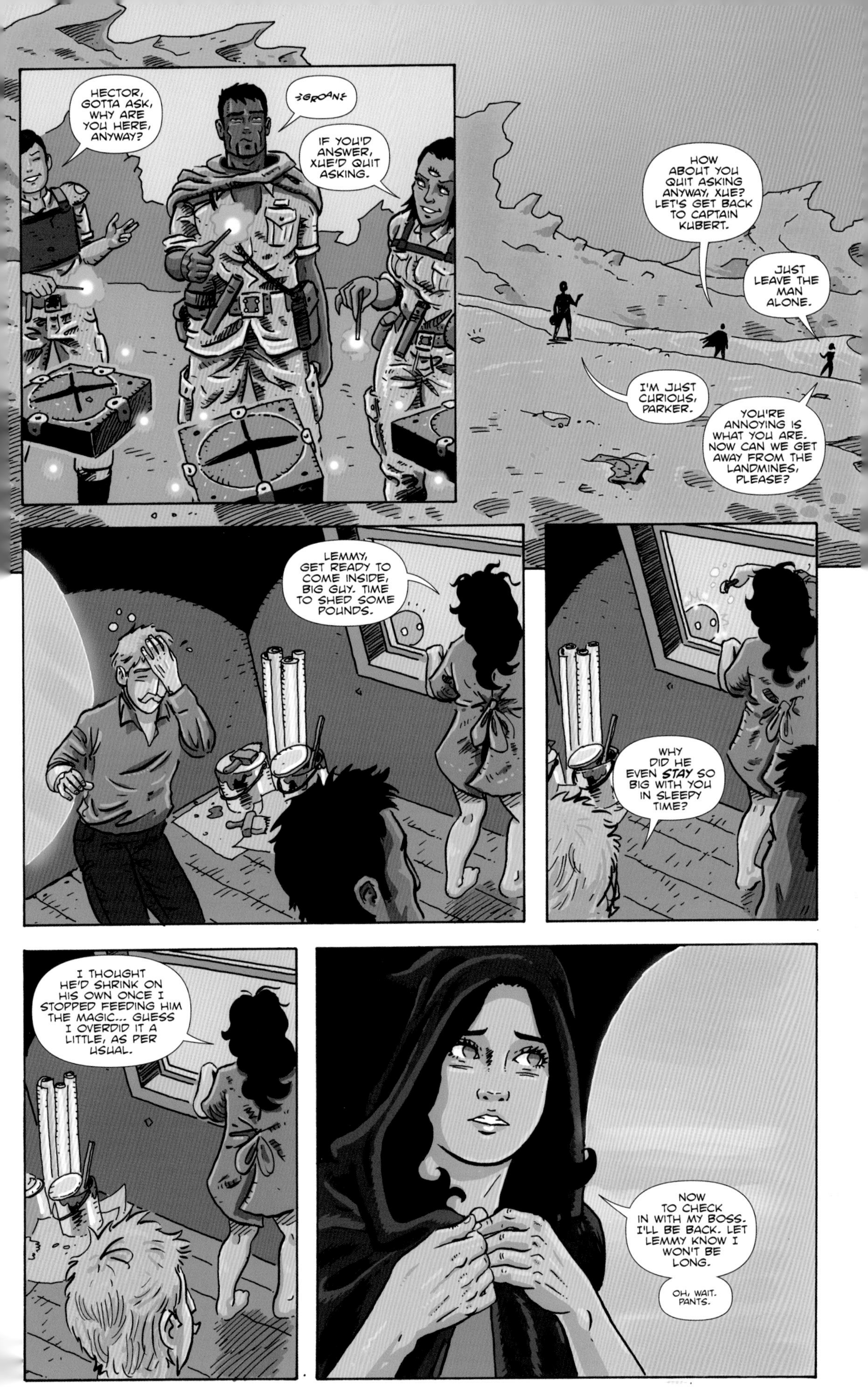
HECTOR, GOTTA ASK, WHY ARE YOU HERE, ANYWAY?
GROAN
IF YOU'D ANSWER, XUE'D QUIT ASKING.
HOW ABOUT YOU QUIT ASKING ANYWAY, XUE? LET'S GET BACK TO CAPTAIN KUBERT.
JUST LEAVE THE MAN ALONE.
I'M JUST CURIOUS, PARKER.
YOU'RE ANNOYING IS WHAT YOU ARE. NOW CAN WE GET AWAY FROM THE LANDMINES, PLEASE?
LEMMY, GET READY TO COME INSIDE, BIG GUY. TIME TO SHED SOME POUNDS.
WHY DID HE EVEN STAY SO BIG WITH YOU IN SLEEPY TIME?
I THOUGHT HE'D SHRINK ON HIS OWN ONCE I STOPPED FEEDING HIM THE MAGIC... GUESS I OVERDID IT A LITTLE, AS PER USUAL.
NOW TO CHECK IN WITH MY BOSS. I'LL BE BACK. LET LEMMY KNOW I WON'T BE LONG.
OH, WAIT. PANTS.

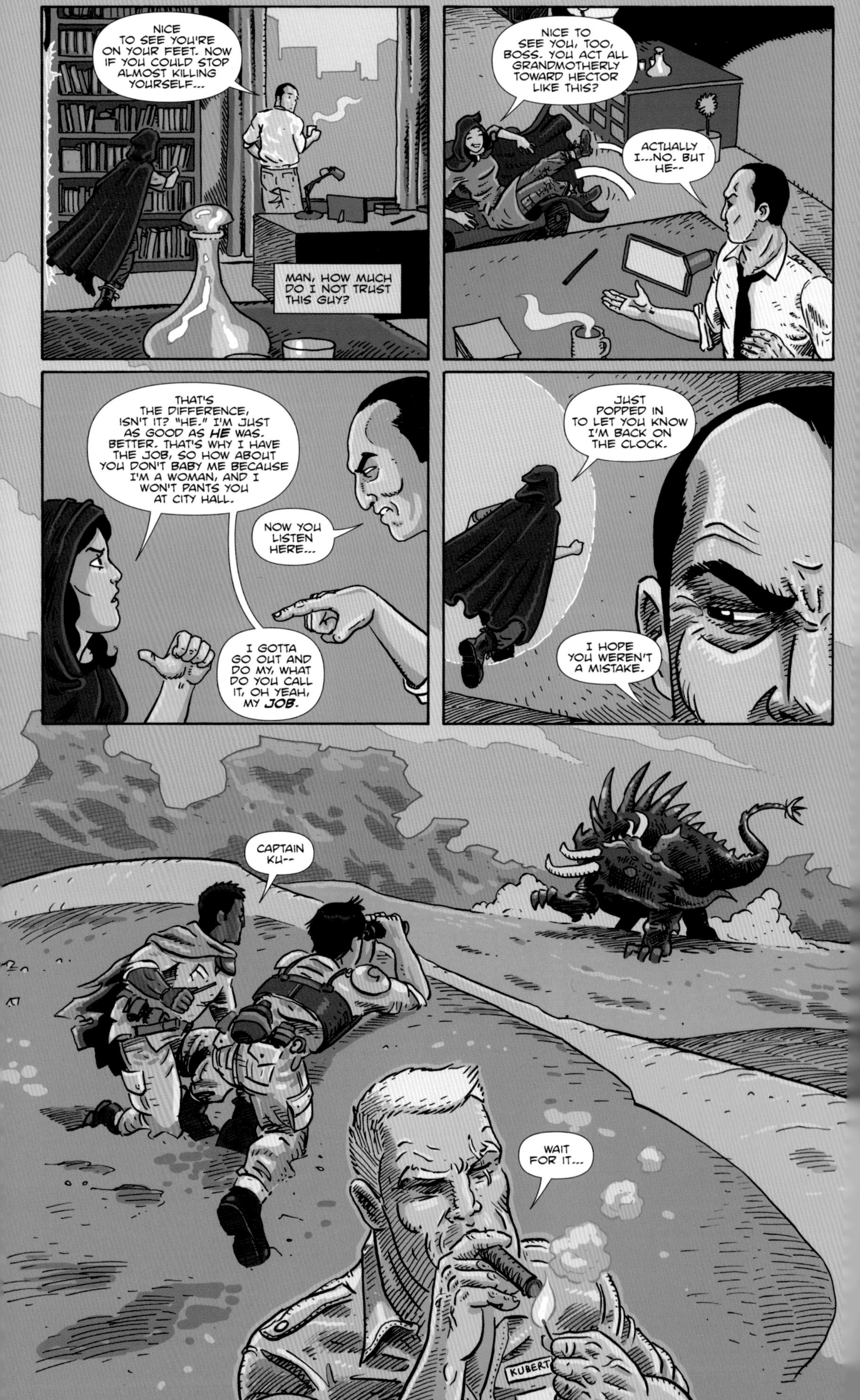
NICE TO SEE YOU'RE ON YOUR FEET. NOW IF YOU COULD STOP ALMOST KILLING YOURSELF...
MAN, HOW MUCH DO I NOT TRUST THIS GUY?
NICE TO SEE YOU, TOO, BOSS. YOU ACT ALL GRANDMOTHERLY TOWARD HECTOR LIKE THIS?
ACTUALLY I...NO. BUT HE--
THAT'S THE DIFFERENCE, ISN'T IT? "HE." I'M JUST AS GOOD AS HE WAS. BETTER. THAT'S WHY I HAVE THE JOB, SO HOW ABOUT YOU DON'T BABY ME BECAUSE I'M A WOMAN, AND I WON'T PANTS YOU AT CITY HALL.
NOW YOU LISTEN HERE...
I GOTTA GO OUT AND DO MY, WHAT DO YOU CALL IT, OH YEAH, MY JOB.
JUST POPPED IN TO LET YOU KNOW I'M BACK ON THE CLOCK.
I HOPE YOU WEREN'T A MISTAKE.
CAPTAIN KU--
WAIT FOR IT...
KUBERT

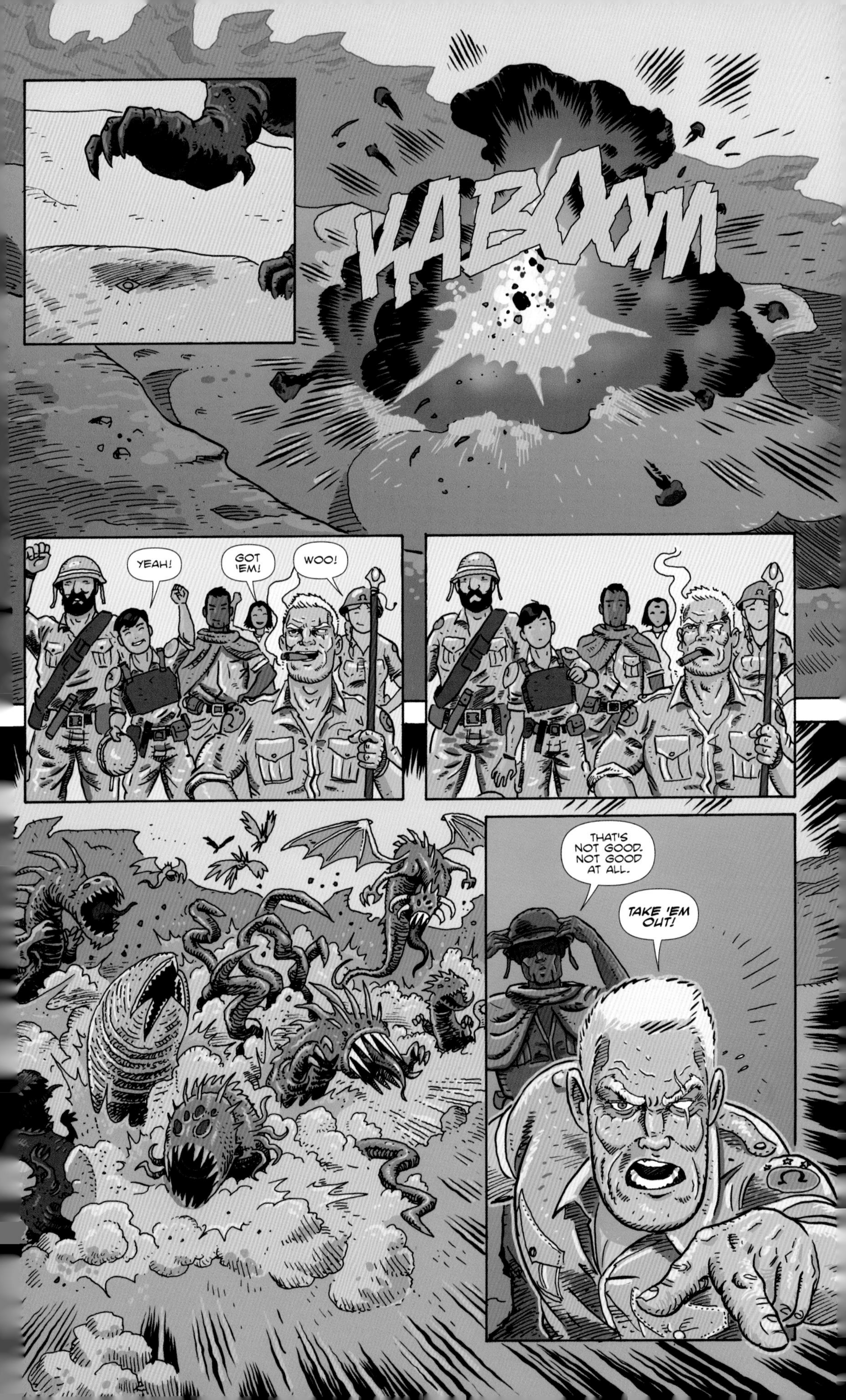
YABOOM
YEAH!
GOT 'EM!
WOO!
THAT'S NOT GOOD. NOT GOOD AT ALL.
TAKE 'EM OUT!

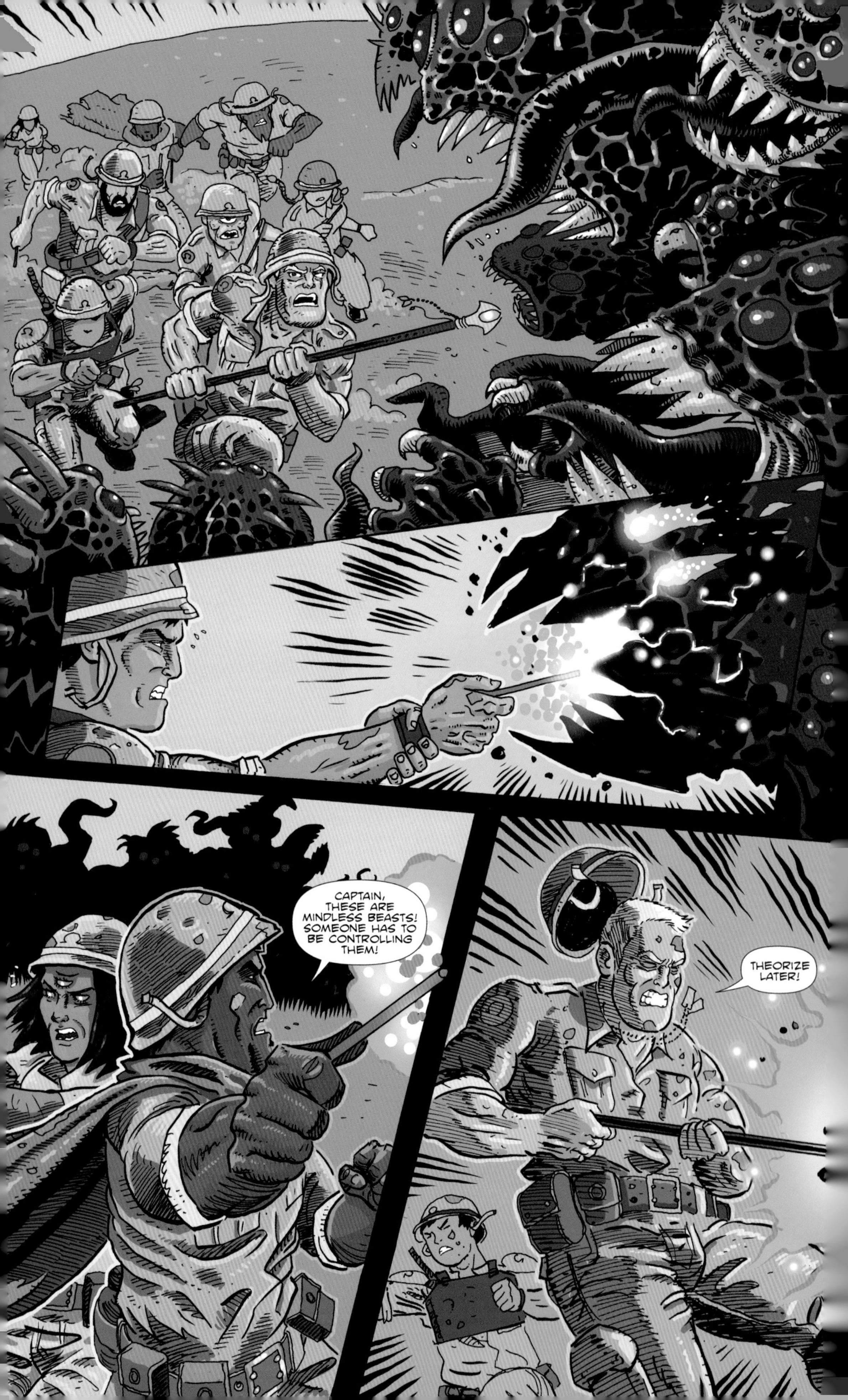
CAPTAIN, THESE ARE MINDLESS BEASTS! SOMEONE HAS TO BE CONTROLLING THEM!
THEORIZE LATER!

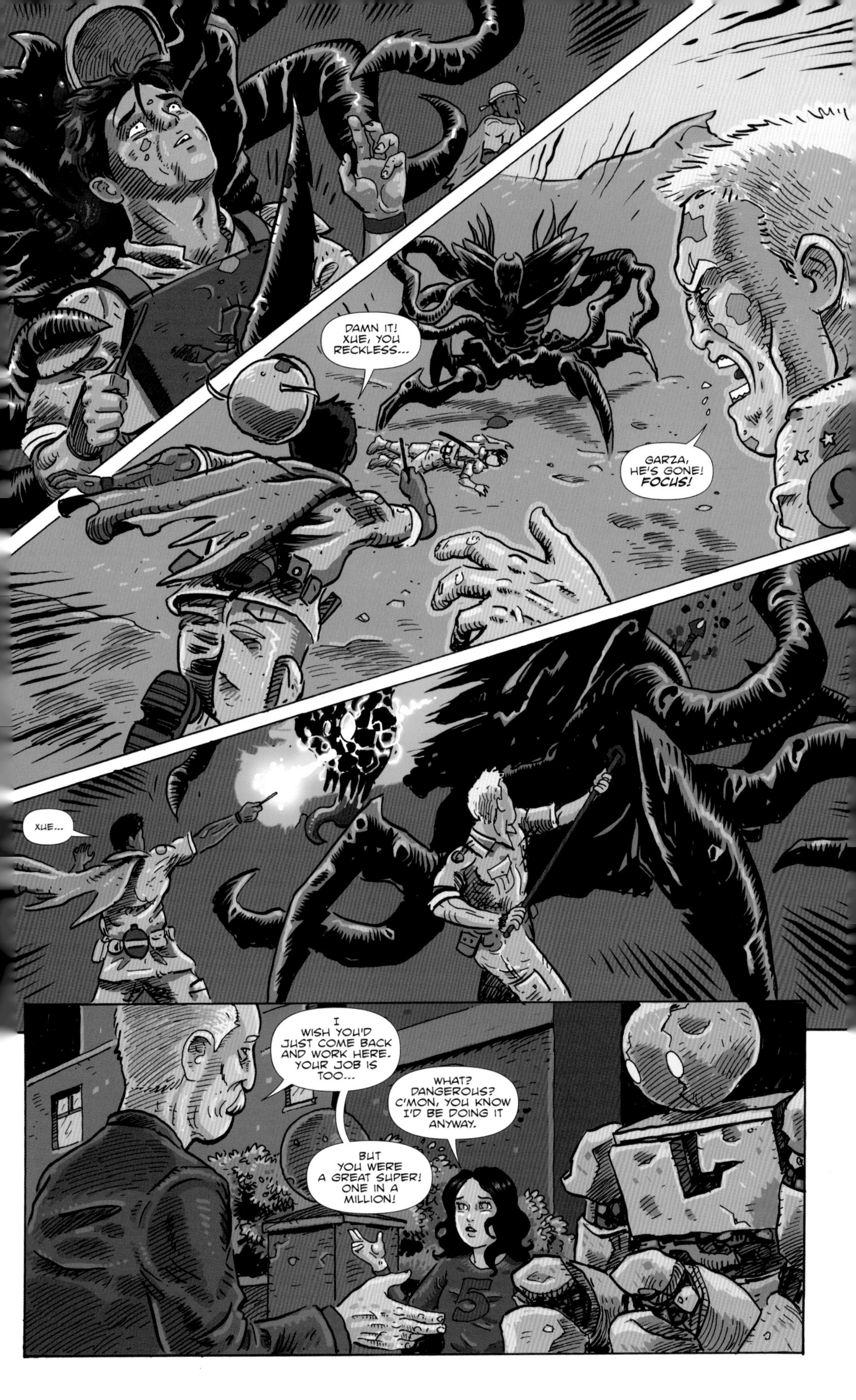
DAMN IT! XUE, YOU RECKLESS...
GARZA, HE'S GONE! FOCUS!
XUE...
I WISH YOU'D JUST COME BACK AND WORK HERE. YOUR JOB IS TOO...
WHAT? DANGEROUS? C'MON, YOU KNOW I'D BE DOING IT ANYWAY.
BUT YOU WERE A GREAT SUPER! ONE IN A MILLION!

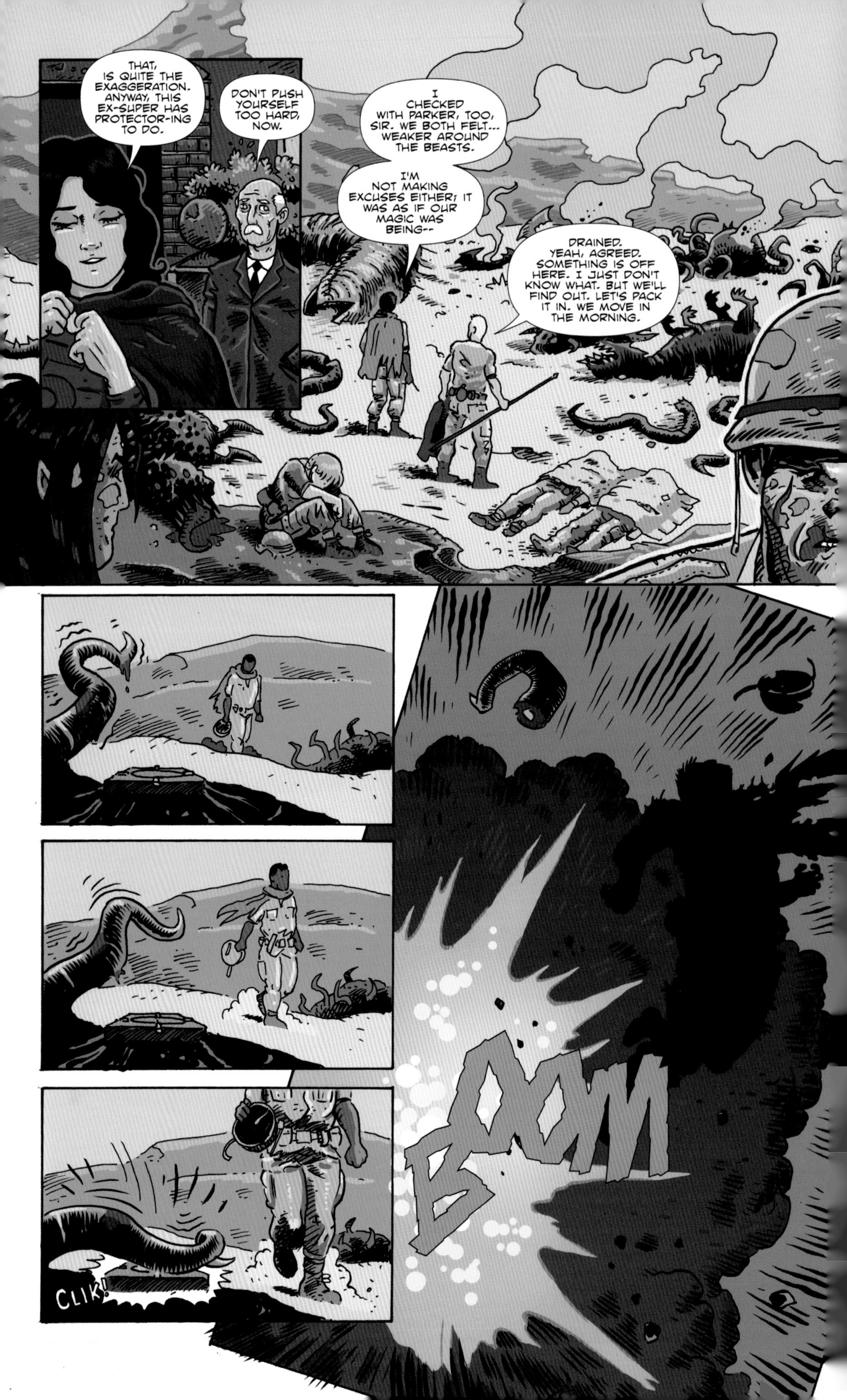
THAT, IS QUITE THE EXAGGERATION. ANYWAY, THIS EX-SUPER HAS PROTECTOR-ING TO DO.
DON'T PUSH YOURSELF TOO HARD, NOW.
I CHECKED WITH PARKER, TOO, SIR. WE BOTH FELT... WEAKER AROUND THE BEASTS.
I'M NOT MAKING EXCUSES EITHER; IT WAS AS IF OUR MAGIC WAS BEING--
DRAINED. YEAH, AGREED. SOMETHING IS OFF HERE. I JUST DON'T KNOW WHAT. BUT WE'LL FIND OUT. LET'S PACK IT IN. WE MOVE IN THE MORNING.
CLIK!
BOOM

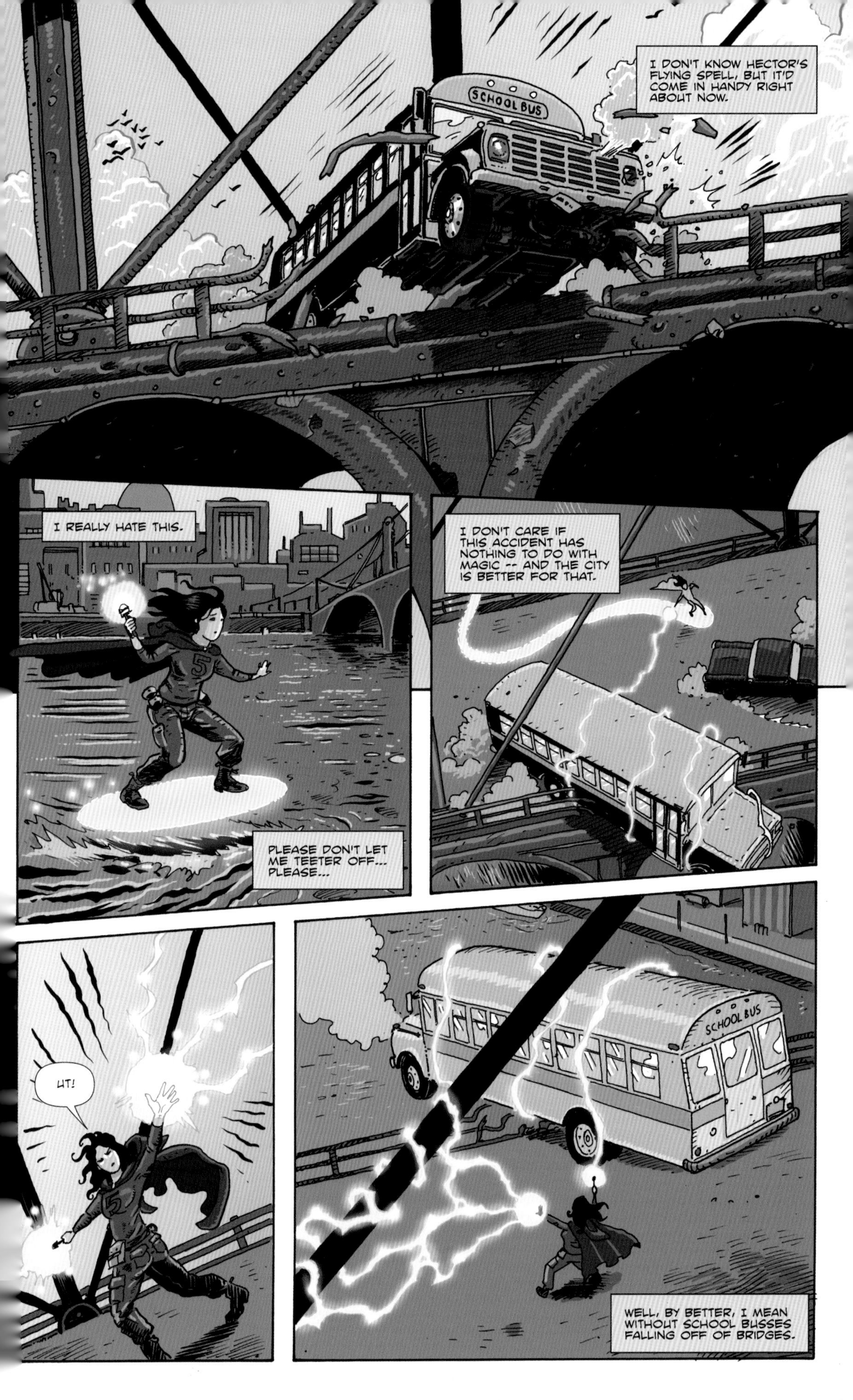

SCHOOL BUS
I DON'T KNOW HECTOR'S FLYING SPELL, BUT IT'D COME IN HANDY RIGHT ABOUT NOW.
I REALLY HATE THIS.
PLEASE DON'T LET ME TEETER OFF... PLEASE...
I DON'T CARE IF THIS ACCIDENT HAS NOTHING TO DO WITH MAGIC -- AND THE CITY IS BETTER FOR THAT.
UT!
SCHOOL BUS
WELL, BY BETTER, I MEAN WITHOUT SCHOOL BUSSES FALLING OFF OF BRIDGES.

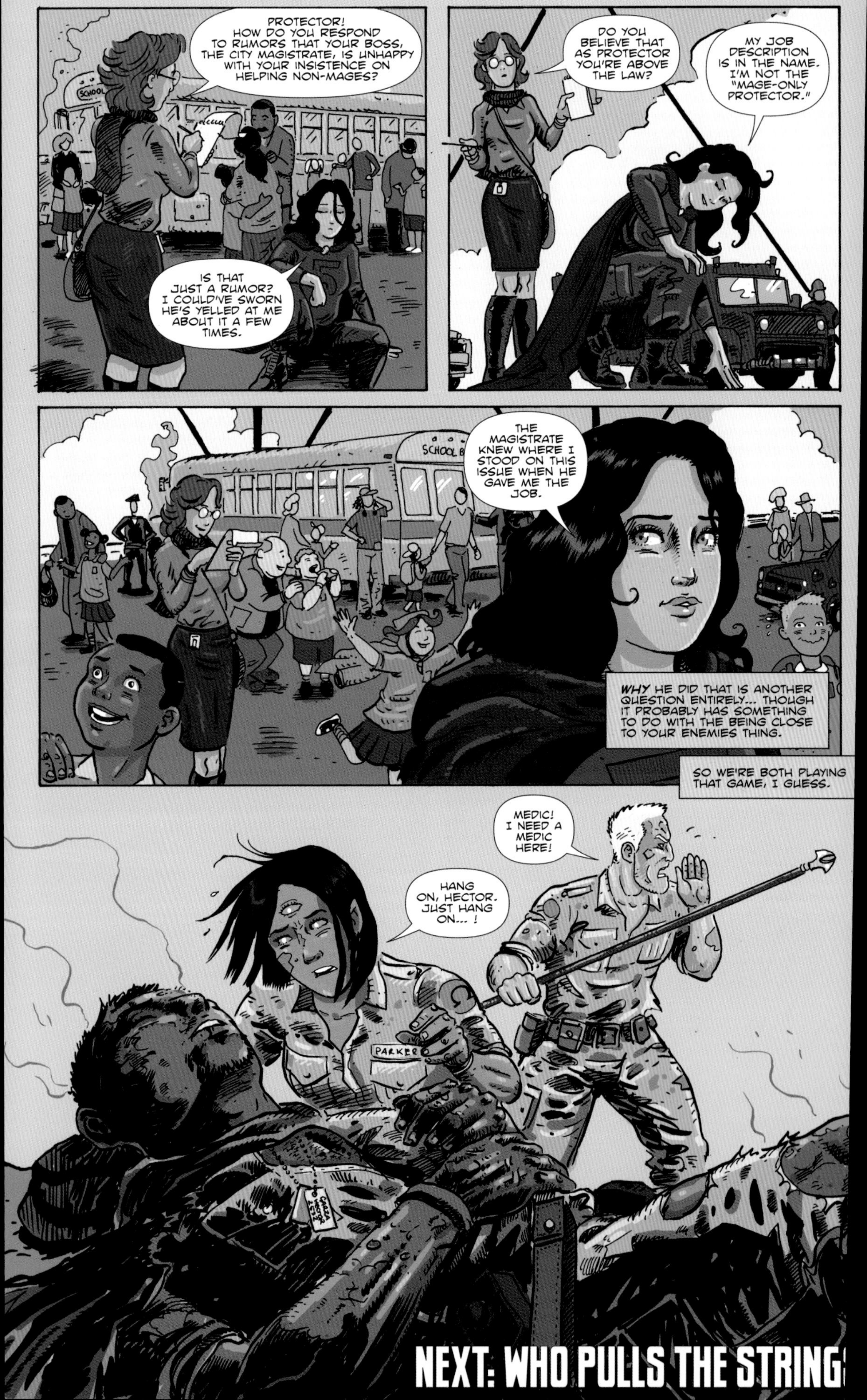
PROTECTOR! HOW DO YOU RESPOND TO RUMORS THAT YOUR BOSS, THE CITY MAGISTRATE, IS UNHAPPY WITH YOUR INSISTENCE ON HELPING NON-MAGES?
SCHOOL
IS THAT JUST A RUMOR? I COULD'VE SWORN HE'S YELLED AT ME ABOUT IT A FEW TIMES.
DO YOU BELIEVE THAT AS PROTECTOR YOU'RE ABOVE THE LAW?
MY JOB DESCRIPTION IS IN THE NAME. I'M NOT THE "MAGE-ONLY PROTECTOR."
SCHOOL B
THE MAGISTRATE KNEW WHERE I STOOD ON THIS ISSUE WHEN HE GAVE ME THE JOB.
WHY HE DID THAT IS ANOTHER QUESTION ENTIRELY... THOUGH IT PROBABLY HAS SOMETHING TO DO WITH THE BEING CLOSE TO YOUR ENEMIES THING.
SO WE'RE BOTH PLAYING THAT GAME, I GUESS.
MEDIC! I NEED A MEDIC HERE!
HANG ON, HECTOR. JUST HANG ON... !
PARKER
NEXT: WHO PULLS THE STRING

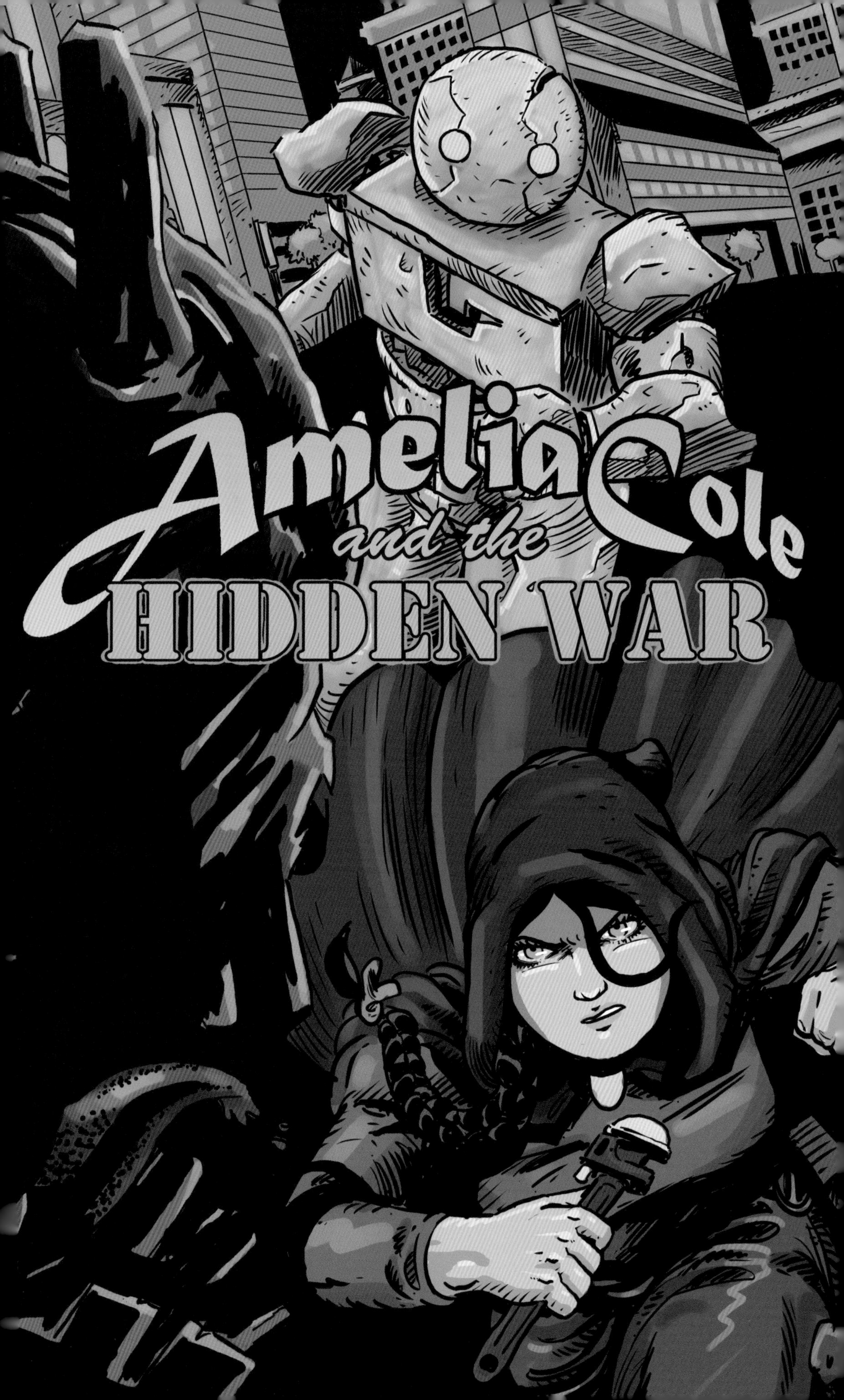
Amelia Cole
and the
HIDDEN WAR

CHAPTER 3

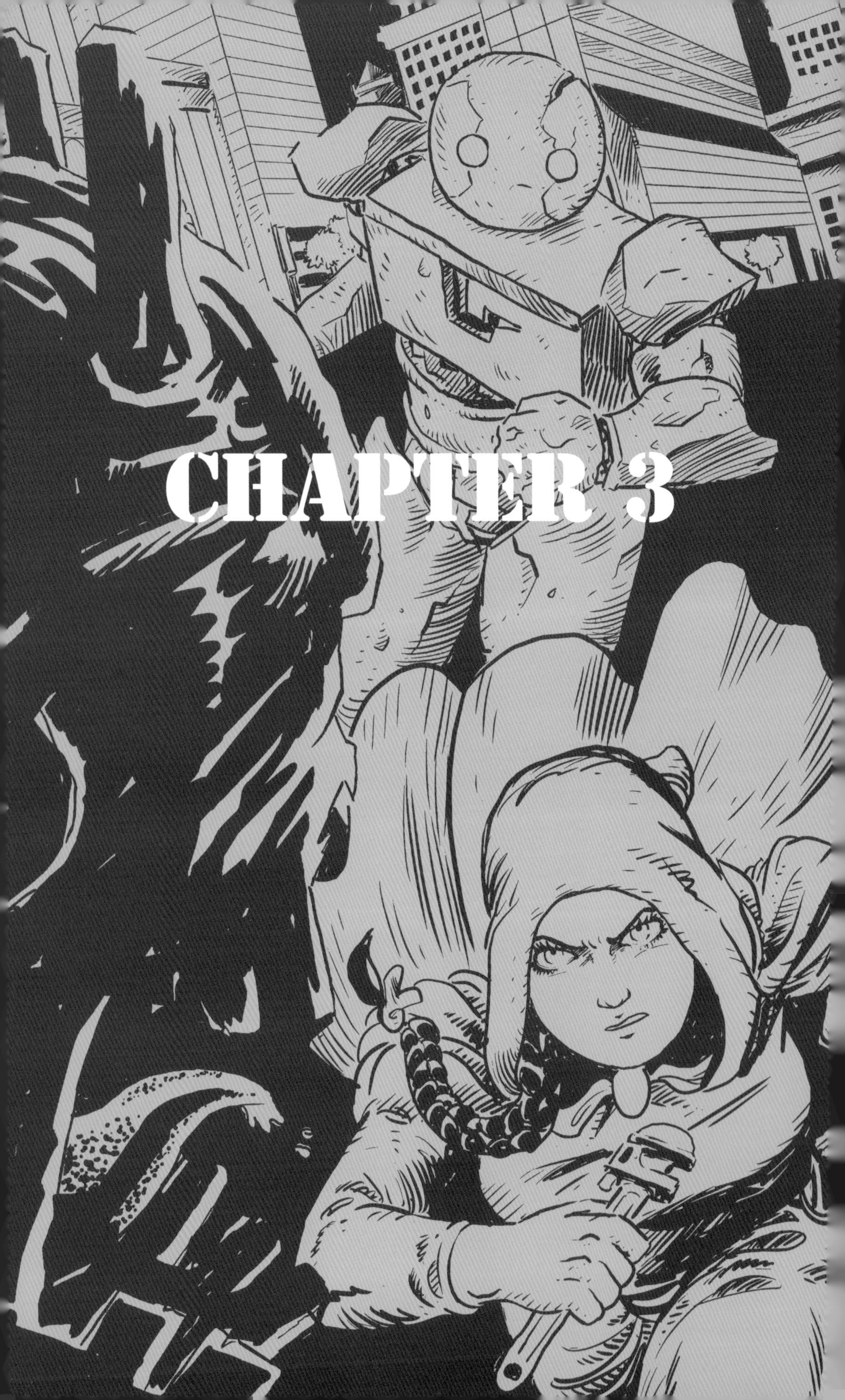

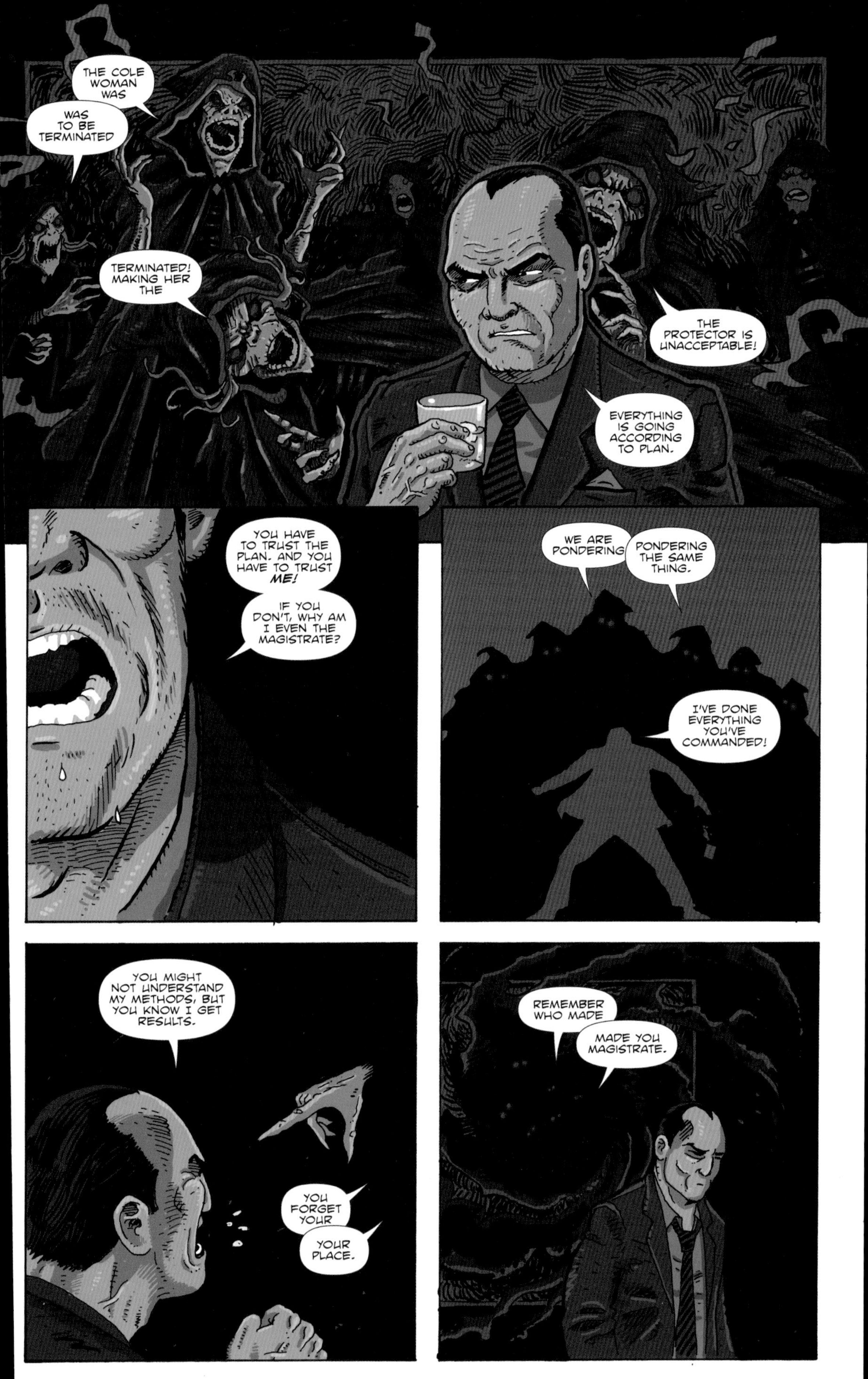
THE COLE WOMAN WAS
WAS TO BE TERMINATED
TERMINATED! MAKING HER THE
THE PROTECTOR IS UNACCEPTABLE!
EVERYTHING IS GOING ACCORDING TO PLAN.
YOU HAVE TO TRUST THE PLAN. AND YOU HAVE TO TRUST ME!
IF YOU DON'T, WHY AM I EVEN THE MAGISTRATE?
WE ARE PONDERING
PONDERING THE SAME THING.
I'VE DONE EVERYTHING YOU'VE COMMANDED!
YOU MIGHT NOT UNDERSTAND MY METHODS, BUT YOU KNOW I GET RESULTS.
YOU FORGET YOUR
YOUR PLACE.
REMEMBER WHO MADE
MADE YOU MAGISTRATE.

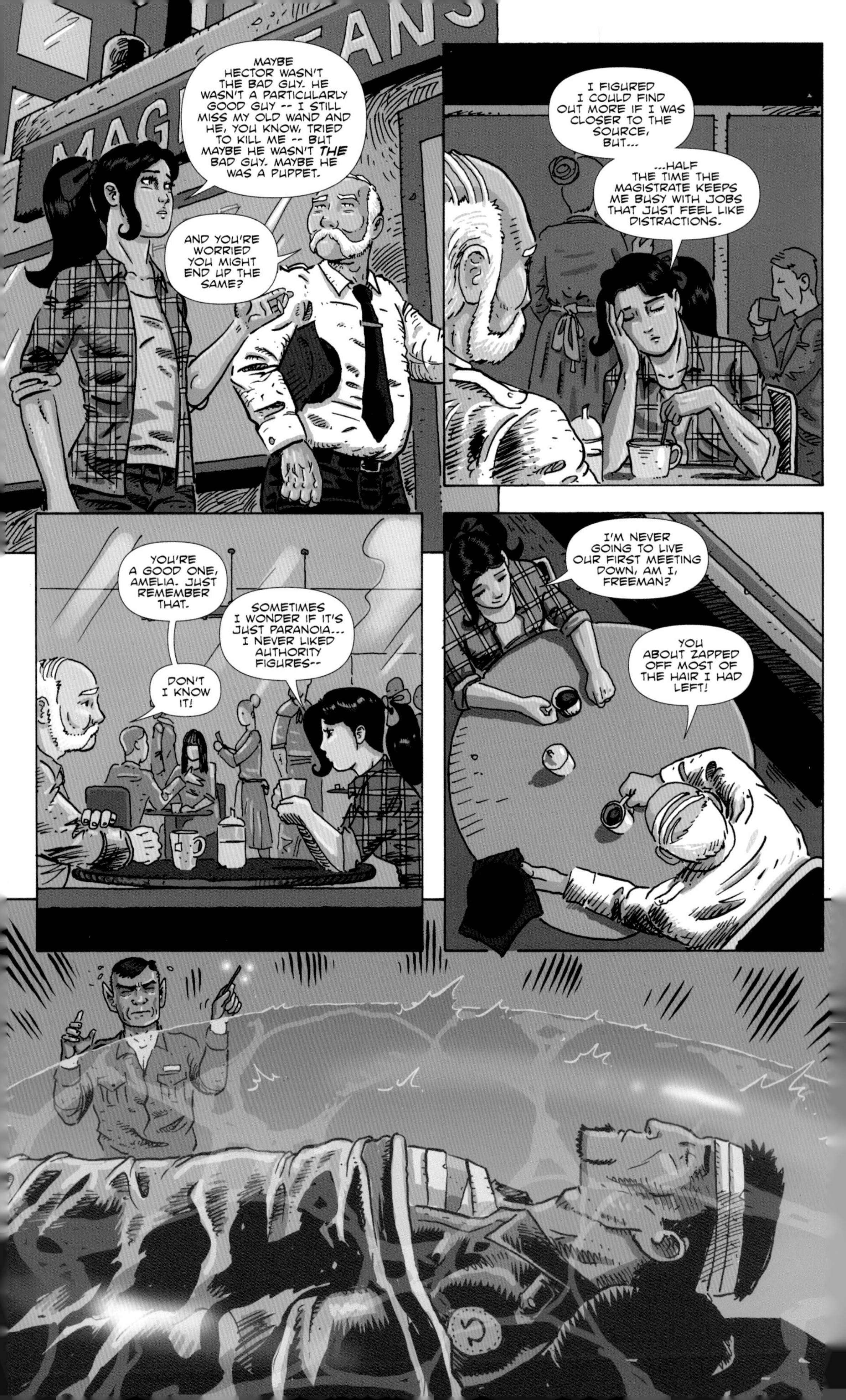
MAGI... EANS
MAYBE HECTOR WASN'T THE BAD GUY. HE WASN'T A PARTICULARLY GOOD GUY -- I STILL MISS MY OLD WAND AND HE, YOU KNOW, TRIED TO KILL ME -- BUT MAYBE HE WASN'T THE BAD GUY. MAYBE HE WAS A PUPPET.
AND YOU'RE WORRIED YOU MIGHT END UP THE SAME?
I FIGURED I COULD FIND OUT MORE IF I WAS CLOSER TO THE SOURCE, BUT...
...HALF THE TIME THE MAGISTRATE KEEPS ME BUSY WITH JOBS THAT JUST FEEL LIKE DISTRACTIONS.
SOMETIMES I WONDER IF IT'S JUST PARANOIA... I NEVER LIKED AUTHORITY FIGURES--
DON'T I KNOW IT!
YOU'RE A GOOD ONE, AMELIA. JUST REMEMBER THAT.
I'M NEVER GOING TO LIVE OUR FIRST MEETING DOWN, AM I, FREEMAN?
YOU ABOUT ZAPPED OFF MOST OF THE HAIR I HAD LEFT!

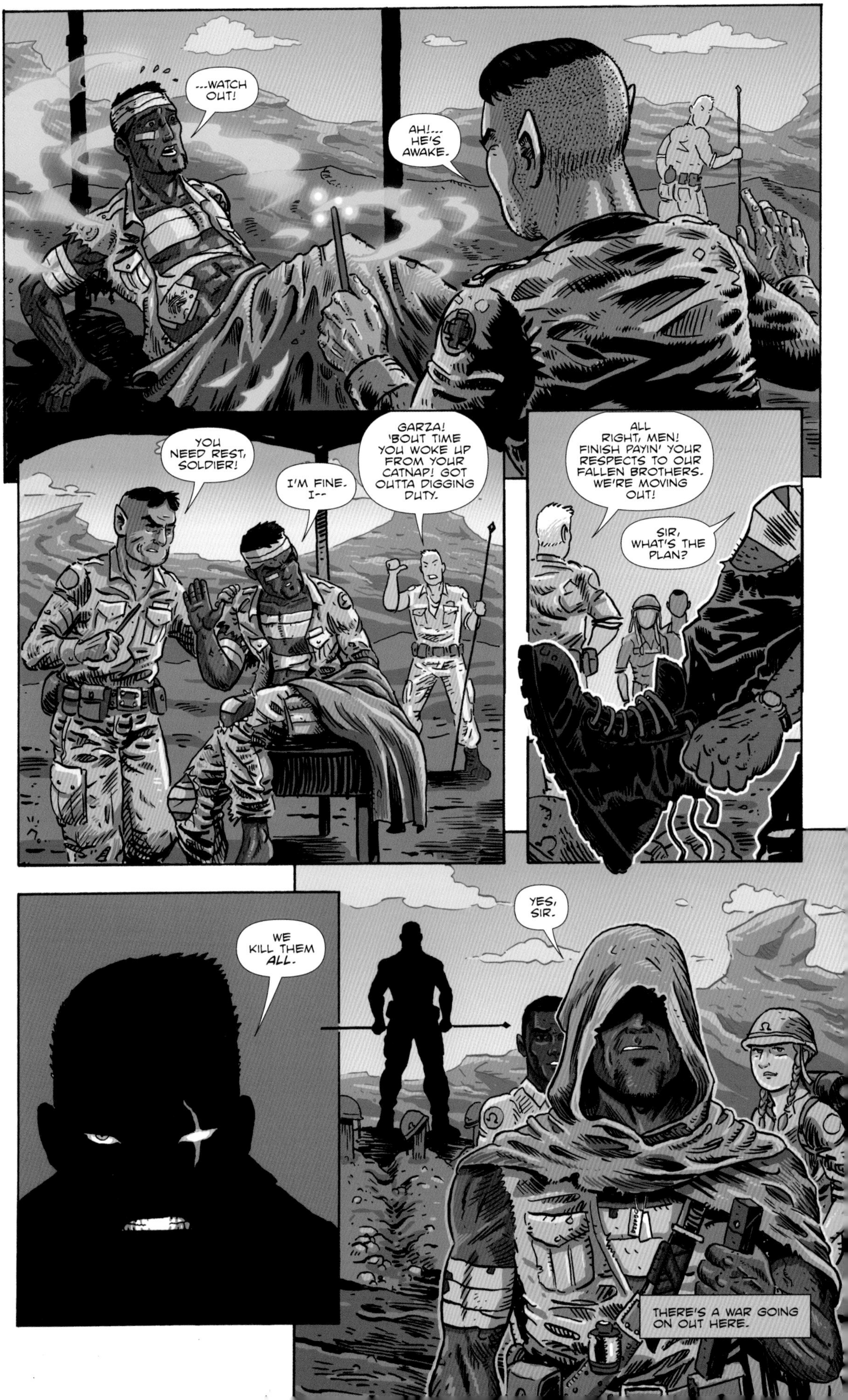
---WATCH OUT!
AH!--- HE'S AWAKE.
YOU NEED REST, SOLDIER!
I'M FINE. I--
GARZA! 'BOUT TIME YOU WOKE UP FROM YOUR CATNAP! GOT OUTTA DIGGING DUTY.
ALL RIGHT, MEN! FINISH PAYIN' YOUR RESPECTS TO OUR FALLEN BROTHERS. WE'RE MOVING OUT!
SIR, WHAT'S THE PLAN?
WE KILL THEM ALL.
YES, SIR.
THERE'S A WAR GOING ON OUT HERE.

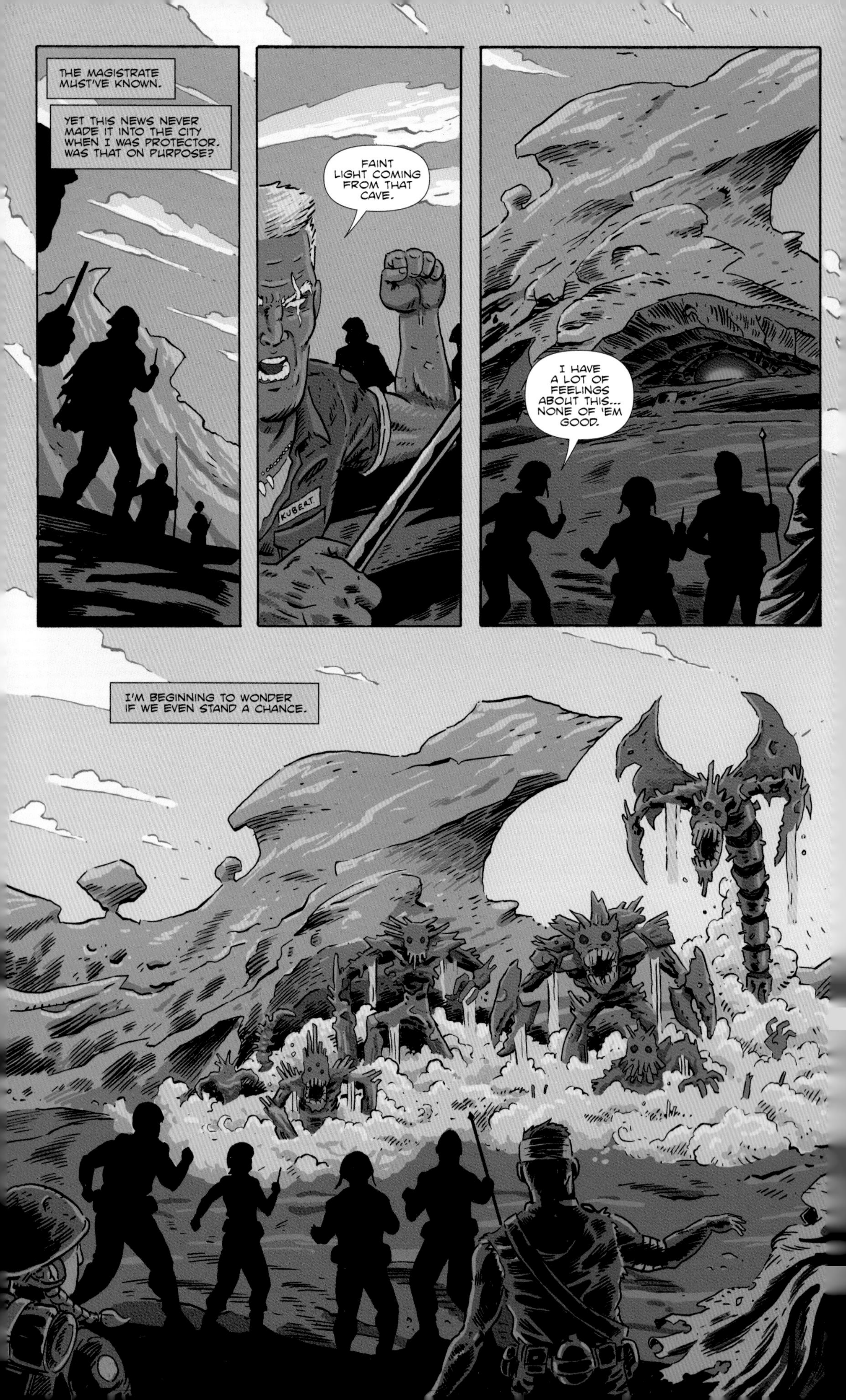
THE MAGISTRATE MUST'VE KNOWN.
YET THIS NEWS NEVER MADE IT INTO THE CITY WHEN I WAS PROTECTOR. WAS THAT ON PURPOSE?
FAINT LIGHT COMING FROM THAT CAVE.
KUBERT.
I HAVE A LOT OF FEELINGS ABOUT THIS... NONE OF 'EM GOOD.
I'M BEGINNING TO WONDER IF WE EVEN STAND A CHANCE.

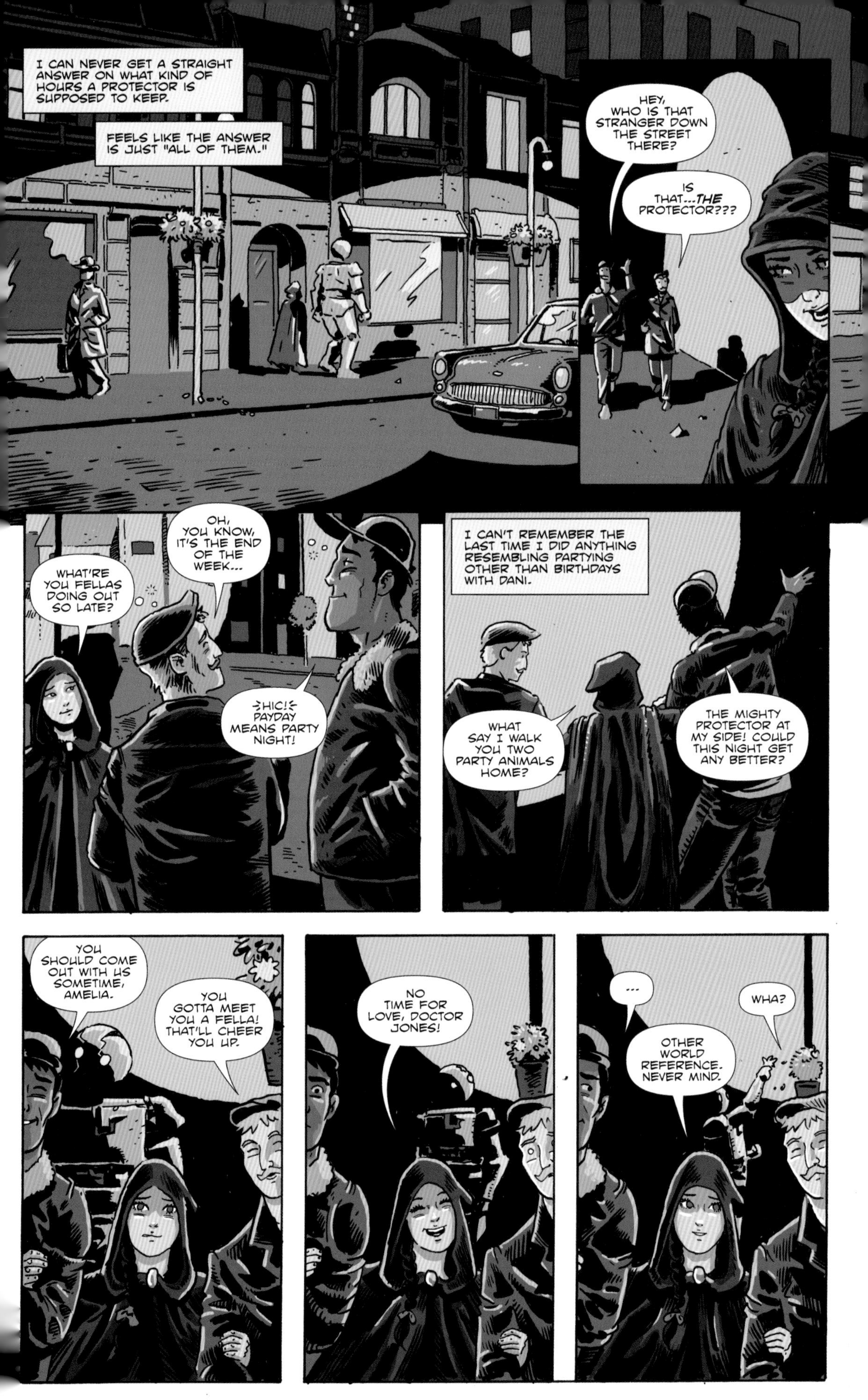
I CAN NEVER GET A STRAIGHT ANSWER ON WHAT KIND OF HOURS A PROTECTOR IS SUPPOSED TO KEEP.
FEELS LIKE THE ANSWER IS JUST "ALL OF THEM."
HEY, WHO IS THAT STRANGER DOWN THE STREET THERE?
IS THAT...THE PROTECTOR???
WHAT'RE YOU FELLAS DOING OUT SO LATE?
OH, YOU KNOW, IT'S THE END OF THE WEEK...
HIC! PAYDAY MEANS PARTY NIGHT!
I CAN'T REMEMBER THE LAST TIME I DID ANYTHING RESEMBLING PARTYING OTHER THAN BIRTHDAYS WITH DANI.
WHAT SAY I WALK YOU TWO PARTY ANIMALS HOME?
THE MIGHTY PROTECTOR AT MY SIDE! COULD THIS NIGHT GET ANY BETTER?
YOU SHOULD COME OUT WITH US SOMETIME, AMELIA.
YOU GOTTA MEET YOU A FELLA! THAT'LL CHEER YOU UP.
NO TIME FOR LOVE, DOCTOR JONES!
...
WHA?
OTHER WORLD REFERENCE. NEVER MIND.

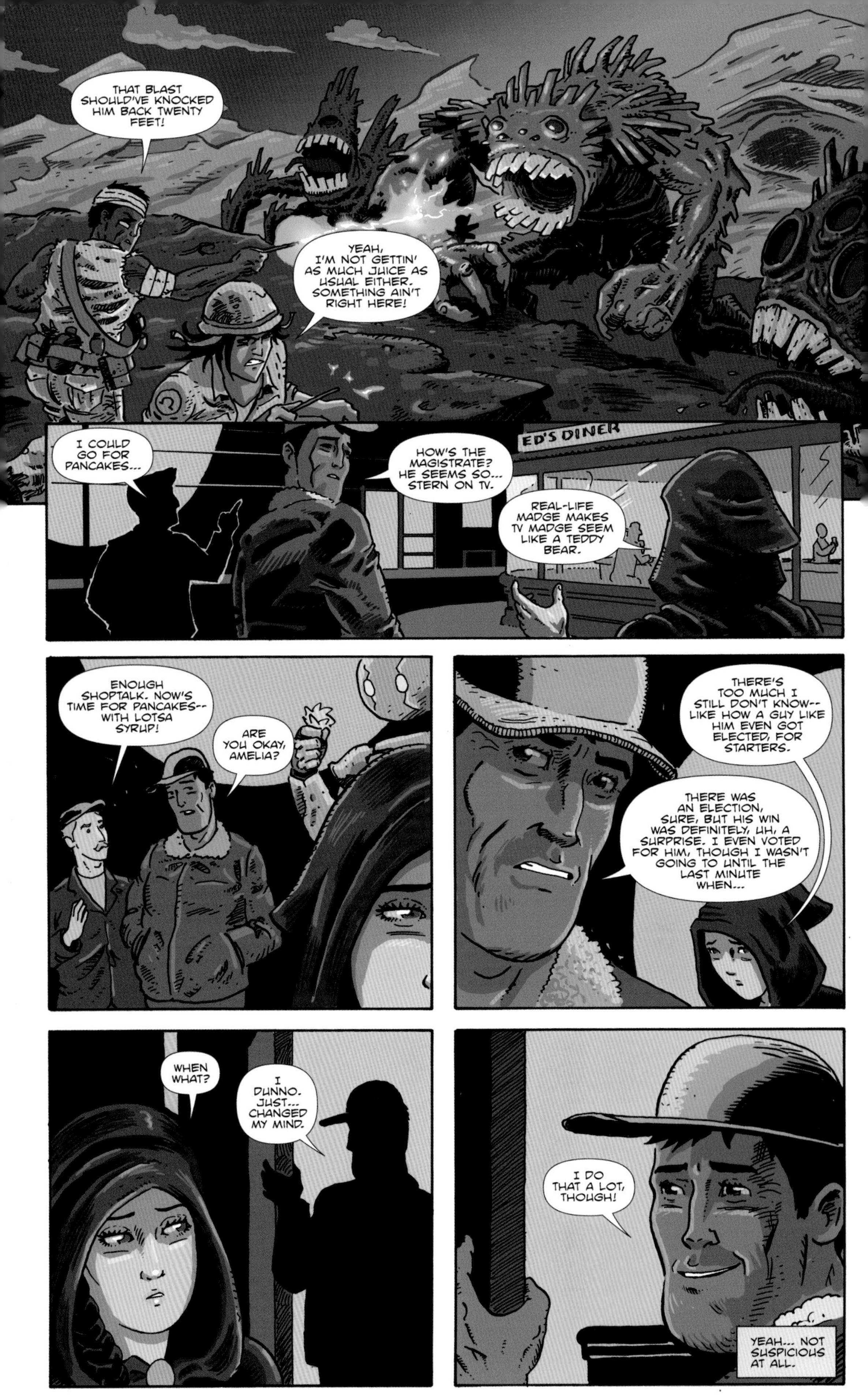
THAT BLAST SHOULD'VE KNOCKED HIM BACK TWENTY FEET!
YEAH, I'M NOT GETTIN' AS MUCH JUICE AS USUAL EITHER. SOMETHING AIN'T RIGHT HERE!
ED'S DINER
I COULD GO FOR PANCAKES...
HOW'S THE MAGISTRATE? HE SEEMS SO... STERN ON TV.
REAL-LIFE MADGE MAKES TV MADGE SEEM LIKE A TEDDY BEAR.
ENOUGH SHOPTALK. NOW'S TIME FOR PANCAKES--WITH LOTSA SYRUP!
ARE YOU OKAY, AMELIA?
THERE'S TOO MUCH I STILL DON'T KNOW--LIKE HOW A GUY LIKE HIM EVEN GOT ELECTED, FOR STARTERS.
THERE WAS AN ELECTION, SURE, BUT HIS WIN WAS DEFINITELY, UH, A SURPRISE. I EVEN VOTED FOR HIM, THOUGH I WASN'T GOING TO UNTIL THE LAST MINUTE WHEN...
WHEN WHAT?
I DUNNO. JUST... CHANGED MY MIND.
I DO THAT A LOT, THOUGH!
YEAH... NOT SUSPICIOUS AT ALL.

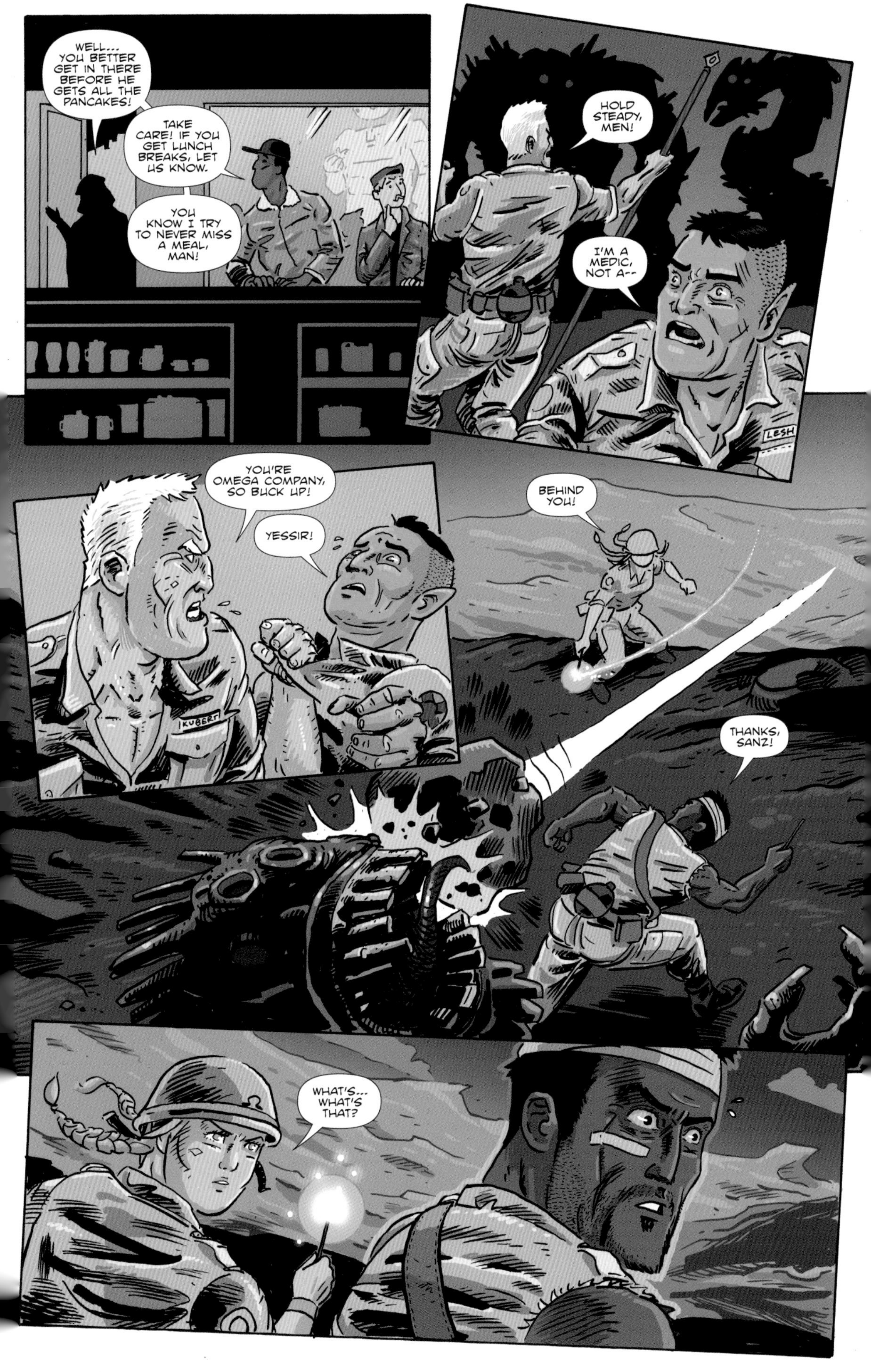
WELL... YOU BETTER GET IN THERE BEFORE HE GETS ALL THE PANCAKES!
TAKE CARE! IF YOU GET LUNCH BREAKS, LET US KNOW.
YOU KNOW I TRY TO NEVER MISS A MEAL, MAN!
HOLD STEADY, MEN!
I'M A MEDIC, NOT A--
LESH
YOU'RE OMEGA COMPANY, SO BUCK UP!
YESSIR!
KUBERT
BEHIND YOU!
THANKS, SANZ!
WHAT'S... WHAT'S THAT?

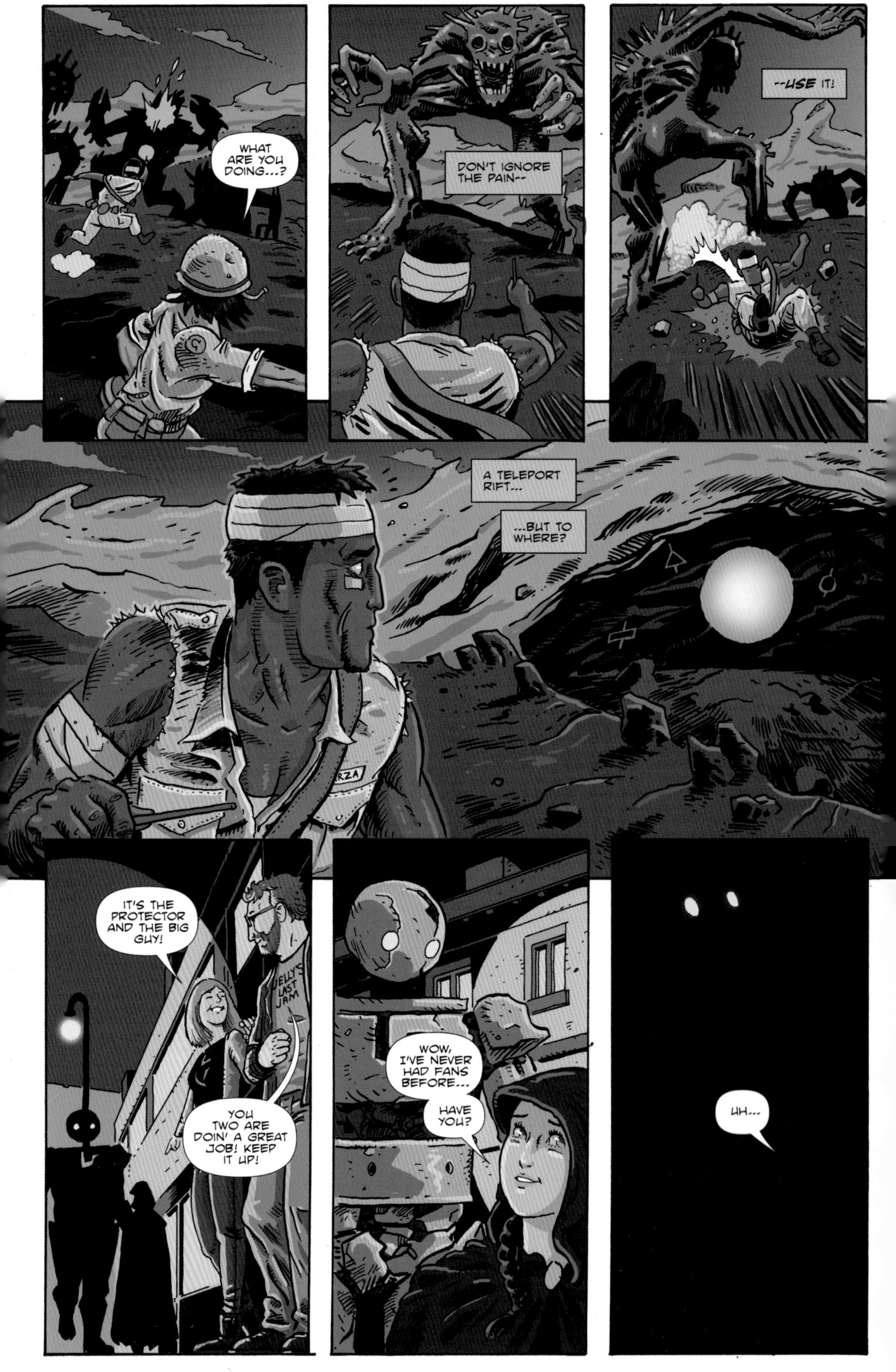
WHAT ARE YOU DOING...?
DON'T IGNORE THE PAIN--
--USE IT!
A TELEPORT RIFT...
...BUT TO WHERE?
IT'S THE PROTECTOR AND THE BIG GUY!
YOU TWO ARE DOIN' A GREAT JOB! KEEP IT UP!
WOW, I'VE NEVER HAD FANS BEFORE...
HAVE YOU?
UH...

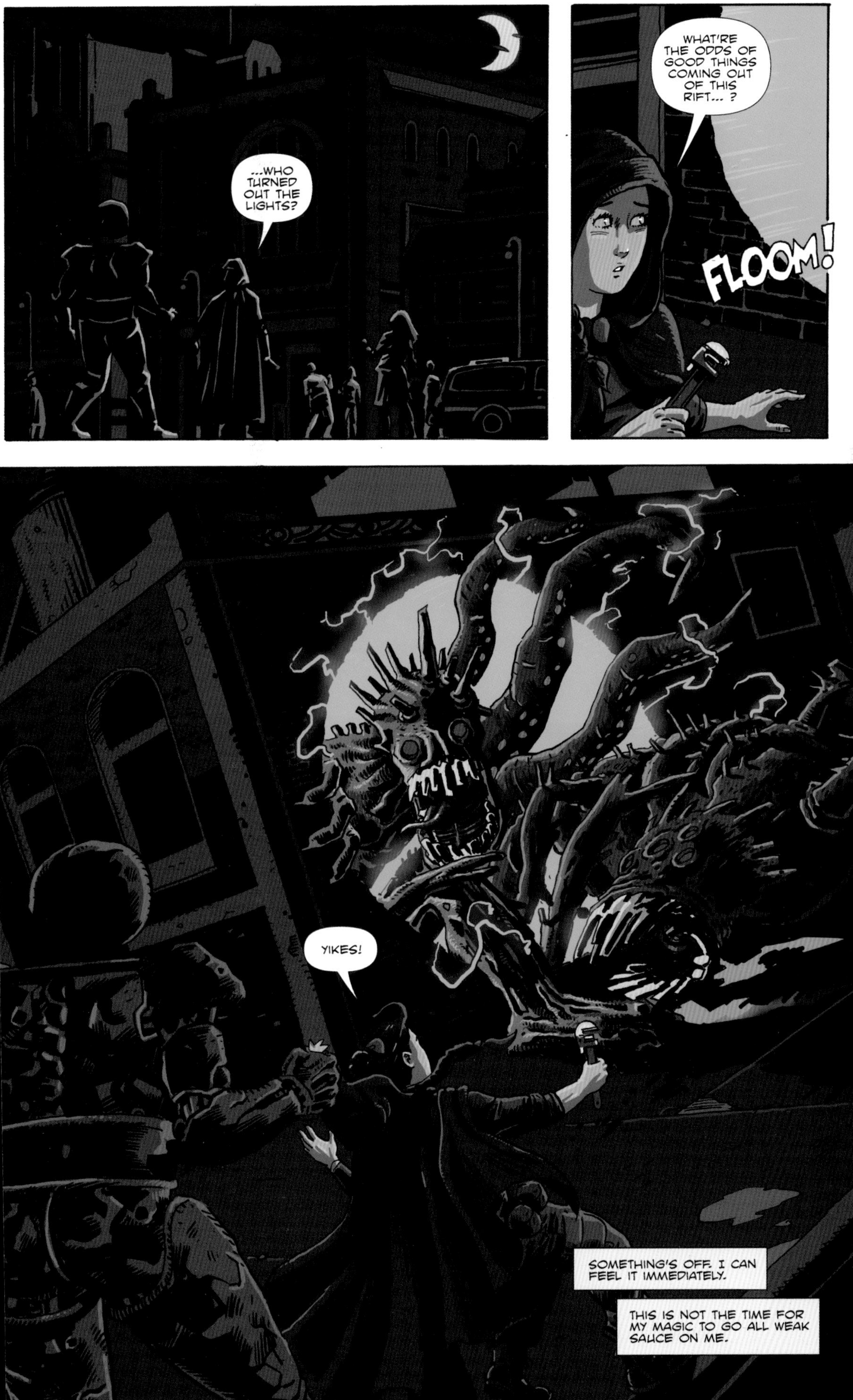
...WHO TURNED OUT THE LIGHTS?
WHAT'RE THE ODDS OF GOOD THINGS COMING OUT OF THIS RIFT... ?
FLOOM!
YIKES!
SOMETHING'S OFF. I CAN FEEL IT IMMEDIATELY.
THIS IS NOT THE TIME FOR MY MAGIC TO GO ALL WEAK SAUCE ON ME.

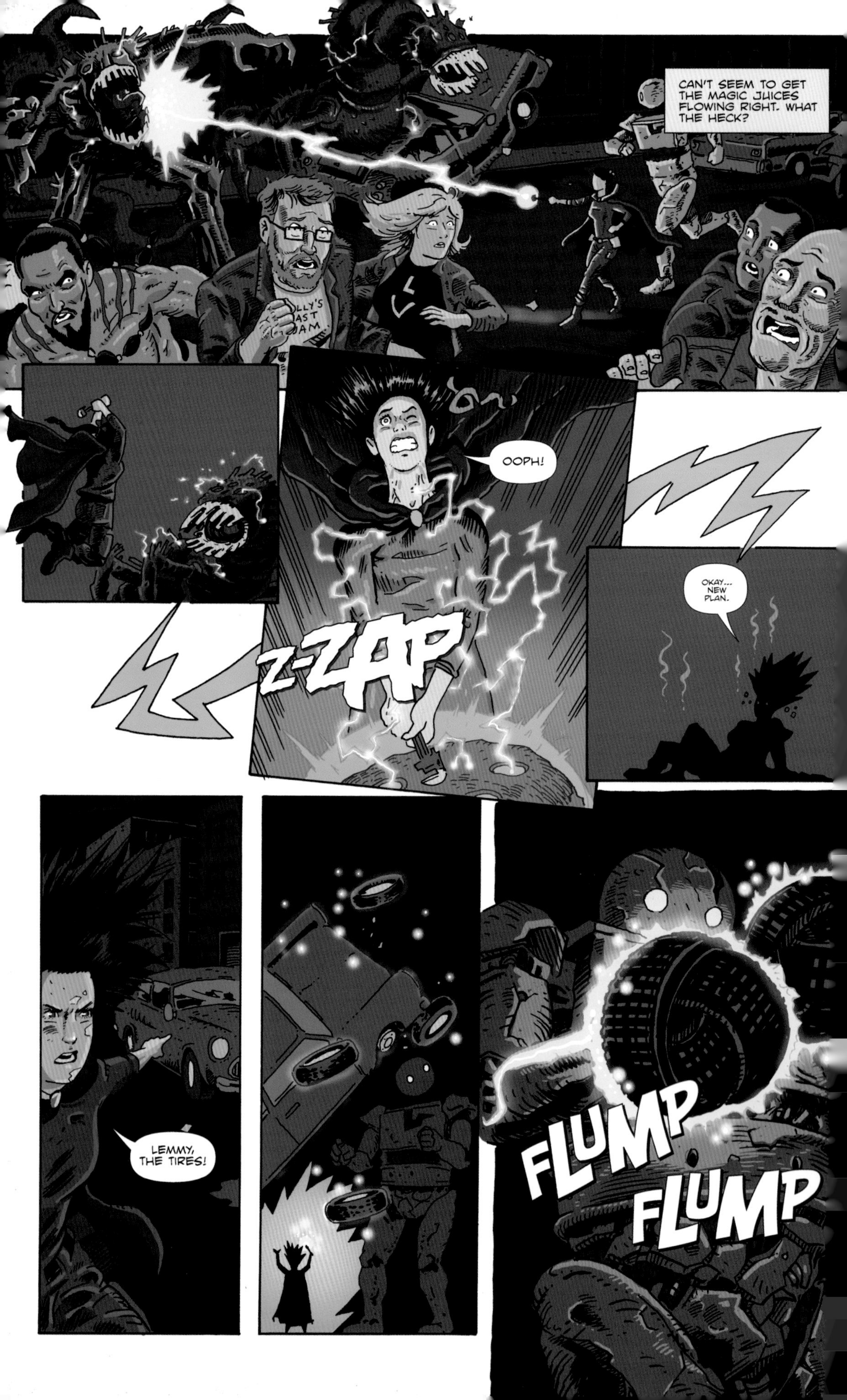
CAN'T SEEM TO GET THE MAGIC JUICES FLOWING RIGHT. WHAT THE HECK?
OOPH!
Z-ZAP
OKAY... NEW PLAN.
LEMMY, THE TIRES!
FLUMP
FLUMP

GET YOUR PUNCH ON, LEMMY!
KA-POW
GOTTA SEND THEM BACK THROUGH BEFORE IT CLOSES...
THINK, AMELIA, THINK!
OKAY, THEIR ENERGY FEELS ELECTRICAL... SO...MAGIC LIGHTNING RODS!
TWICE THE EFFORT FOR HALF THE RESULTS.
THEY'RE ABSORBING MY MAGIC. MUST BE. BUT HOW?
THIS SHOULD WORK... MAYBE DRAIN THEM IN THE PROCESS!
LEMMY! KNOCK 'EM TOWARD THE PORTAL!
I KNOW YOU'RE FEELING WEAKER, TOO...
...BUT YOU CAN DO IT, BIG GUY!

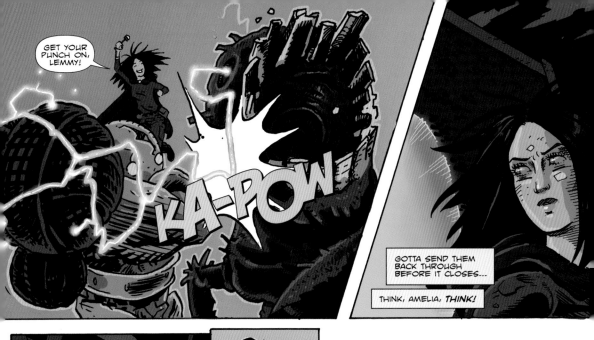

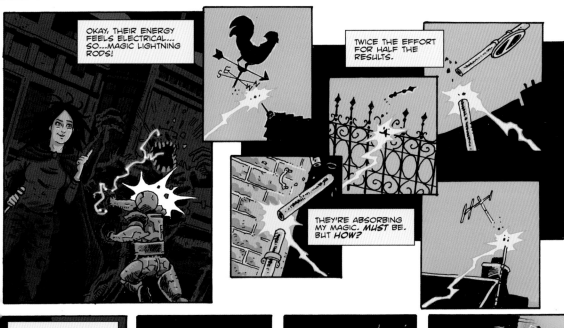

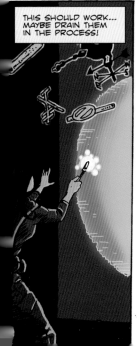

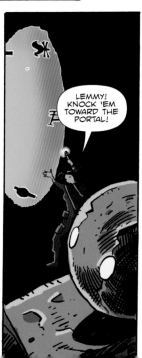

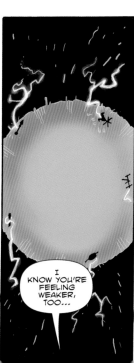

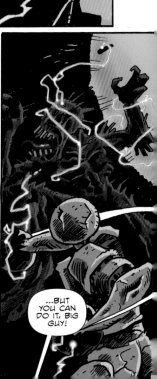

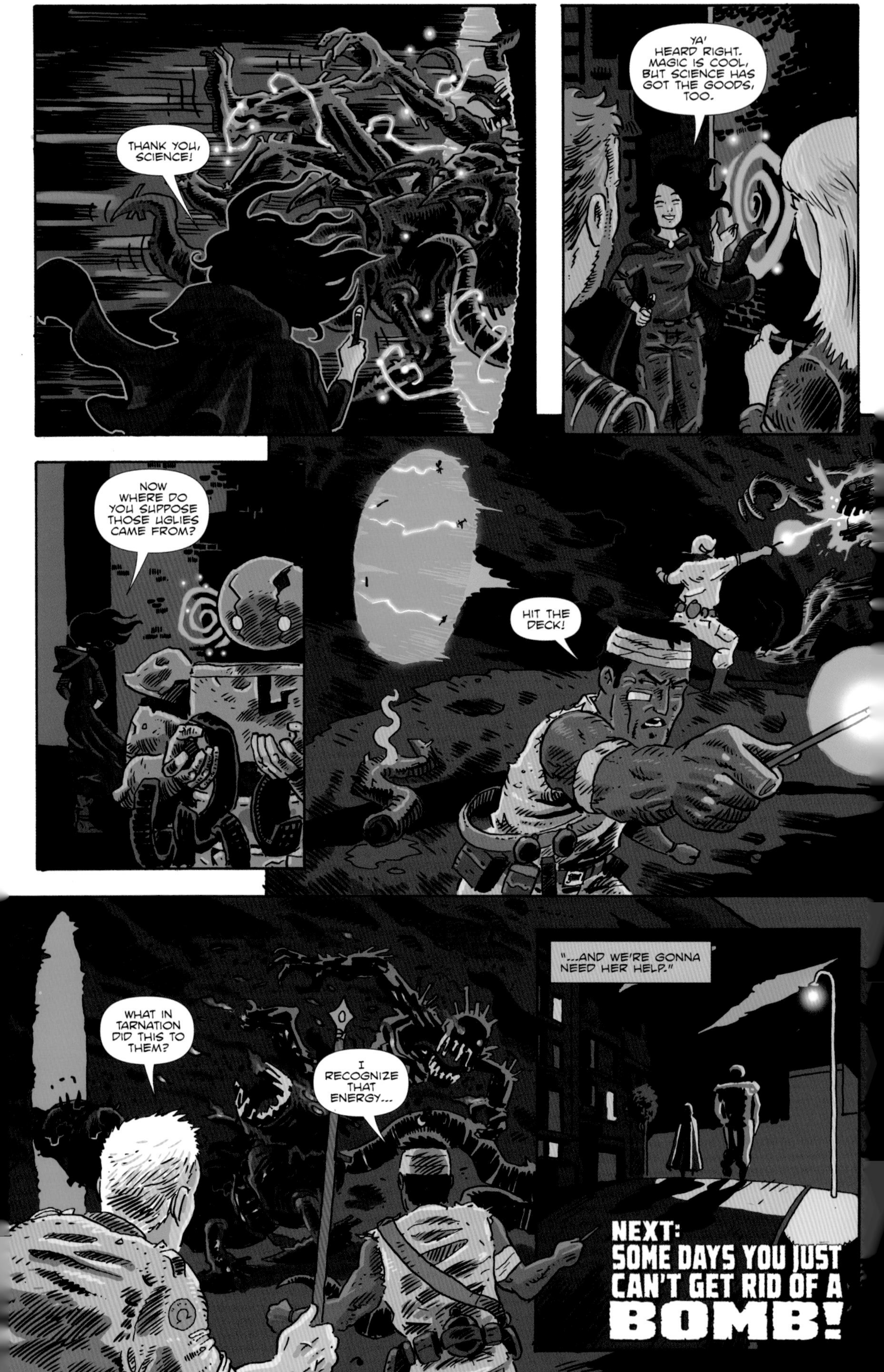
THANK YOU, SCIENCE!
YA' HEARD RIGHT. MAGIC IS COOL, BUT SCIENCE HAS GOT THE GOODS, TOO.
NOW WHERE DO YOU SUPPOSE THOSE UGLIES CAME FROM?
HIT THE DECK!
WHAT IN TARNATION DID THIS TO THEM?
I RECOGNIZE THAT ENERGY...
"...AND WE'RE GONNA NEED HER HELP."
NEXT:
SOME DAYS YOU JUST CAN'T GET RID OF A
BOMB!

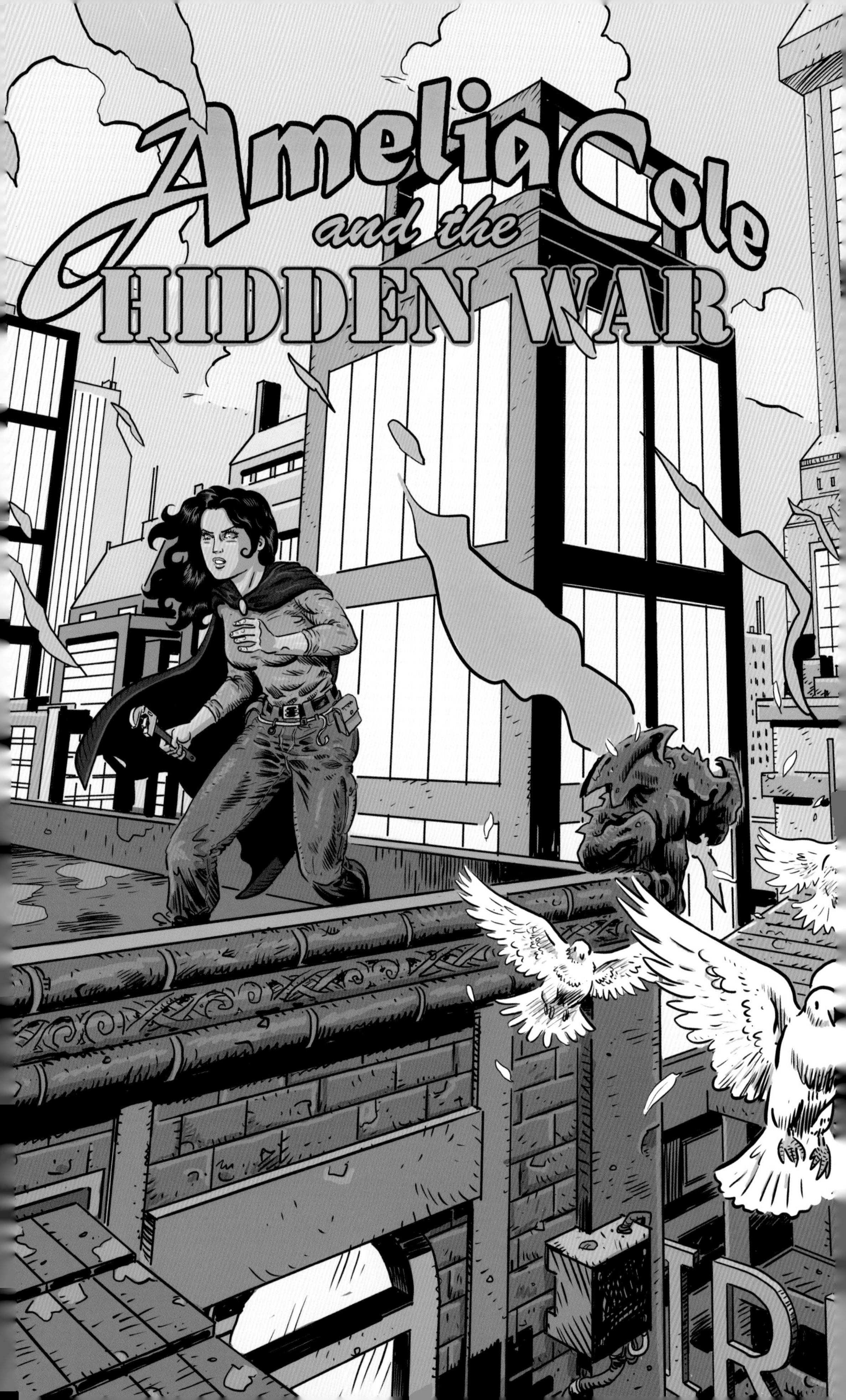
Amelia Cole
and the
HIDDEN WAR

CHAPTER 4

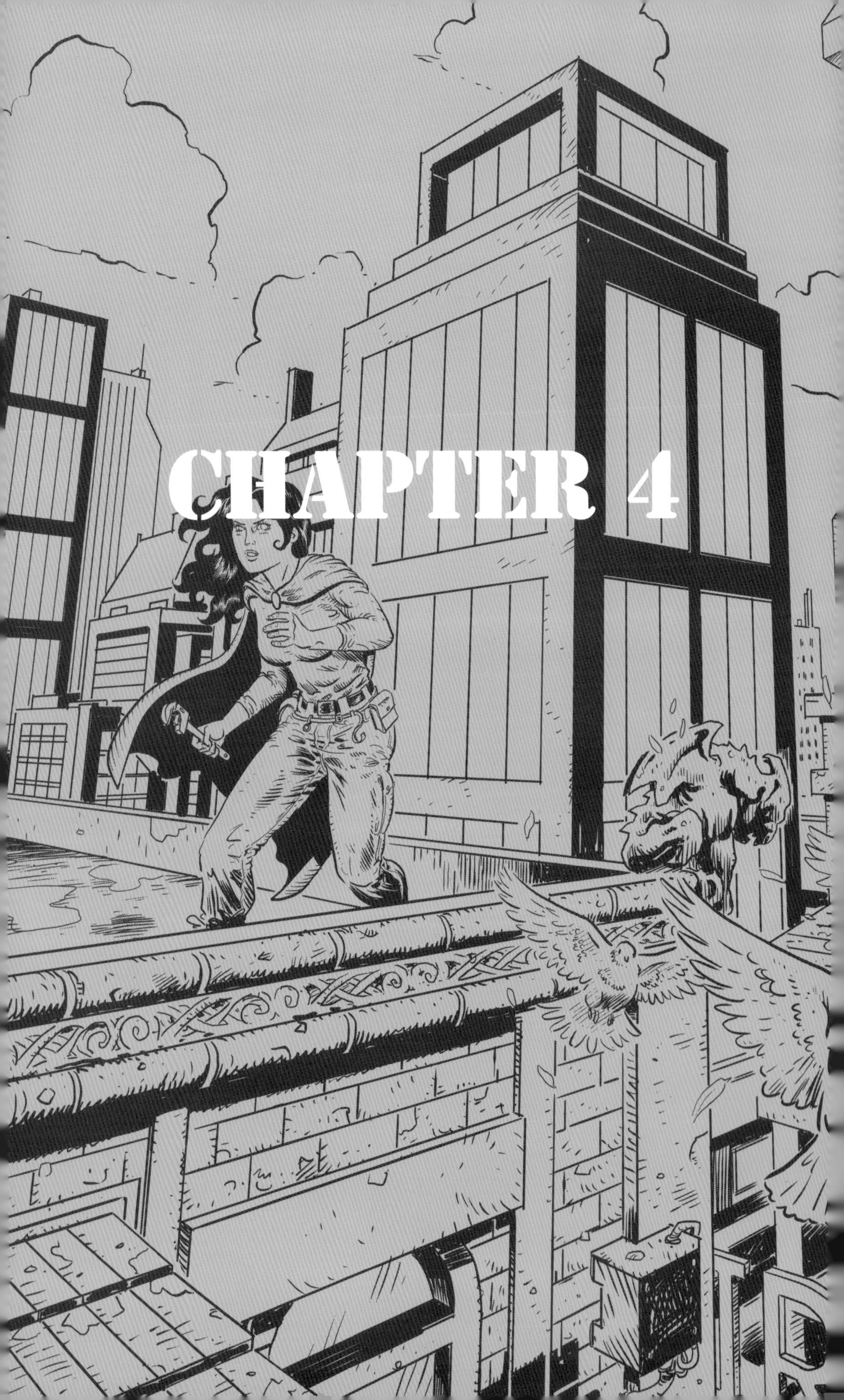

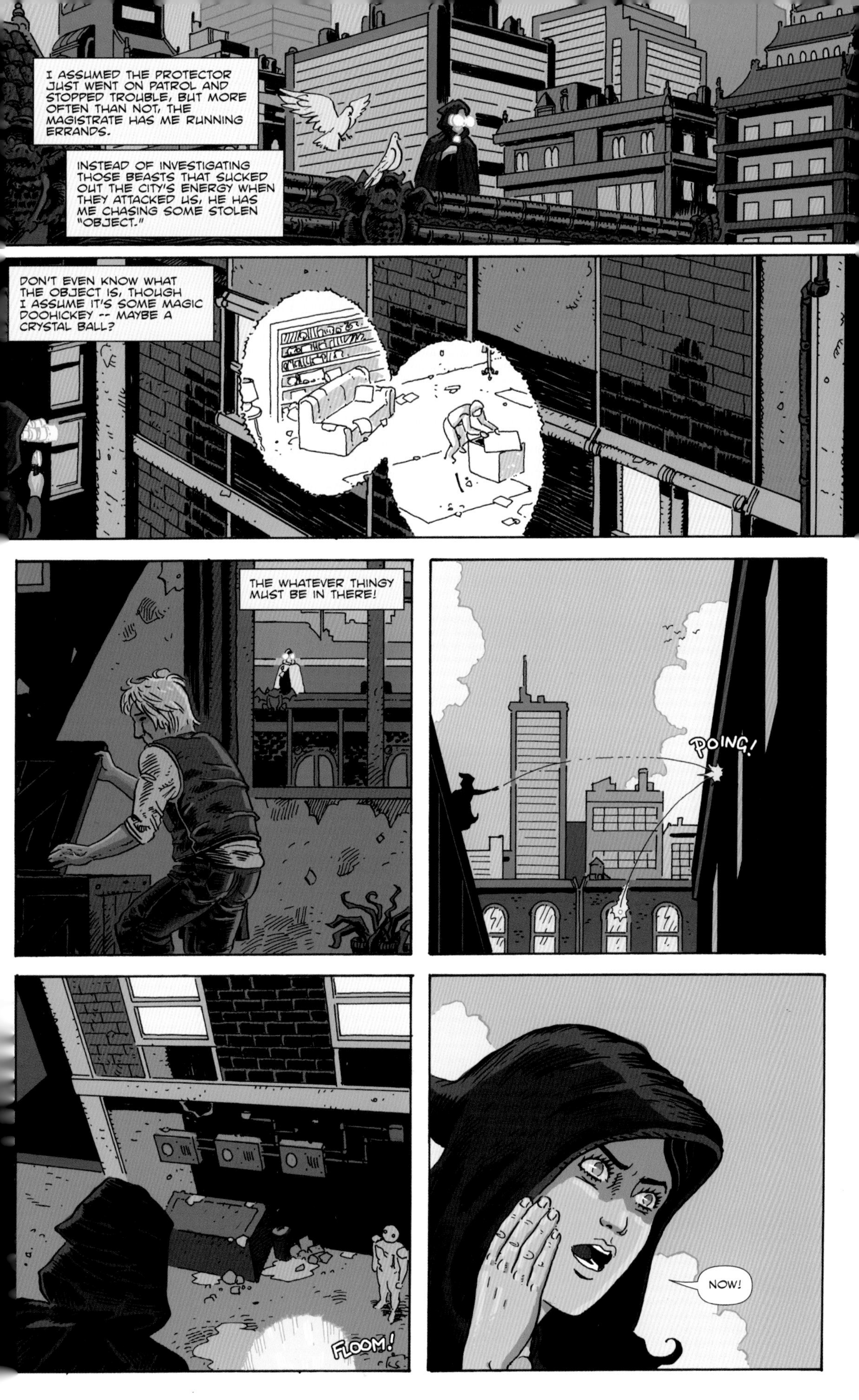
I ASSUMED THE PROTECTOR JUST WENT ON PATROL AND STOPPED TROUBLE, BUT MORE OFTEN THAN NOT, THE MAGISTRATE HAS ME RUNNING ERRANDS.
INSTEAD OF INVESTIGATING THOSE BEASTS THAT SUCKED OUT THE CITY'S ENERGY WHEN THEY ATTACKED US, HE HAS ME CHASING SOME STOLEN "OBJECT."
DON'T EVEN KNOW WHAT THE OBJECT IS, THOUGH I ASSUME IT'S SOME MAGIC DOOHICKEY -- MAYBE A CRYSTAL BALL?
THE WHATEVER THINGY MUST BE IN THERE!
POING!
FLOOM!
NOW!

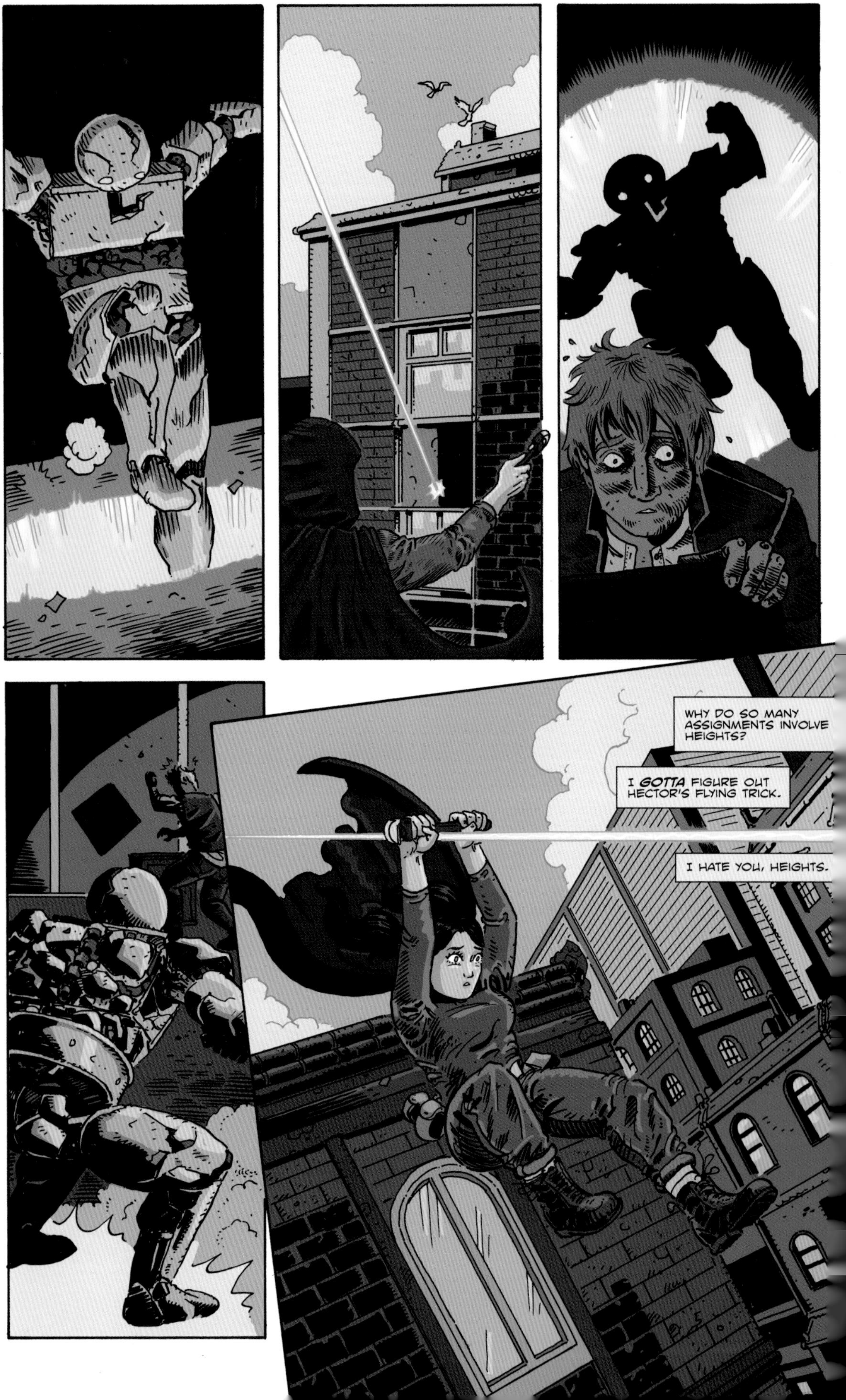
WHY DO SO MANY ASSIGNMENTS INVOLVE HEIGHTS?
I GOTTA FIGURE OUT HECTOR'S FLYING TRICK.
I HATE YOU, HEIGHTS.

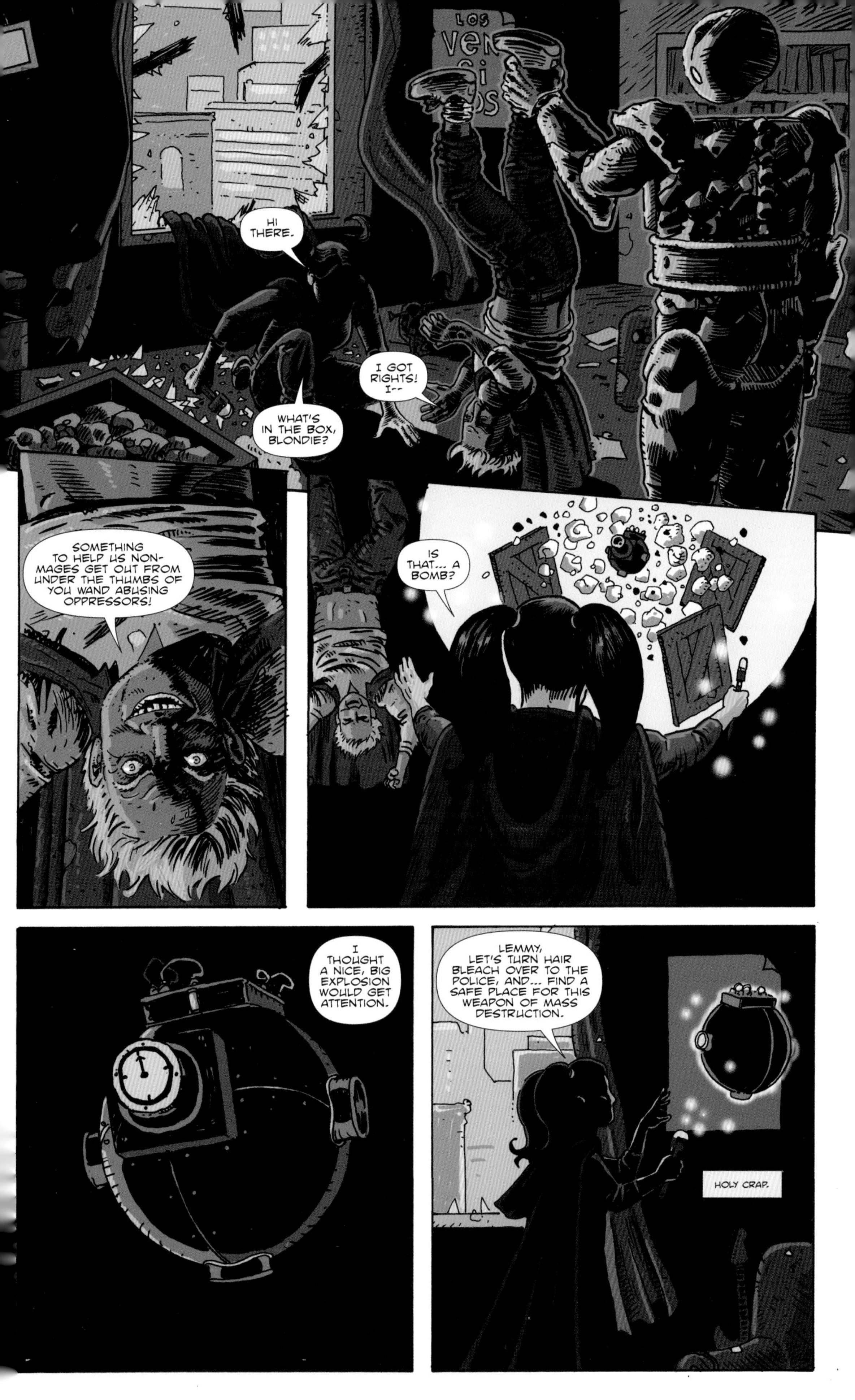
LOS VEN GI OS
HI THERE.
WHAT'S IN THE BOX, BLONDIE?
I GOT RIGHTS! I--
SOMETHING TO HELP US NON-MAGES GET OUT FROM UNDER THE THUMBS OF YOU WAND ABUSING OPPRESSORS!
IS THAT... A BOMB?
I THOUGHT A NICE, BIG EXPLOSION WOULD GET ATTENTION.
LEMMY, LET'S TURN HAIR BLEACH OVER TO THE POLICE, AND... FIND A SAFE PLACE FOR THIS WEAPON OF MASS DESTRUCTION.
HOLY CRAP.

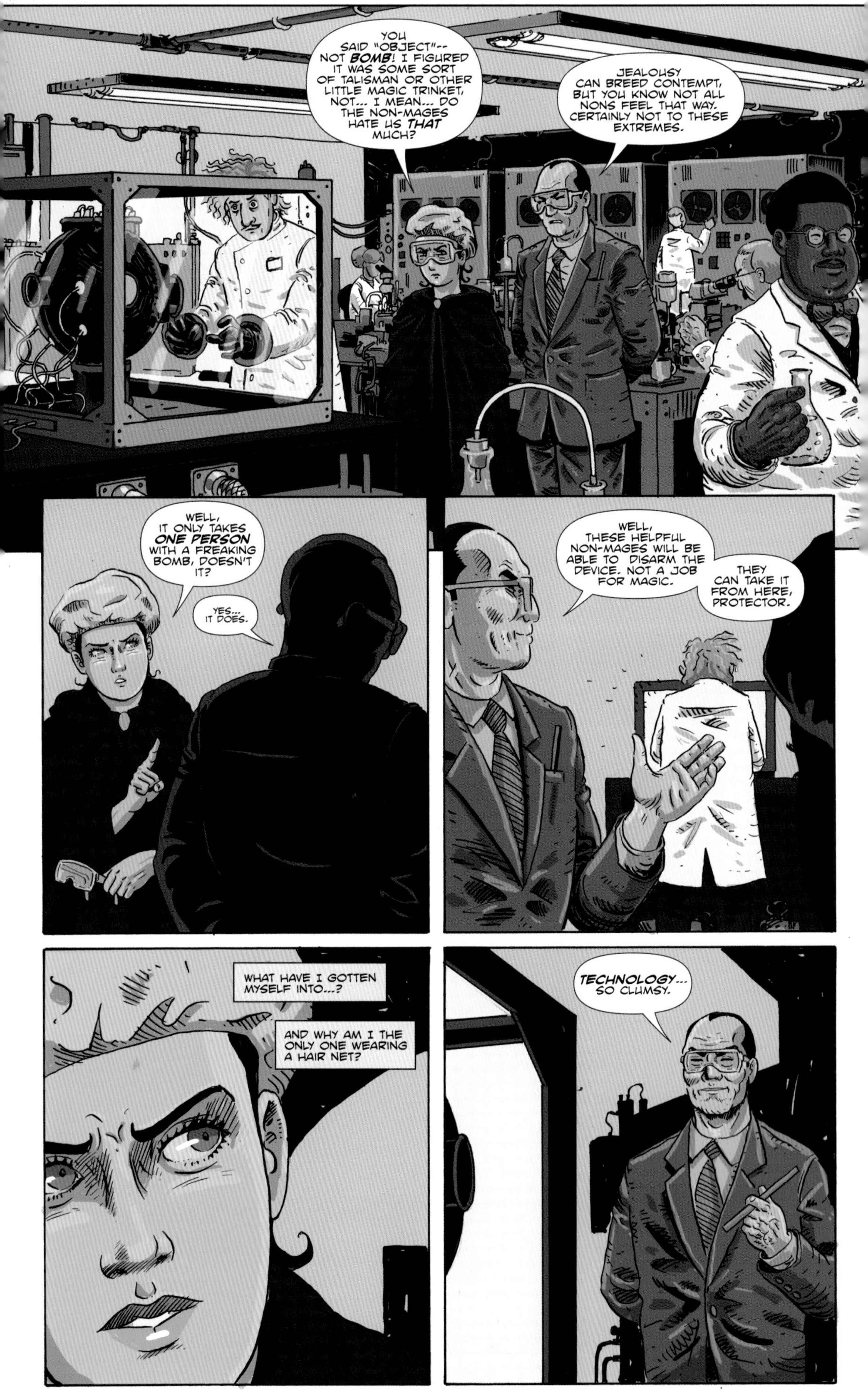
YOU SAID "OBJECT"-- NOT BOMB! I FIGURED IT WAS SOME SORT OF TALISMAN OR OTHER LITTLE MAGIC TRINKET, NOT... I MEAN... DO THE NON-MAGES HATE US THAT MUCH?
JEALOUSY CAN BREED CONTEMPT, BUT YOU KNOW NOT ALL NONS FEEL THAT WAY. CERTAINLY NOT TO THESE EXTREMES.
WELL, IT ONLY TAKES ONE PERSON WITH A FREAKING BOMB, DOESN'T IT?
YES... IT DOES.
WELL, THESE HELPFUL NON-MAGES WILL BE ABLE TO DISARM THE DEVICE. NOT A JOB FOR MAGIC.
THEY CAN TAKE IT FROM HERE, PROTECTOR.
WHAT HAVE I GOTTEN MYSELF INTO...?
AND WHY AM I THE ONLY ONE WEARING A HAIR NET?
TECHNOLOGY... SO CLUMSY.

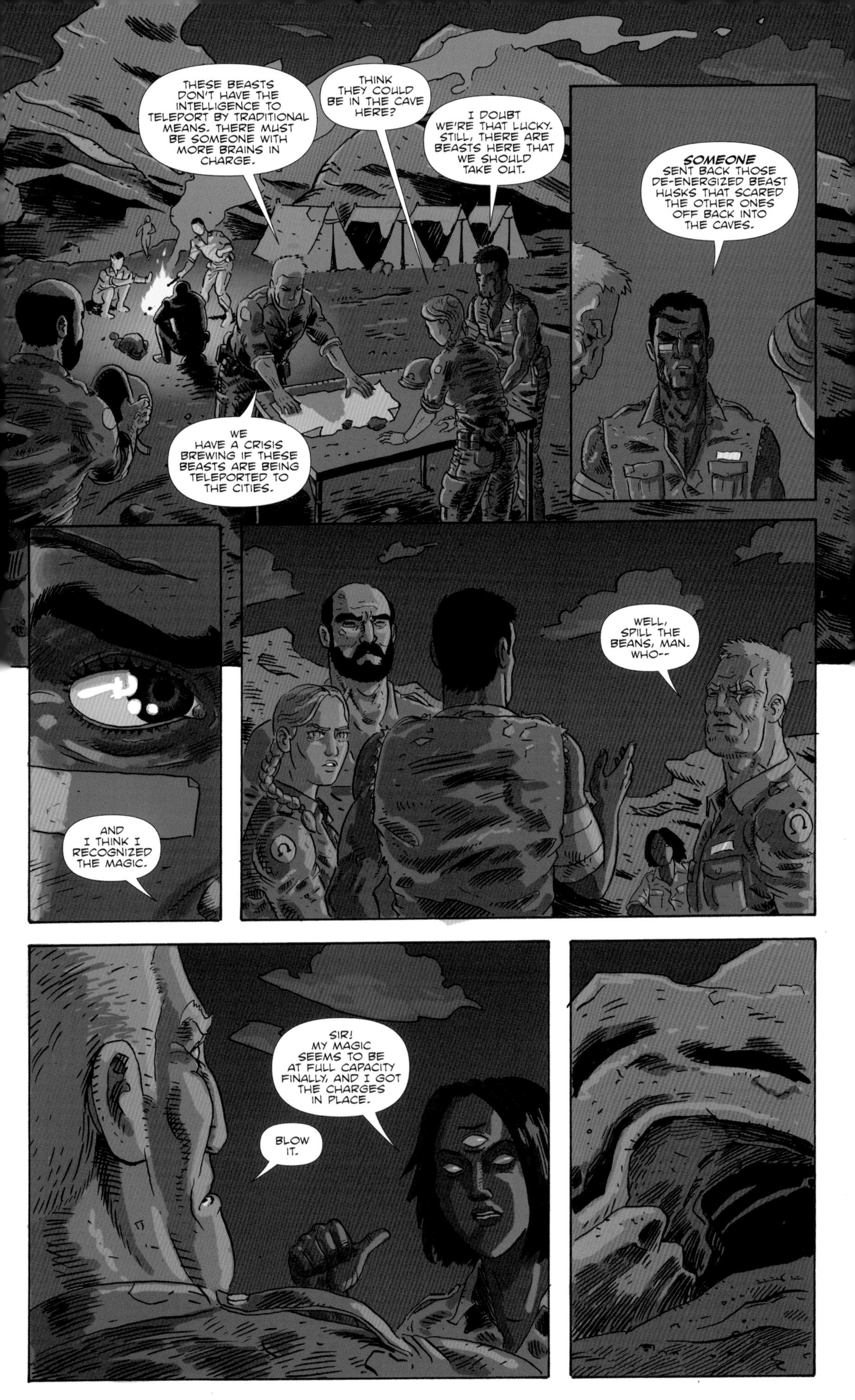
THESE BEASTS DON'T HAVE THE INTELLIGENCE TO TELEPORT BY TRADITIONAL MEANS. THERE MUST BE SOMEONE WITH MORE BRAINS IN CHARGE.
THINK THEY COULD BE IN THE CAVE HERE?
I DOUBT WE'RE THAT LUCKY. STILL, THERE ARE BEASTS HERE THAT WE SHOULD TAKE OUT.
WE HAVE A CRISIS BREWING IF THESE BEASTS ARE BEING TELEPORTED TO THE CITIES.
SOMEONE SENT BACK THOSE DE-ENERGIZED BEAST HUSKS THAT SCARED THE OTHER ONES OFF BACK INTO THE CAVES.
AND I THINK I RECOGNIZED THE MAGIC.
WELL, SPILL THE BEANS, MAN. WHO--
SIR! MY MAGIC SEEMS TO BE AT FULL CAPACITY FINALLY, AND I GOT THE CHARGES IN PLACE.
BLOW IT.

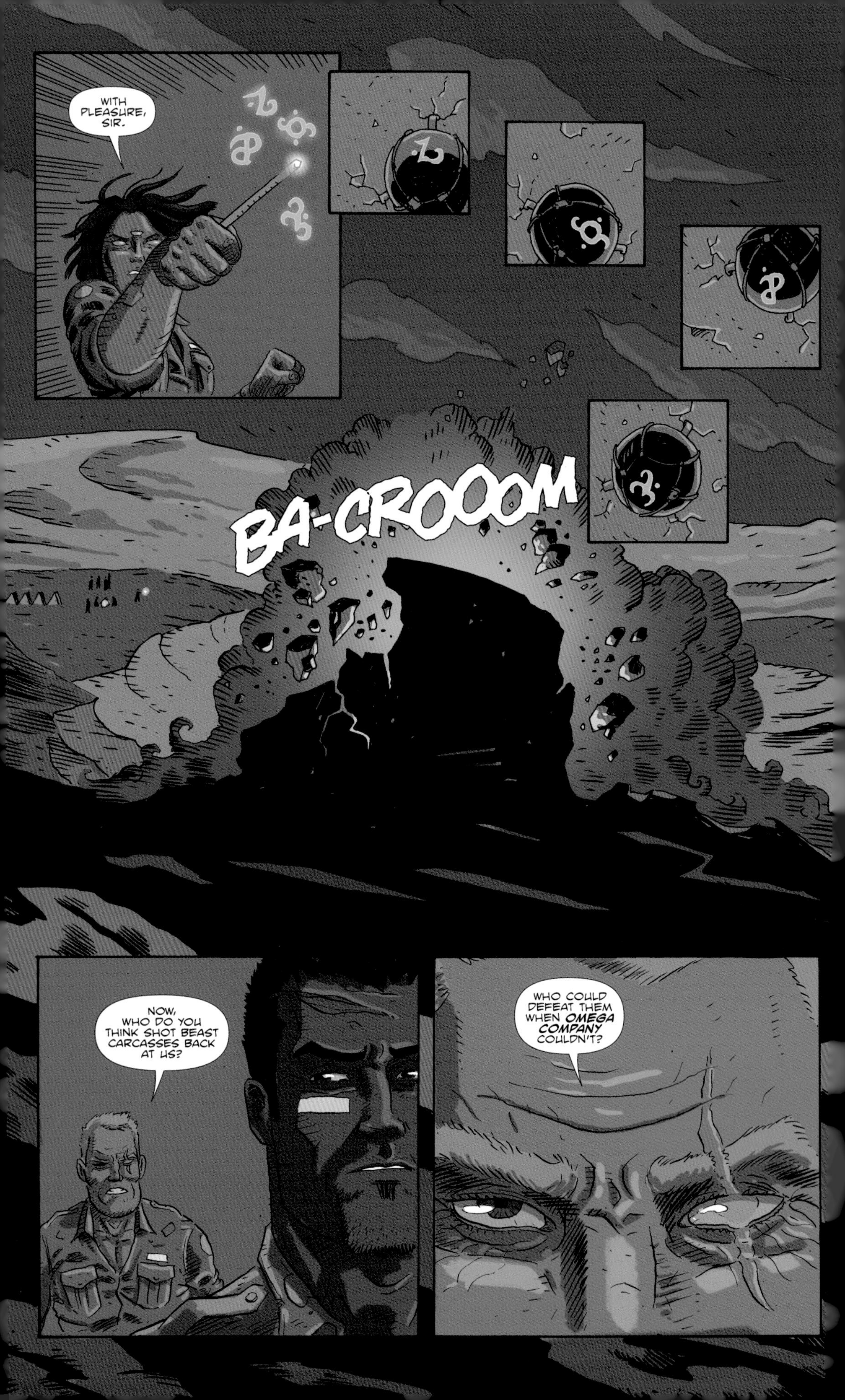
WITH PLEASURE, SIR.
BA-CROOOM
NOW, WHO DO YOU THINK SHOT BEAST CARCASSES BACK AT US?
WHO COULD DEFEAT THEM WHEN *OMEGA COMPANY* COULDN'T?

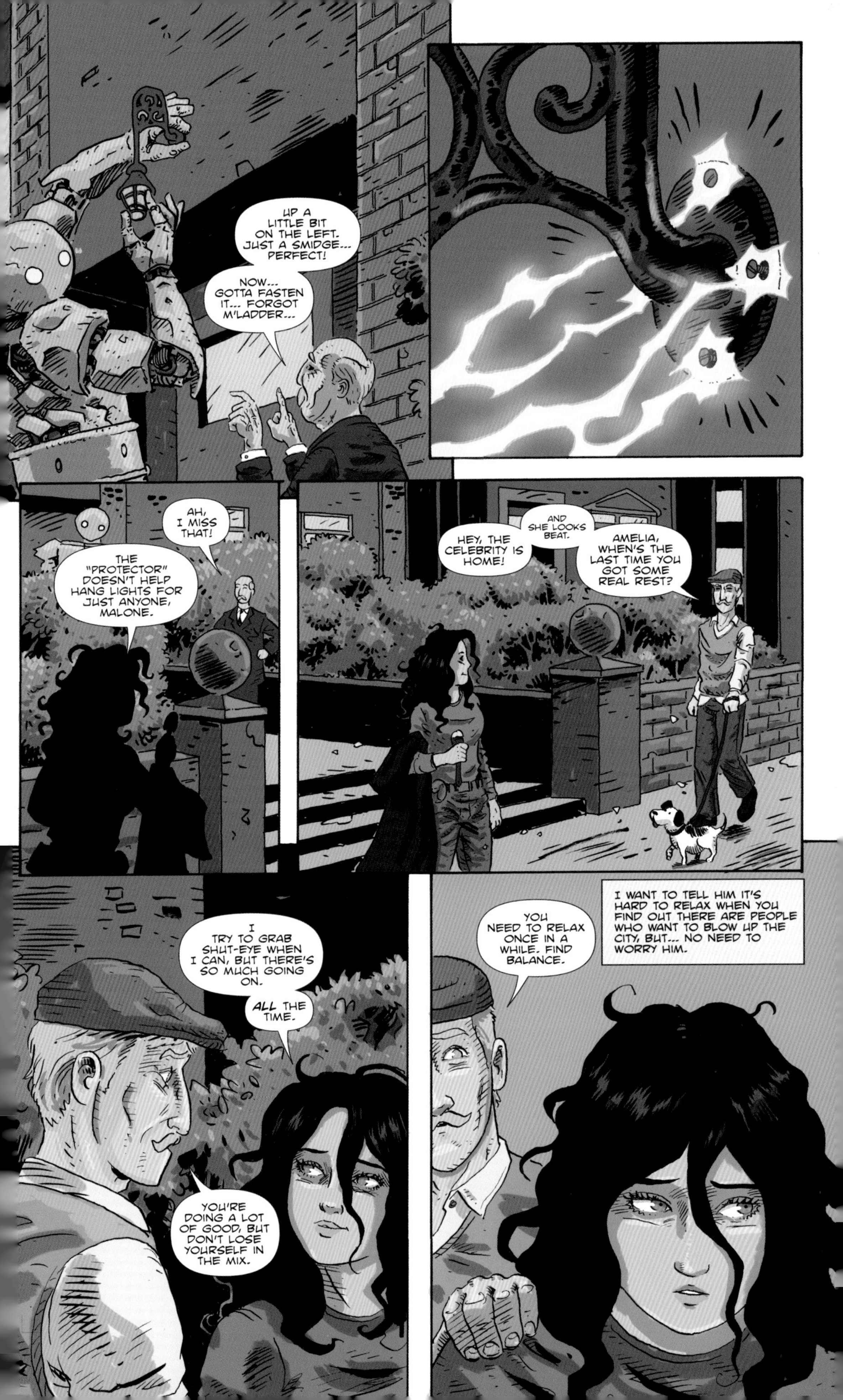
UP A LITTLE BIT ON THE LEFT. JUST A SMIDGE... PERFECT!
NOW... GOTTA FASTEN IT... FORGOT M'LADDER...
AH, I MISS THAT!
THE "PROTECTOR" DOESN'T HELP HANG LIGHTS FOR JUST ANYONE, MALONE.
HEY, THE CELEBRITY IS HOME!
AND SHE LOOKS BEAT.
AMELIA, WHEN'S THE LAST TIME YOU GOT SOME REAL REST?
I TRY TO GRAB SHUT-EYE WHEN I CAN, BUT THERE'S SO MUCH GOING ON.
ALL THE TIME.
YOU'RE DOING A LOT OF GOOD, BUT DON'T LOSE YOURSELF IN THE MIX.
YOU NEED TO RELAX ONCE IN A WHILE. FIND BALANCE.
I WANT TO TELL HIM IT'S HARD TO RELAX WHEN YOU FIND OUT THERE ARE PEOPLE WHO WANT TO BLOW UP THE CITY, BUT... NO NEED TO WORRY HIM.

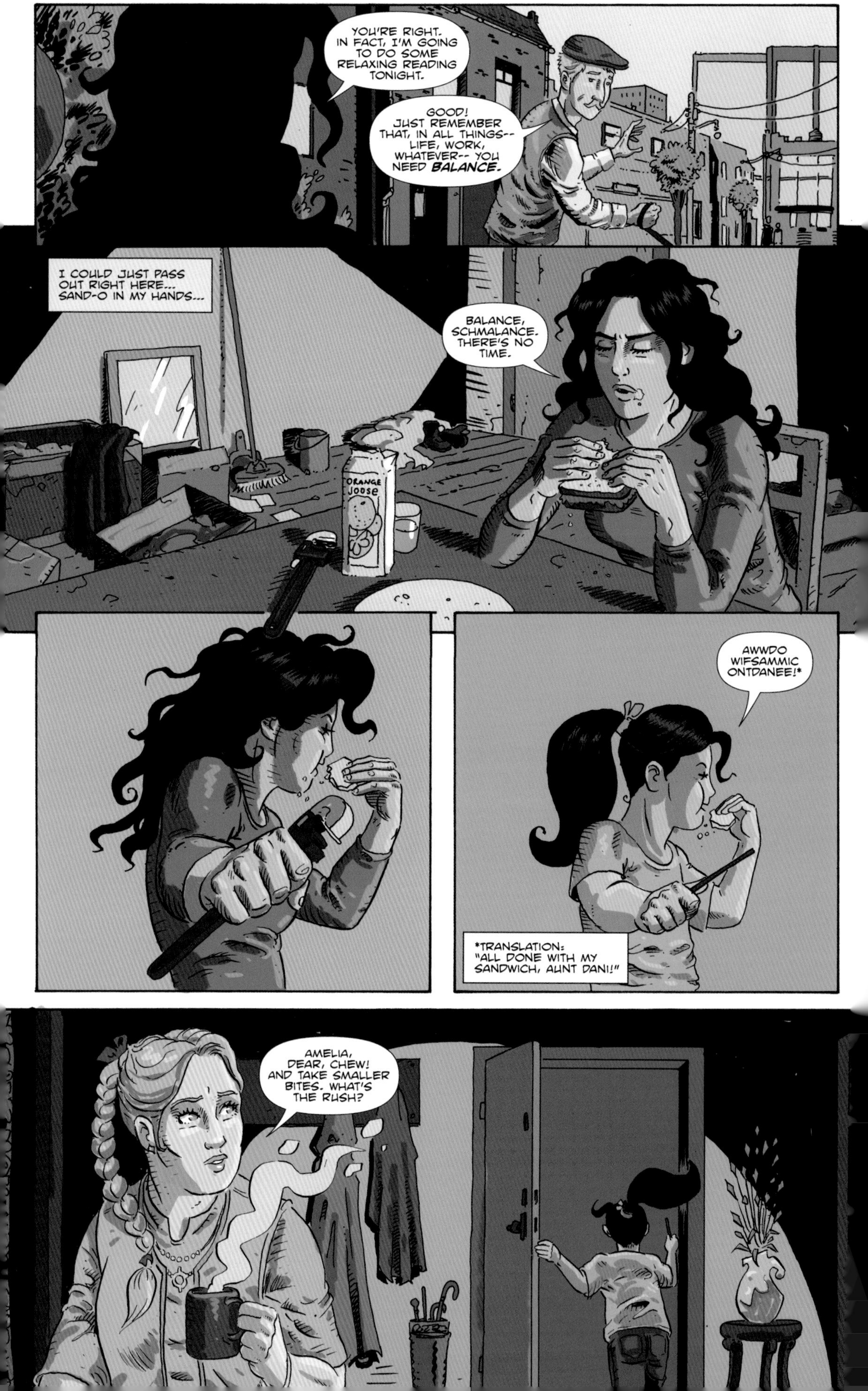
YOU'RE RIGHT. IN FACT, I'M GOING TO DO SOME RELAXING READING TONIGHT.
GOOD! JUST REMEMBER THAT, IN ALL THINGS-- LIFE, WORK, WHATEVER-- YOU NEED BALANCE.
I COULD JUST PASS OUT RIGHT HERE... SAND-O IN MY HANDS...
BALANCE, SCHMALANCE. THERE'S NO TIME.
ORANGE JOOSE
AWWDO WIFSAMMIC ONTDANEE!*
*TRANSLATION: "ALL DONE WITH MY SANDWICH, AUNT DANI!"
AMELIA, DEAR, CHEW! AND TAKE SMALLER BITES. WHAT'S THE RUSH?

I DON'T WANNA WASTE TIME!

OH, AMELIA, WHAT TIME IS WASTING?

I THOUGHT MAYBE I COULD GO AND... AND--

GO AND WALK UP AND DOWN THE STREET AGAIN STOPPING ANYONE FROM DOING ANYTHING POSSIBLY DANGEROUS?

YOU KNOW MISTER HENSHAW COMPLAINED TO ME YESTERDAY THAT YOU PUT A SHIELD UP TO STOP HIM FROM CROSSING THE STREET.

I KNOW YOU MISS LEMMY, HONEY, WE BOTH DO...

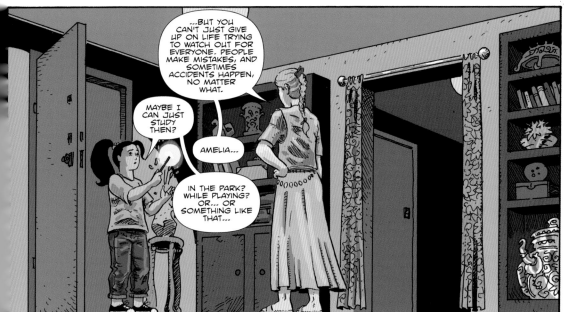

...BUT YOU CAN'T JUST GIVE UP ON LIFE TRYING TO WATCH OUT FOR EVERYONE. PEOPLE MAKE MISTAKES, AND SOMETIMES ACCIDENTS HAPPEN, NO MATTER WHAT.

MAYBE I CAN JUST STUDY THEN?

AMELIA...

IN THE PARK? WHILE PLAYING? OR... OR SOMETHING LIKE THAT...

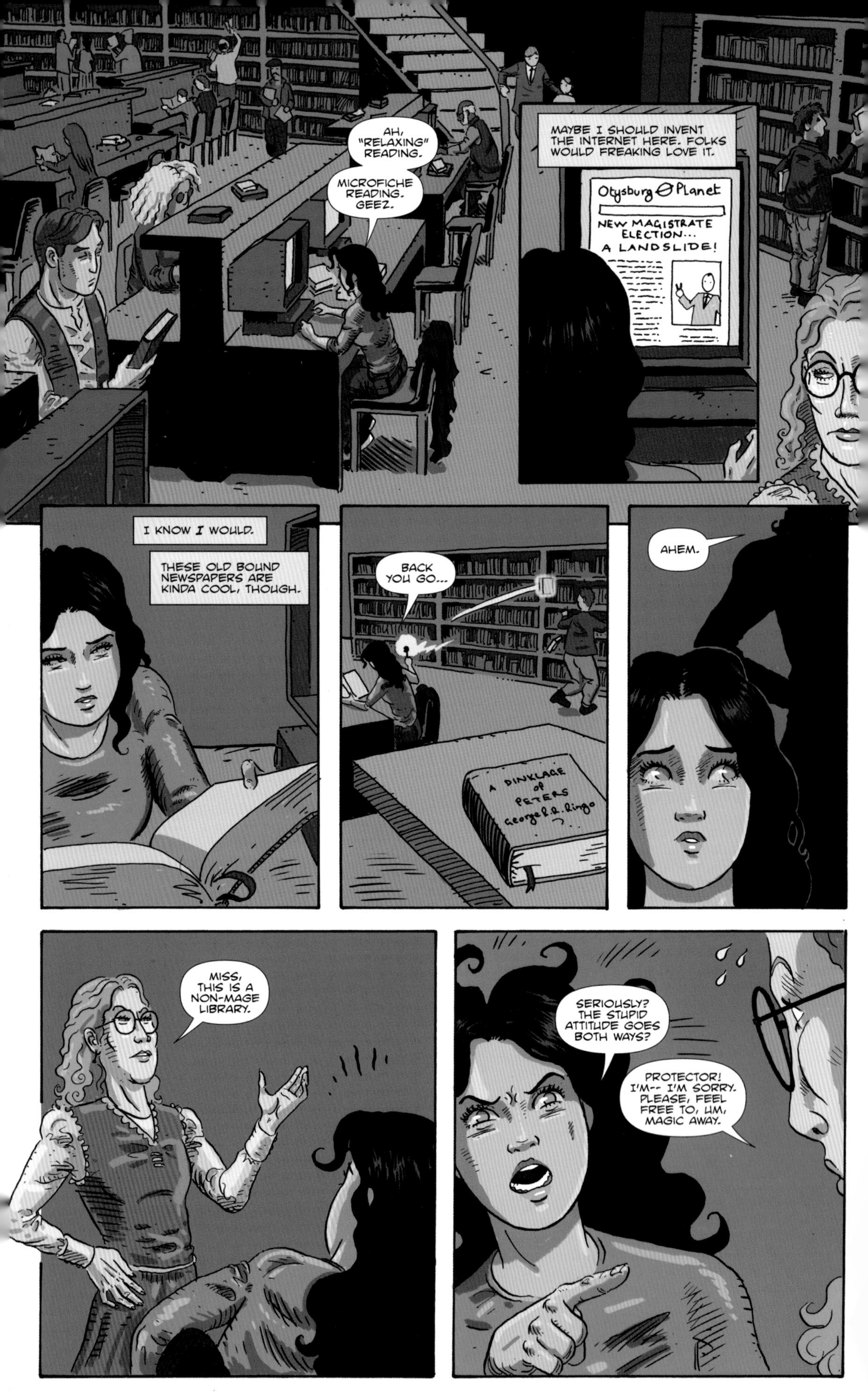
AH, "RELAXING" READING.
MICROFICHE READING. GEEZ.
MAYBE I SHOULD INVENT THE INTERNET HERE. FOLKS WOULD FREAKING LOVE IT.
Otysburg Planet
NEW MAGISTRATE ELECTION... A LANDSLIDE!
I KNOW I WOULD.
THESE OLD BOUND NEWSPAPERS ARE KINDA COOL, THOUGH.
BACK YOU GO...
A DINKLAGE of PETERS George R. R. Ringo
AHEM.
MISS, THIS IS A NON-MAGE LIBRARY.
SERIOUSLY? THE STUPID ATTITUDE GOES BOTH WAYS?
PROTECTOR! I'M-- I'M SORRY. PLEASE, FEEL FREE TO, UM, MAGIC AWAY.

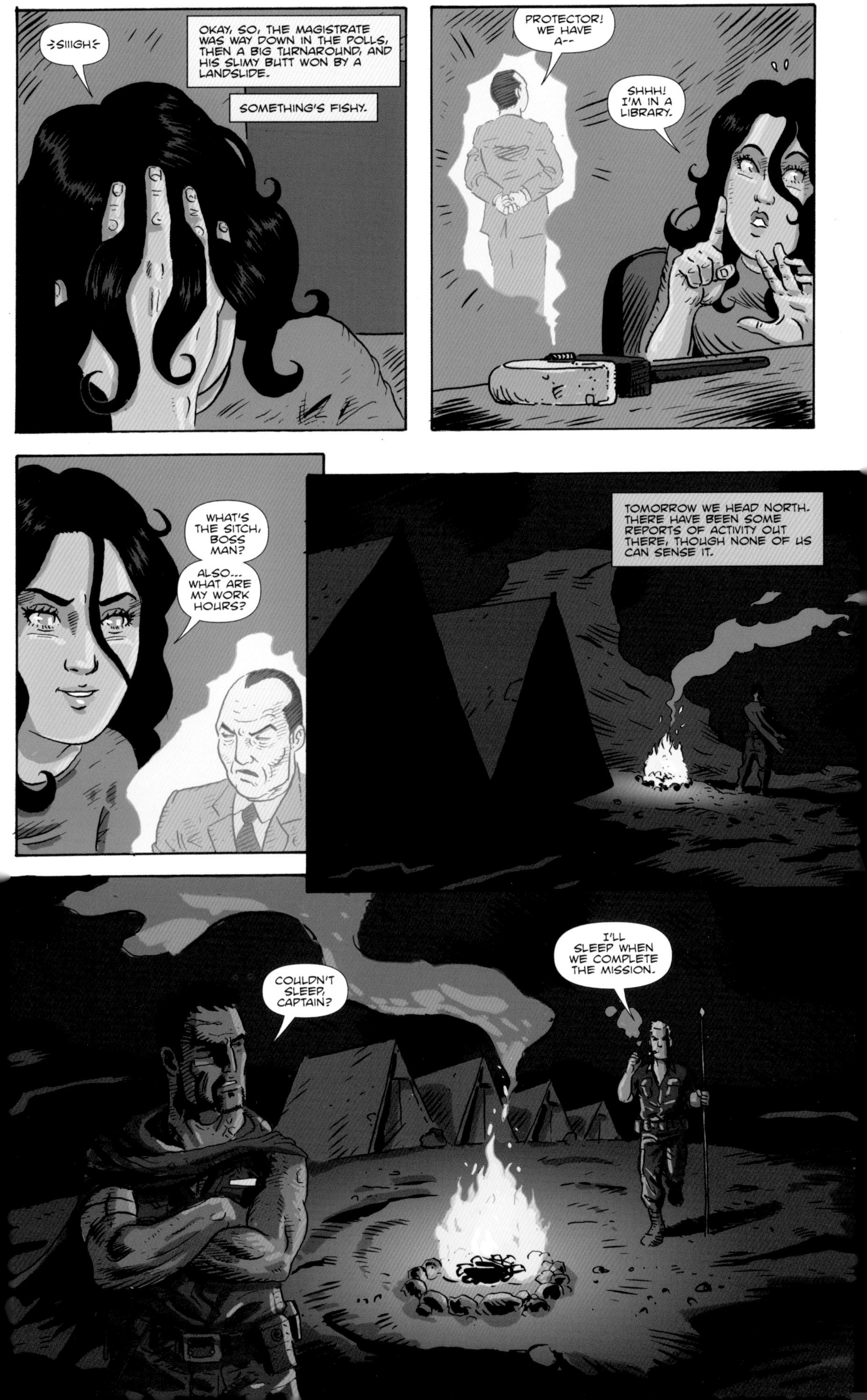
⁃SIIIGH⁃
OKAY, SO, THE MAGISTRATE WAS WAY DOWN IN THE POLLS, THEN A BIG TURNAROUND, AND HIS SLIMY BUTT WON BY A LANDSLIDE.
SOMETHING'S FISHY.
PROTECTOR! WE HAVE A--
SHHH! I'M IN A LIBRARY.
WHAT'S THE SITCH, BOSS MAN?
ALSO... WHAT ARE MY WORK HOURS?
TOMORROW WE HEAD NORTH. THERE HAVE BEEN SOME REPORTS OF ACTIVITY OUT THERE, THOUGH NONE OF US CAN SENSE IT.
COULDN'T SLEEP, CAPTAIN?
I'LL SLEEP WHEN WE COMPLETE THE MISSION.

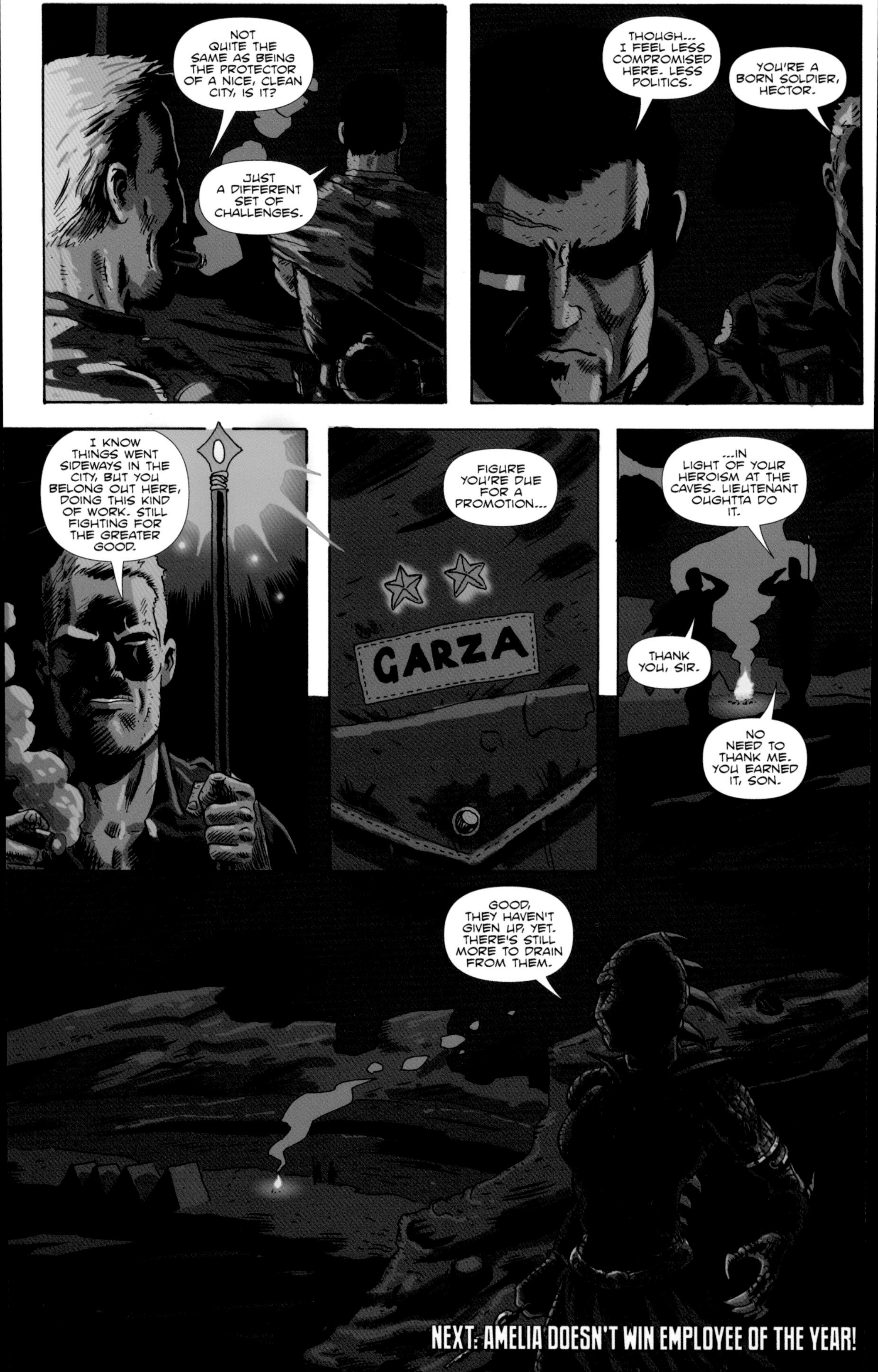
NOT QUITE THE SAME AS BEING THE PROTECTOR OF A NICE, CLEAN CITY, IS IT?
JUST A DIFFERENT SET OF CHALLENGES.
THOUGH... I FEEL LESS COMPROMISED HERE. LESS POLITICS.
YOU'RE A BORN SOLDIER, HECTOR.
I KNOW THINGS WENT SIDEWAYS IN THE CITY, BUT YOU BELONG OUT HERE, DOING THIS KIND OF WORK. STILL FIGHTING FOR THE GREATER GOOD.
FIGURE YOU'RE DUE FOR A PROMOTION...
GARZA
...IN LIGHT OF YOUR HEROISM AT THE CAVES. LIEUTENANT OUGHTTA DO IT.
THANK YOU, SIR.
NO NEED TO THANK ME. YOU EARNED IT, SON.
GOOD, THEY HAVEN'T GIVEN UP, YET. THERE'S STILL MORE TO DRAIN FROM THEM.
NEXT: AMELIA DOESN'T WIN EMPLOYEE OF THE YEAR!

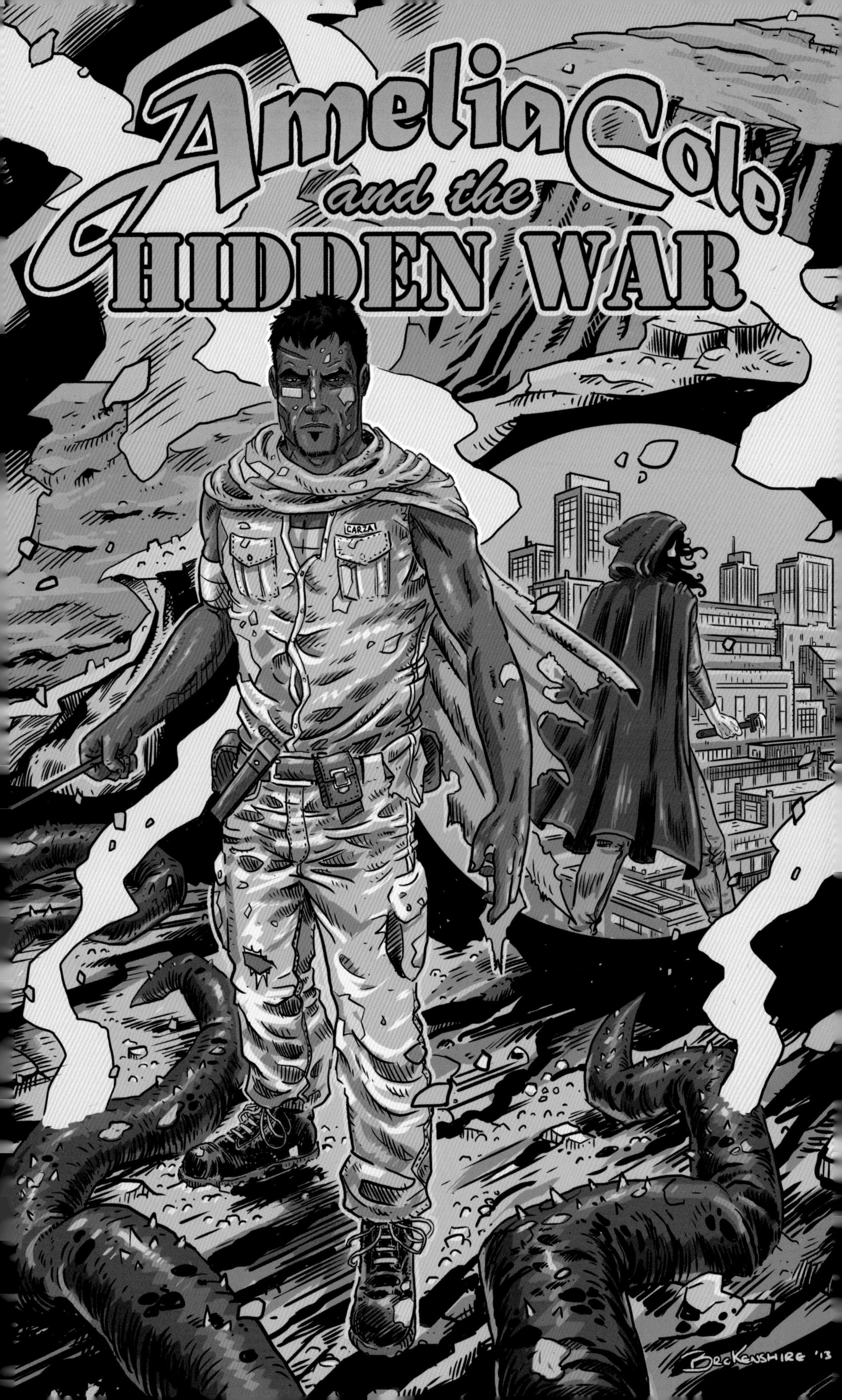

Amelia Cole
and the
HIDDEN WAR
CARZA
BRoKENSHIRE '13

CHAPTER 5

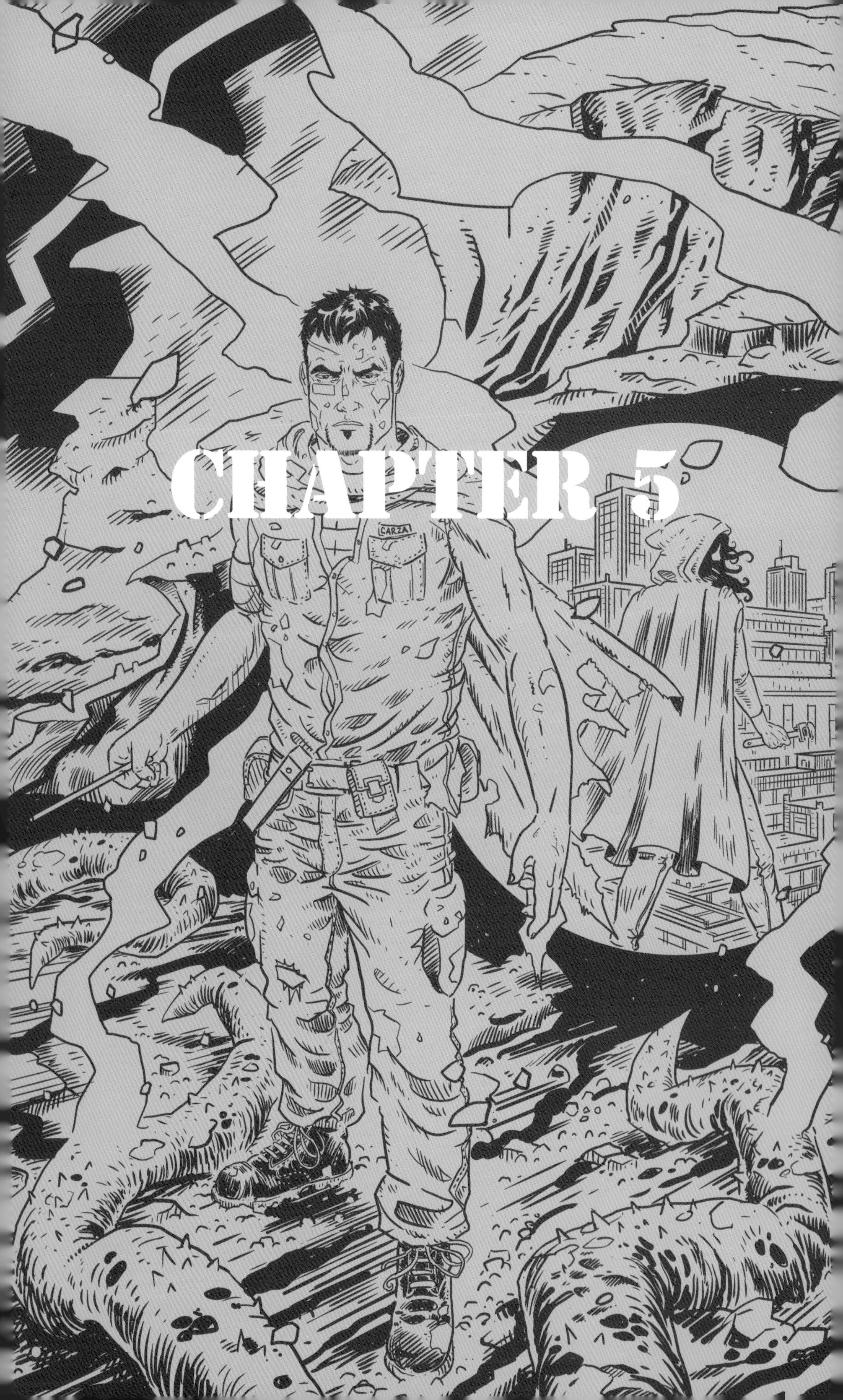
CARZA

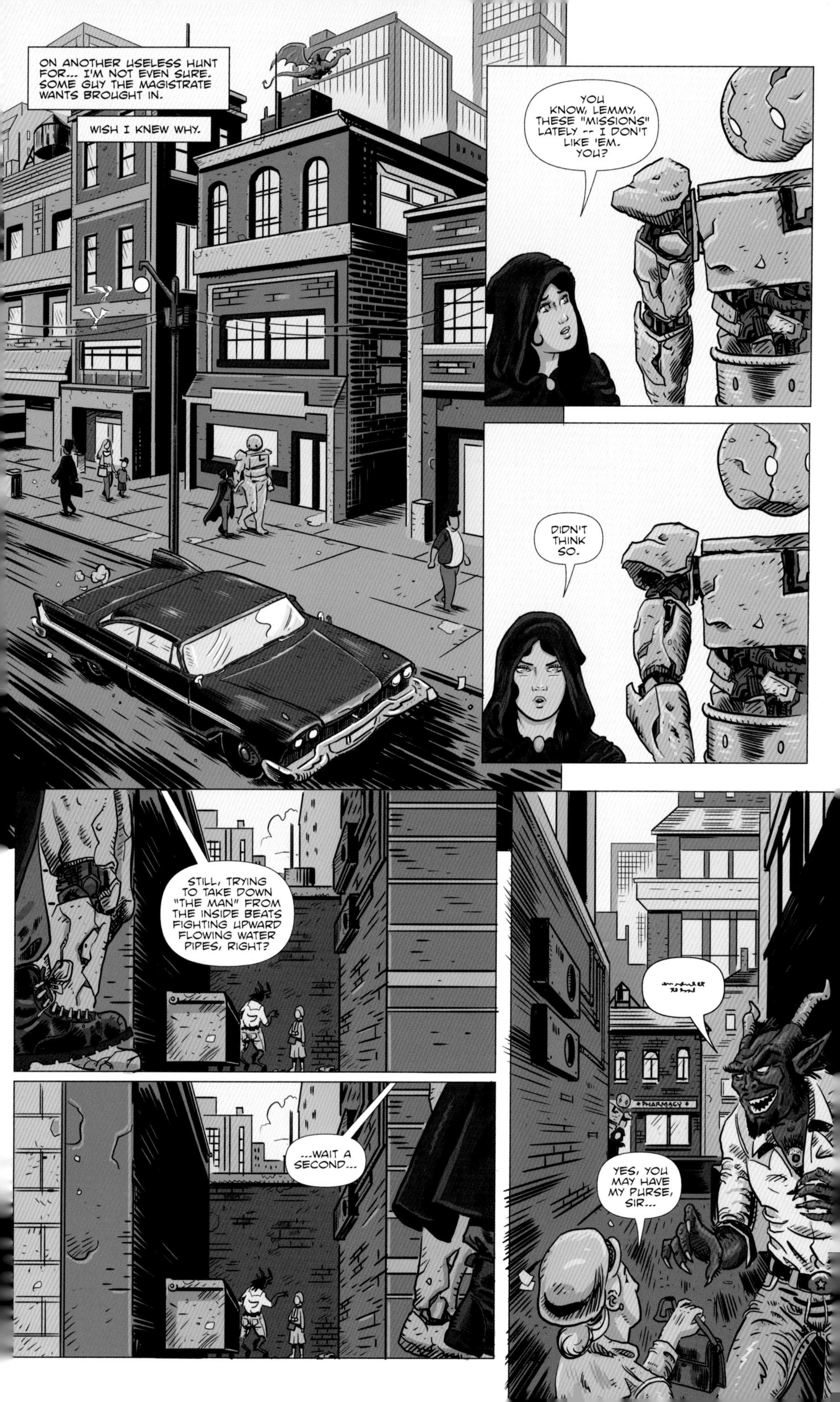
ON ANOTHER USELESS HUNT FOR... I'M NOT EVEN SURE. SOME GUY THE MAGISTRATE WANTS BROUGHT IN.
WISH I KNEW WHY.
YOU KNOW, LEMMY, THESE "MISSIONS" LATELY -- I DON'T LIKE 'EM. YOU?
DIDN'T THINK SO.
STILL, TRYING TO TAKE DOWN "THE MAN" FROM THE INSIDE BEATS FIGHTING UPWARD FLOWING WATER PIPES, RIGHT?
...WAIT A SECOND...
PHARMACY
YES, YOU MAY HAVE MY PURSE, SIR...

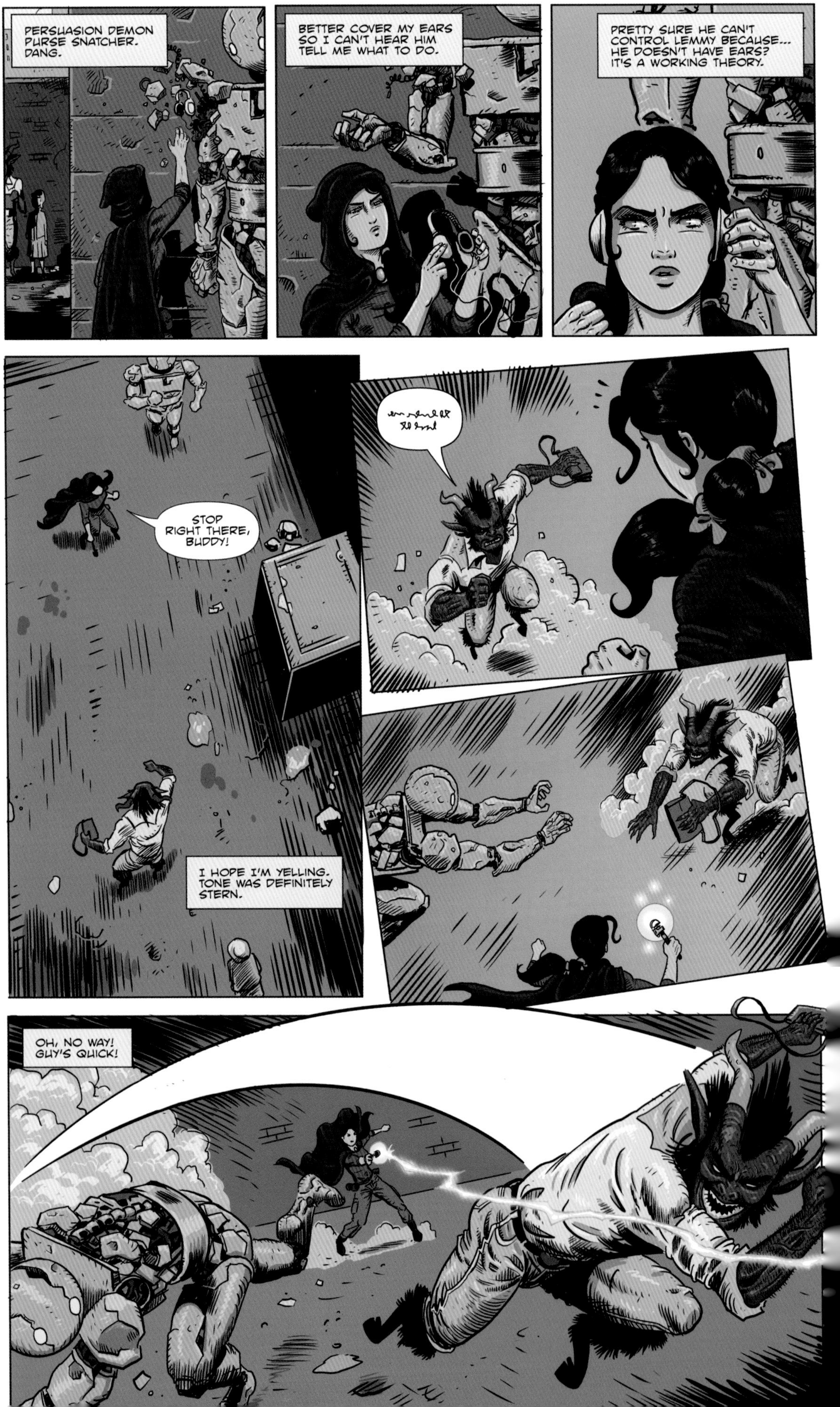
PERSUASION DEMON PURSE SNATCHER. DANG.
BETTER COVER MY EARS SO I CAN'T HEAR HIM TELL ME WHAT TO DO.
PRETTY SURE HE CAN'T CONTROL LEMMY BECAUSE... HE DOESN'T HAVE EARS? IT'S A WORKING THEORY.
STOP RIGHT THERE, BUDDY!
I HOPE I'M YELLING. TONE WAS DEFINITELY STERN.
OH, NO WAY! GUY'S QUICK!

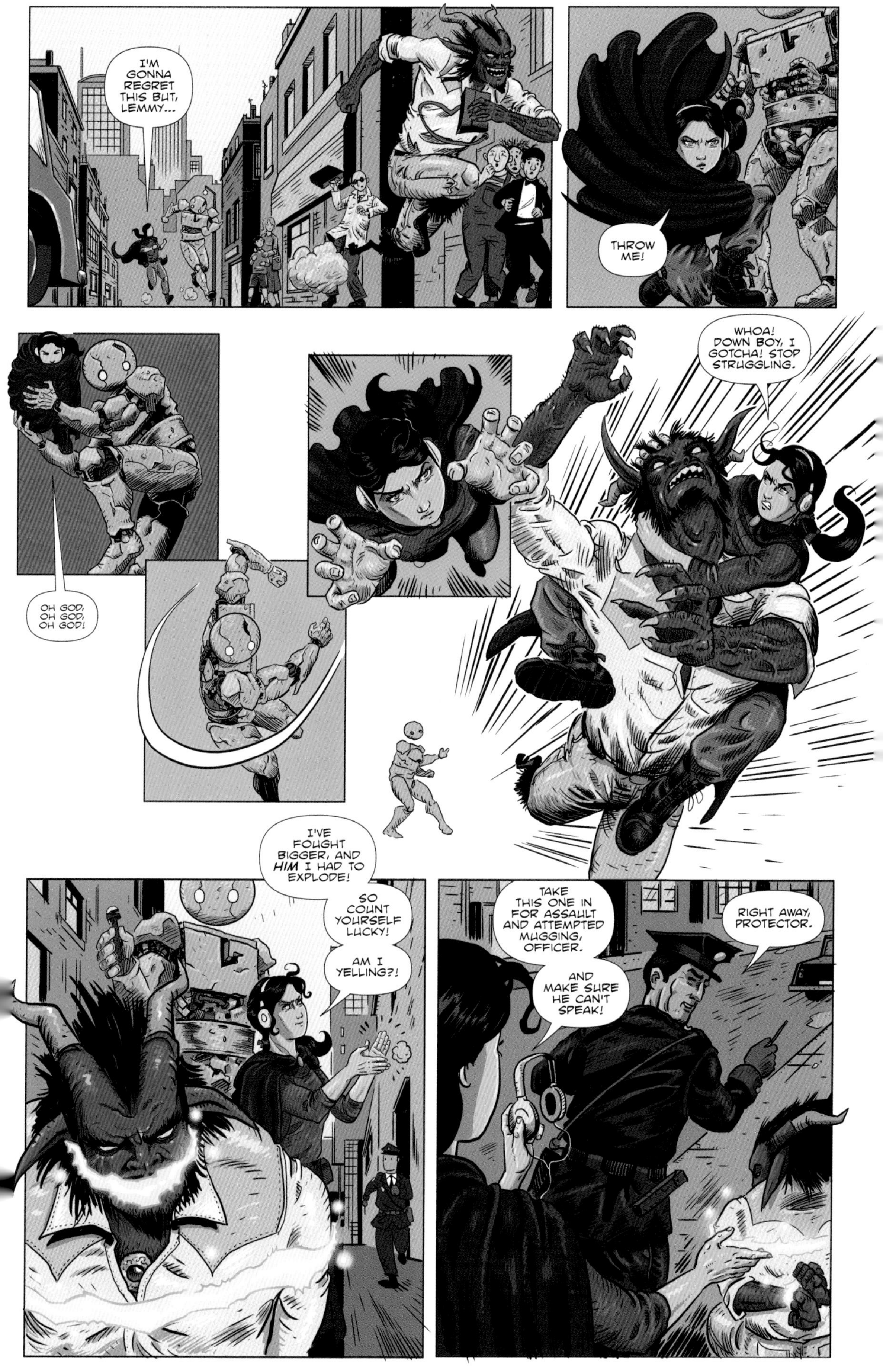
I'M GONNA REGRET THIS BUT, LEMMY...
THROW ME!
OH GOD, OH GOD, OH GOD!
WHOA! DOWN BOY, I GOTCHA! STOP STRUGGLING.
I'VE FOUGHT BIGGER, AND *HIM* I HAD TO EXPLODE!
SO COUNT YOURSELF LUCKY!
AM I YELLING?!
TAKE THIS ONE IN FOR ASSAULT AND ATTEMPTED MUGGING, OFFICER.
AND MAKE SURE HE CAN'T SPEAK!
RIGHT AWAY, PROTECTOR.

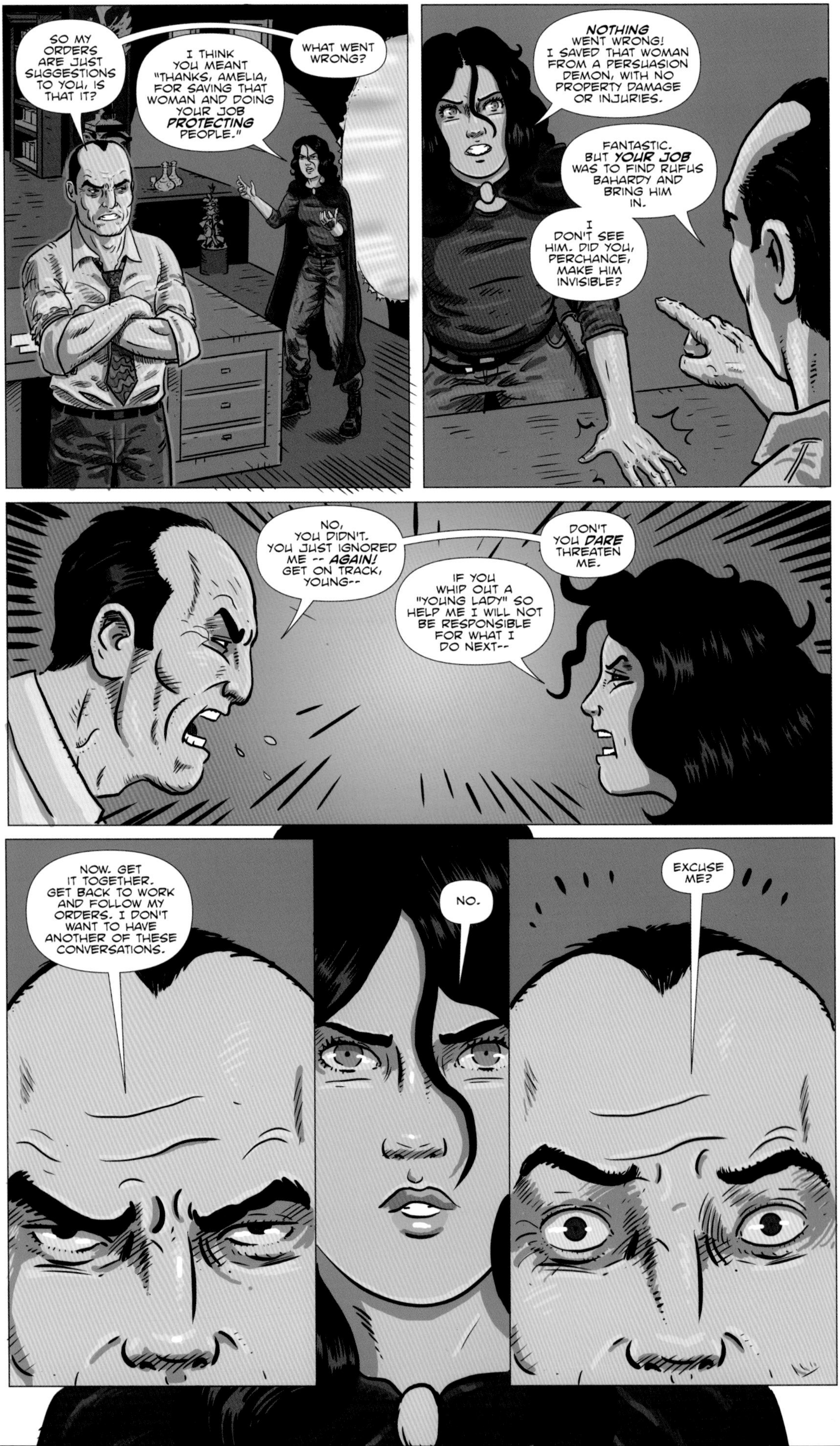
SO MY ORDERS ARE JUST SUGGESTIONS TO YOU, IS THAT IT?
WHAT WENT WRONG?
I THINK YOU MEANT "THANKS, AMELIA, FOR SAVING THAT WOMAN AND DOING YOUR JOB PROTECTING PEOPLE."
NOTHING WENT WRONG! I SAVED THAT WOMAN FROM A PERSUASION DEMON, WITH NO PROPERTY DAMAGE OR INJURIES.
FANTASTIC. BUT YOUR JOB WAS TO FIND RUFUS BAHARDY AND BRING HIM IN.
I DON'T SEE HIM. DID YOU, PERCHANCE, MAKE HIM INVISIBLE?
NO, YOU DIDN'T. YOU JUST IGNORED ME -- AGAIN! GET ON TRACK, YOUNG--
DON'T YOU DARE THREATEN ME.
IF YOU WHIP OUT A "YOUNG LADY" SO HELP ME I WILL NOT BE RESPONSIBLE FOR WHAT I DO NEXT--
NOW. GET IT TOGETHER. GET BACK TO WORK AND FOLLOW MY ORDERS. I DON'T WANT TO HAVE ANOTHER OF THESE CONVERSATIONS.
NO.
EXCUSE ME?

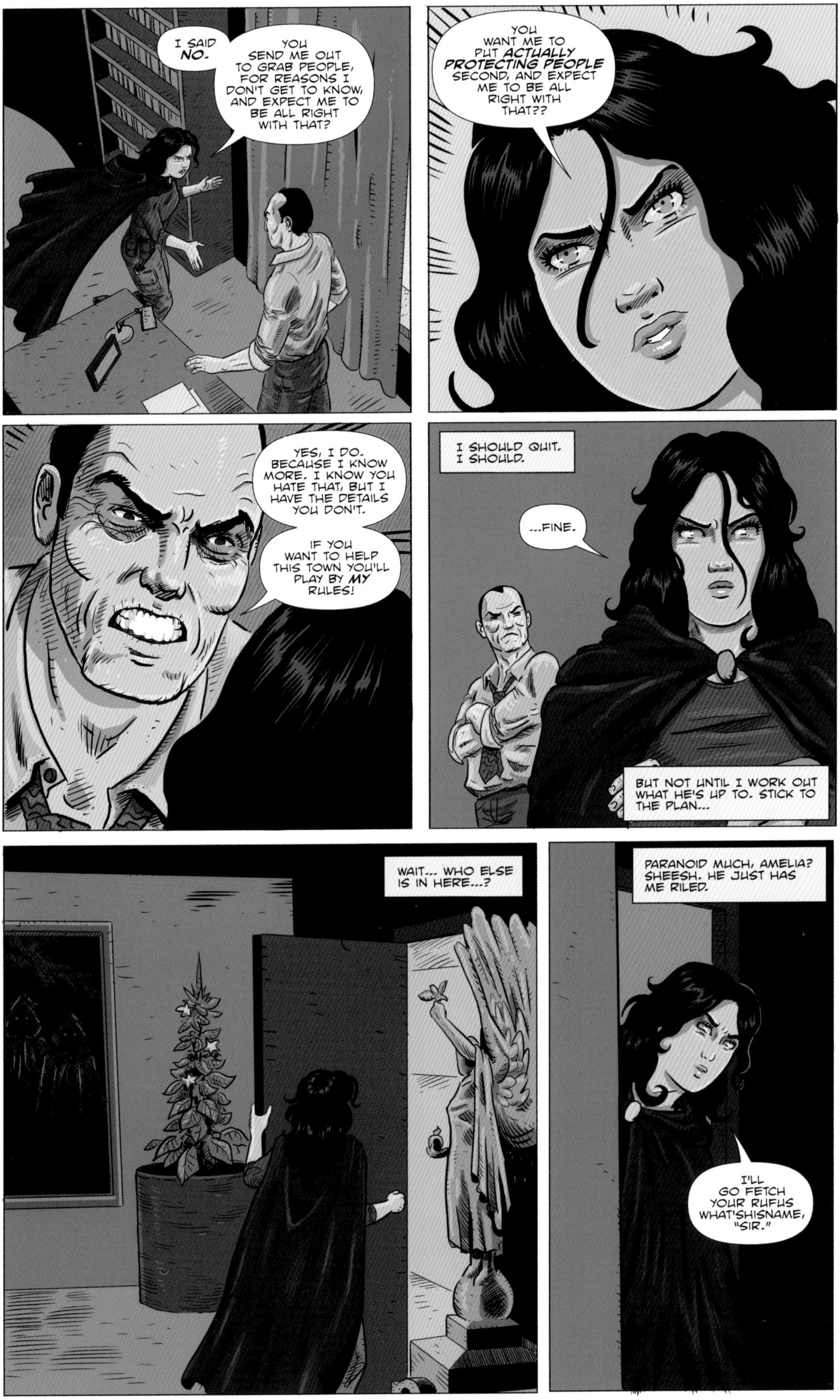
I SAID NO.
YOU SEND ME OUT TO GRAB PEOPLE, FOR REASONS I DON'T GET TO KNOW, AND EXPECT ME TO BE ALL RIGHT WITH THAT?
YOU WANT ME TO PUT ACTUALLY PROTECTING PEOPLE SECOND, AND EXPECT ME TO BE ALL RIGHT WITH THAT??
YES, I DO. BECAUSE I KNOW MORE. I KNOW YOU HATE THAT, BUT I HAVE THE DETAILS YOU DON'T.
IF YOU WANT TO HELP THIS TOWN YOU'LL PLAY BY MY RULES!
I SHOULD QUIT. I SHOULD.
...FINE.
BUT NOT UNTIL I WORK OUT WHAT HE'S UP TO. STICK TO THE PLAN...
WAIT... WHO ELSE IS IN HERE...?
PARANOID MUCH, AMELIA? SHEESH. HE JUST HAS ME RILED.
I'LL GO FETCH YOUR RUFUS WHAT'SHISNAME, "SIR."

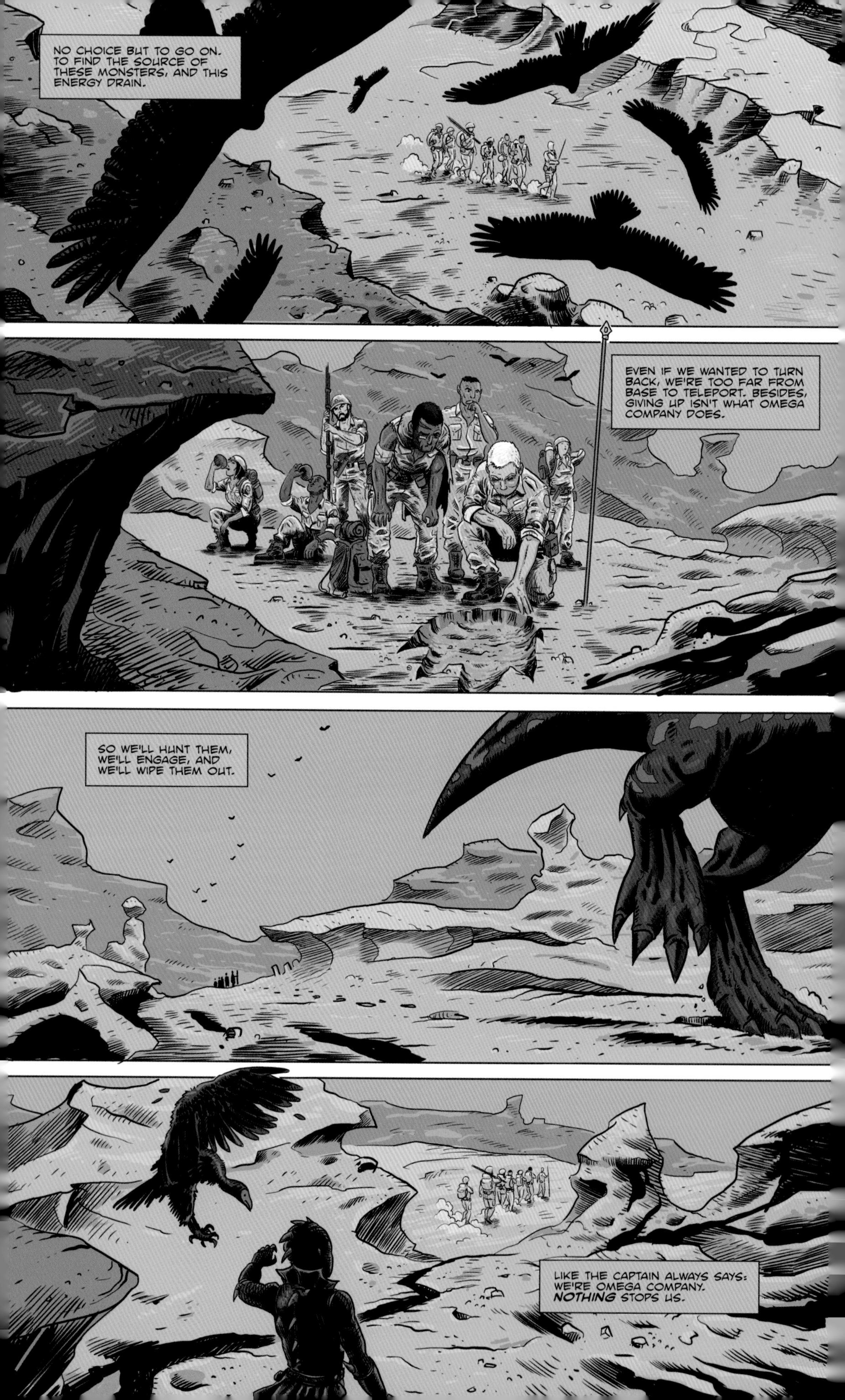
NO CHOICE BUT TO GO ON. TO FIND THE SOURCE OF THESE MONSTERS, AND THIS ENERGY DRAIN.
EVEN IF WE WANTED TO TURN BACK, WE'RE TOO FAR FROM BASE TO TELEPORT. BESIDES, GIVING UP ISN'T WHAT OMEGA COMPANY DOES.
SO WE'LL HUNT THEM, WE'LL ENGAGE, AND WE'LL WIPE THEM OUT.
LIKE THE CAPTAIN ALWAYS SAYS: WE'RE OMEGA COMPANY. ***NOTHING*** STOPS US.

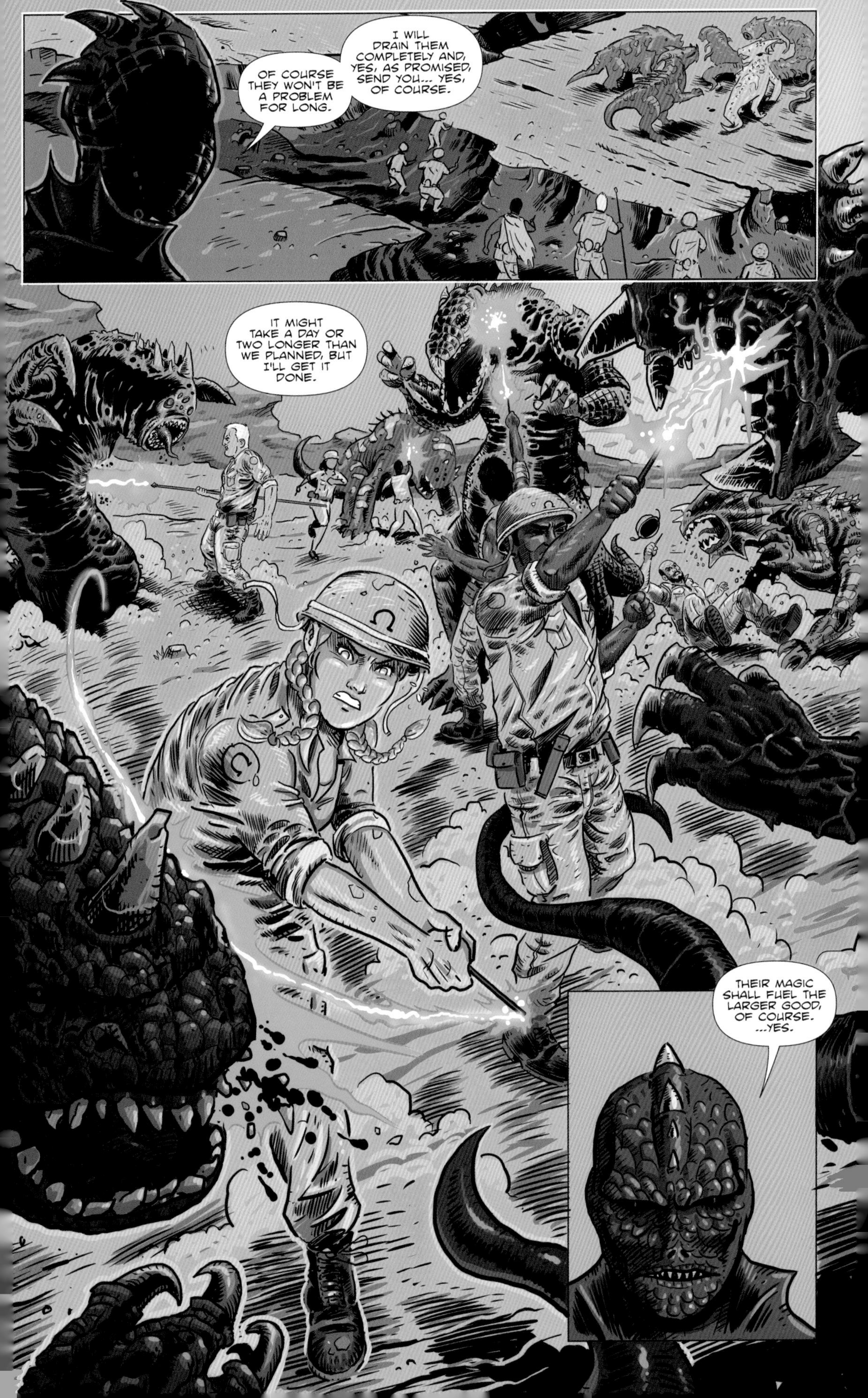

OF COURSE THEY WON'T BE A PROBLEM FOR LONG.
I WILL DRAIN THEM COMPLETELY AND, YES, AS PROMISED, SEND YOU... YES, OF COURSE.
IT MIGHT TAKE A DAY OR TWO LONGER THAN WE PLANNED, BUT I'LL GET IT DONE.
THEIR MAGIC SHALL FUEL THE LARGER GOOD, OF COURSE. ...YES.

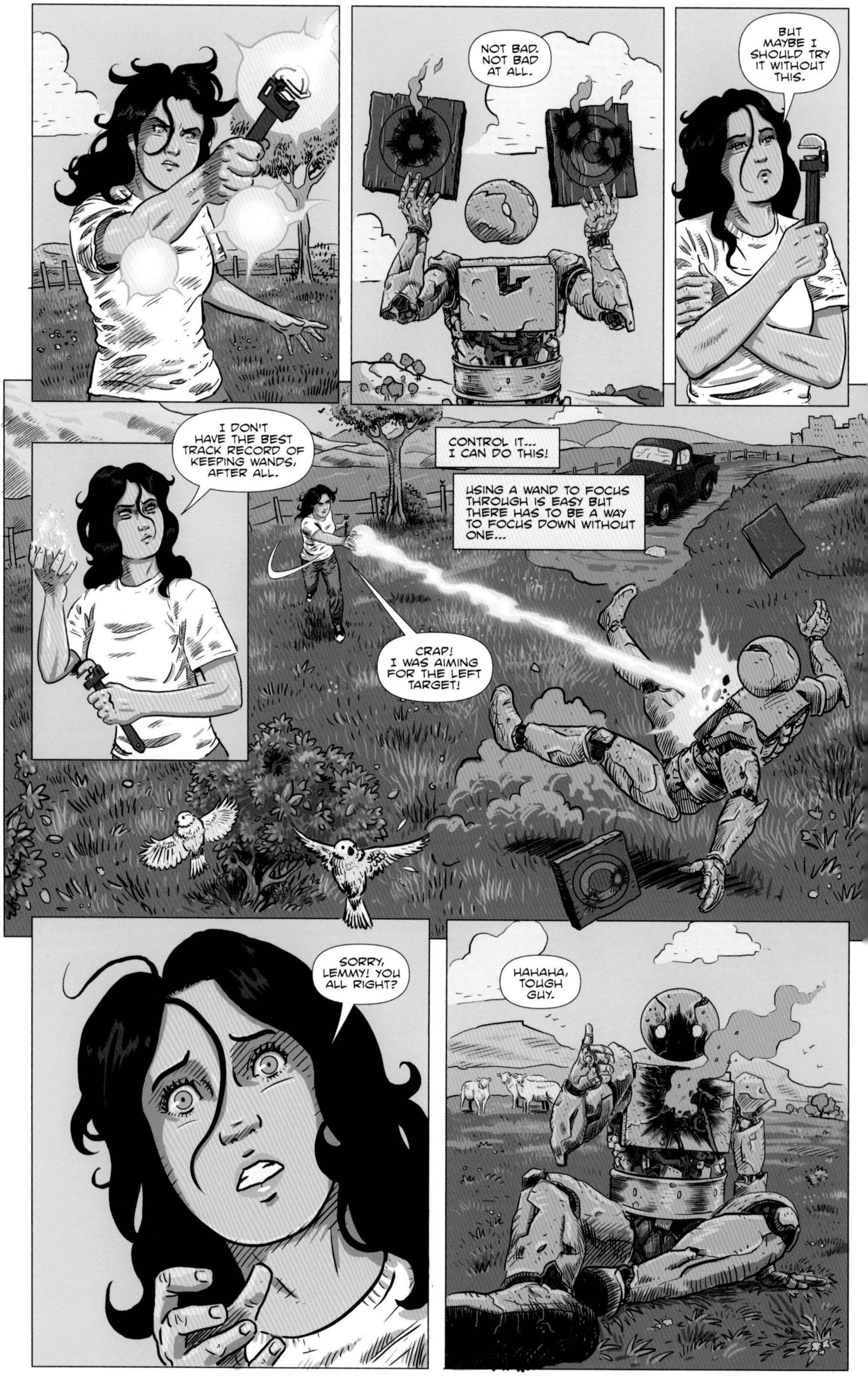
NOT BAD. NOT BAD AT ALL.
BUT MAYBE I SHOULD TRY IT WITHOUT THIS.
I DON'T HAVE THE BEST TRACK RECORD OF KEEPING WANDS, AFTER ALL.
CONTROL IT... I CAN DO THIS!
USING A WAND TO FOCUS THROUGH IS EASY BUT THERE HAS TO BE A WAY TO FOCUS DOWN WITHOUT ONE...
CRAP! I WAS AIMING FOR THE LEFT TARGET!
SORRY, LEMMY! YOU ALL RIGHT?
HAHAHA, TOUGH GUY.

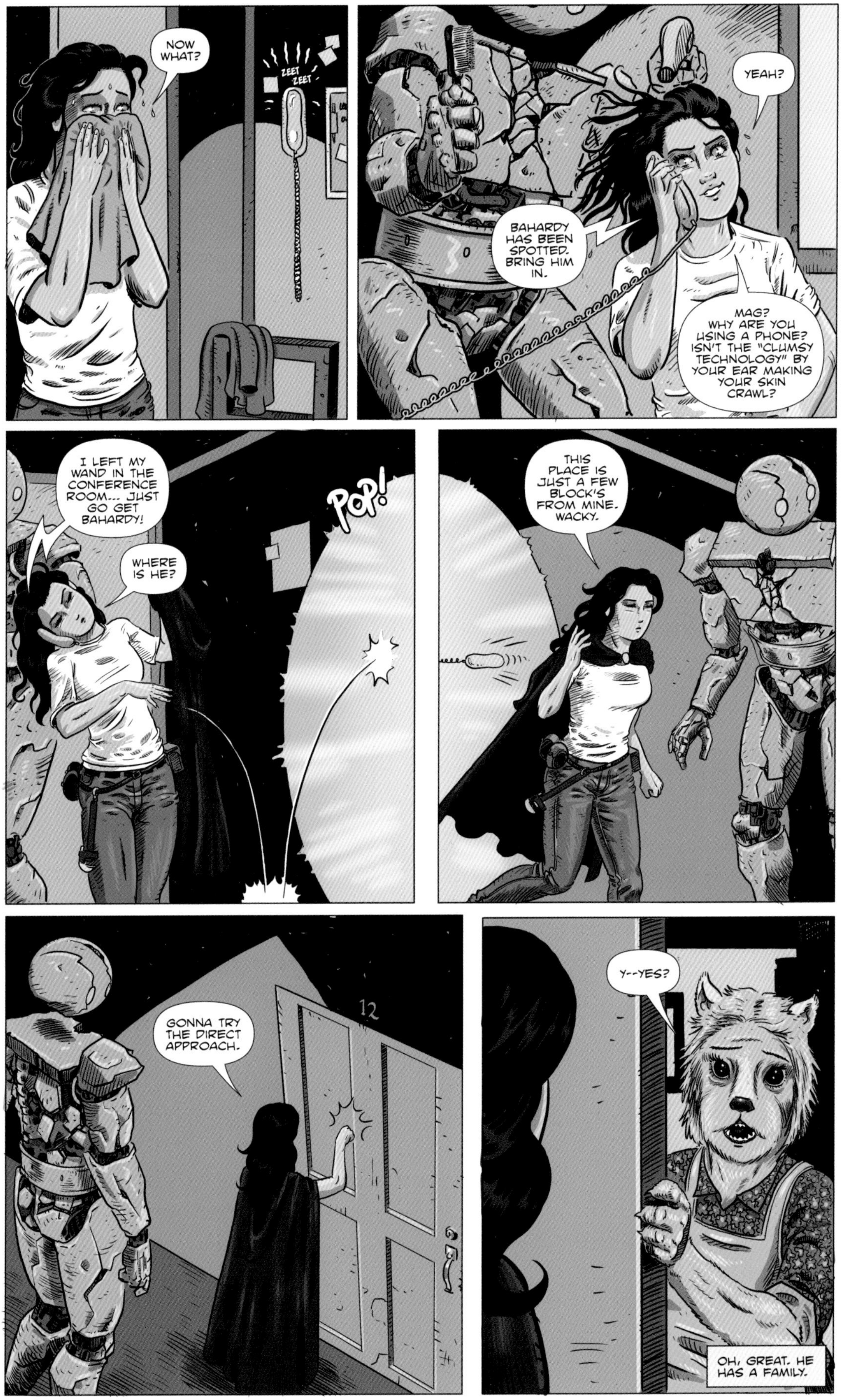
NOW WHAT?
ZEET ZEET
YEAH?
BAHARDY HAS BEEN SPOTTED. BRING HIM IN.
MAG? WHY ARE YOU USING A PHONE? ISN'T THE "CLUMSY TECHNOLOGY" BY YOUR EAR MAKING YOUR SKIN CRAWL?
I LEFT MY WAND IN THE CONFERENCE ROOM... JUST GO GET BAHARDY!
WHERE IS HE?
POP!
THIS PLACE IS JUST A FEW BLOCK'S FROM MINE. WACKY.
GONNA TRY THE DIRECT APPROACH.
12
Y--YES?
OH, GREAT. HE HAS A FAMILY.

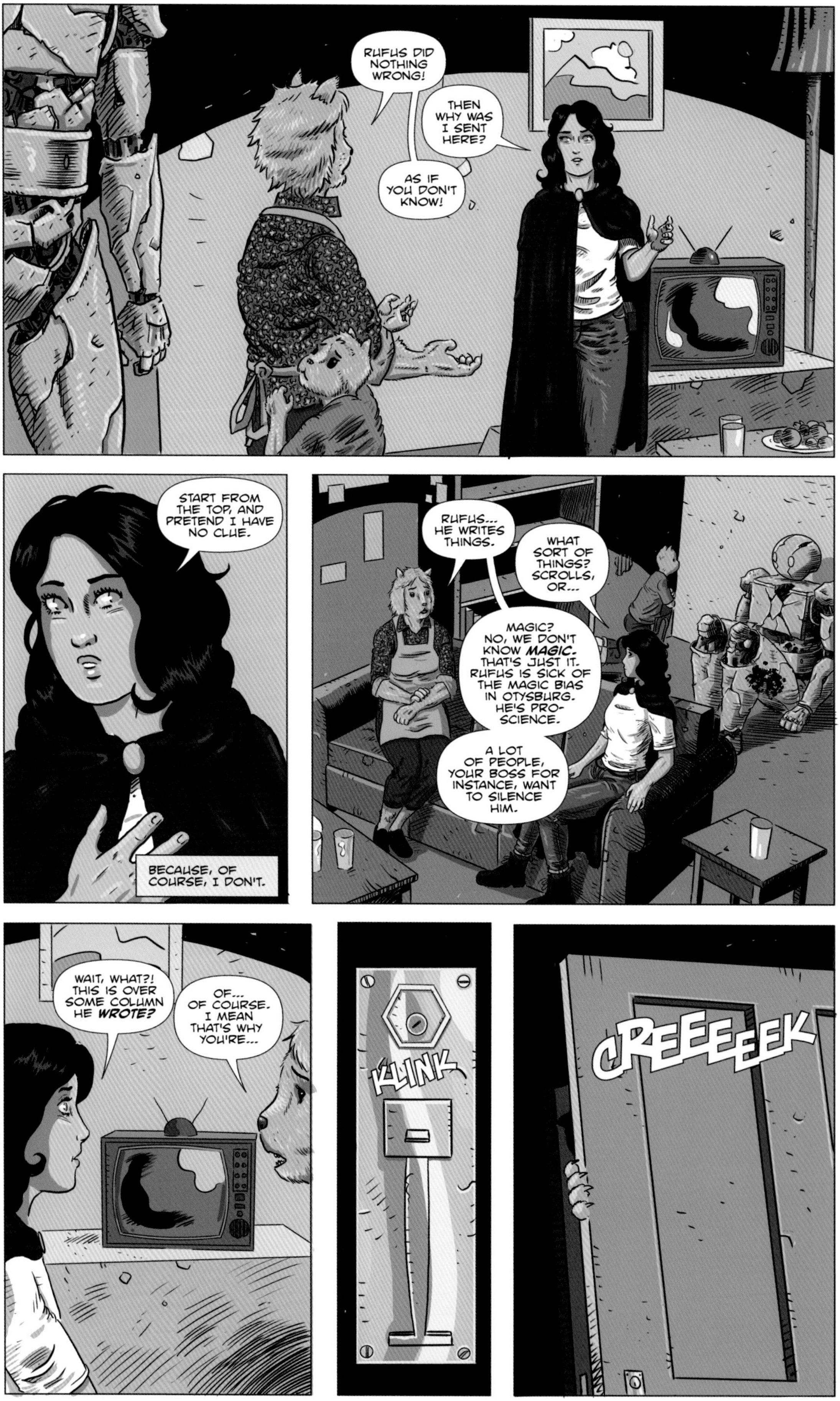
RUFUS DID NOTHING WRONG!
THEN WHY WAS I SENT HERE?
AS IF YOU DON'T KNOW!
START FROM THE TOP, AND PRETEND I HAVE NO CLUE.
BECAUSE, OF COURSE, I DON'T.
RUFUS... HE WRITES THINGS.
WHAT SORT OF THINGS? SCROLLS, OR...
MAGIC? NO, WE DON'T KNOW MAGIC. THAT'S JUST IT. RUFUS IS SICK OF THE MAGIC BIAS IN OTYSBURG. HE'S PRO-SCIENCE.
A LOT OF PEOPLE, YOUR BOSS FOR INSTANCE, WANT TO SILENCE HIM.
WAIT, WHAT?! THIS IS OVER SOME COLUMN HE WROTE?
OF... OF COURSE. I MEAN THAT'S WHY YOU'RE...
KLINK
CREEEEEEK

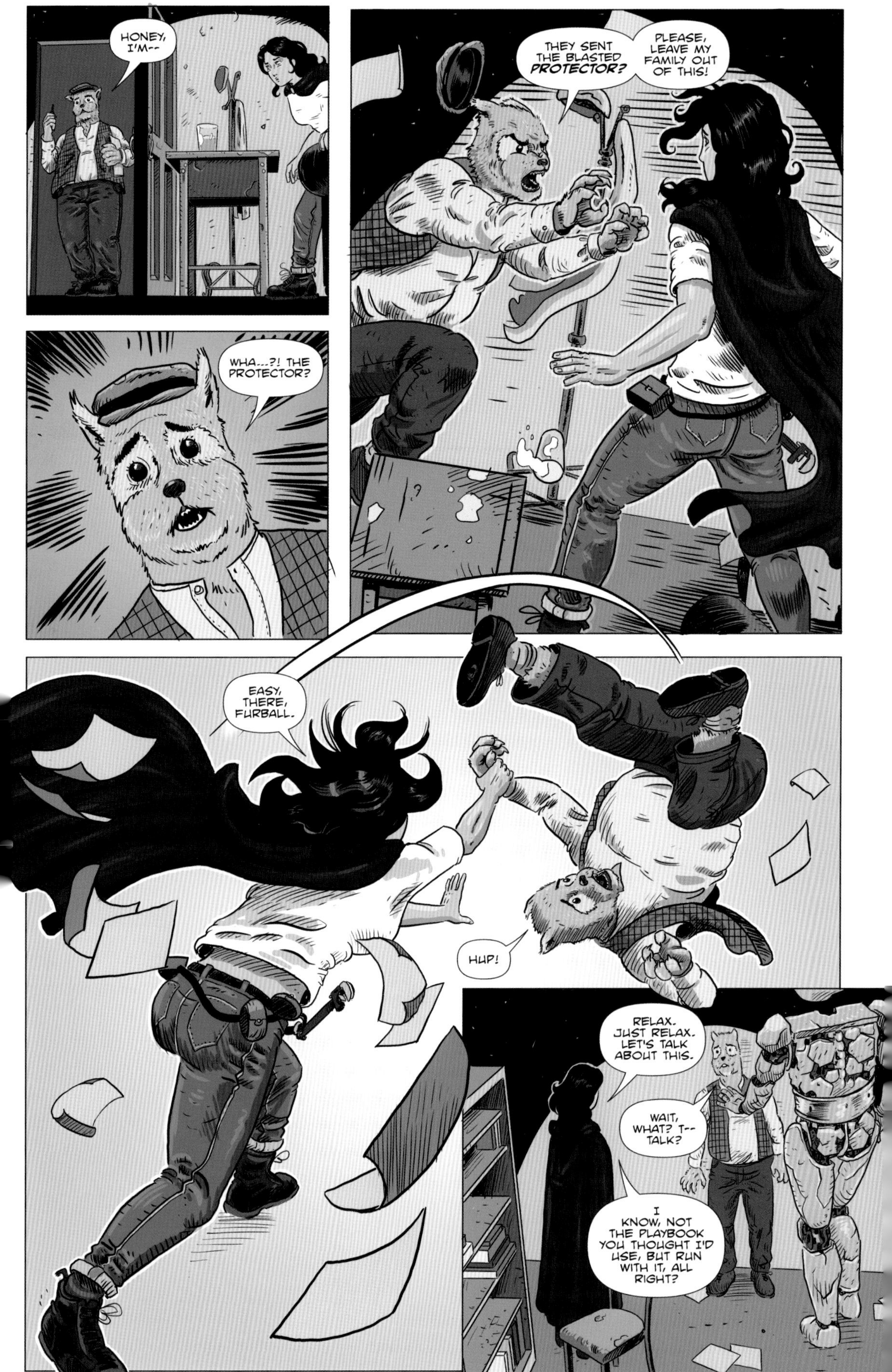
HONEY, I'M--
THEY SENT THE BLASTED PROTECTOR?
PLEASE, LEAVE MY FAMILY OUT OF THIS!
WHA...?! THE PROTECTOR?
EASY, THERE, FURBALL.
HUP!
RELAX. JUST RELAX. LET'S TALK ABOUT THIS.
WAIT, WHAT? T--TALK?
I KNOW, NOT THE PLAYBOOK YOU THOUGHT I'D USE, BUT RUN WITH IT, ALL RIGHT?

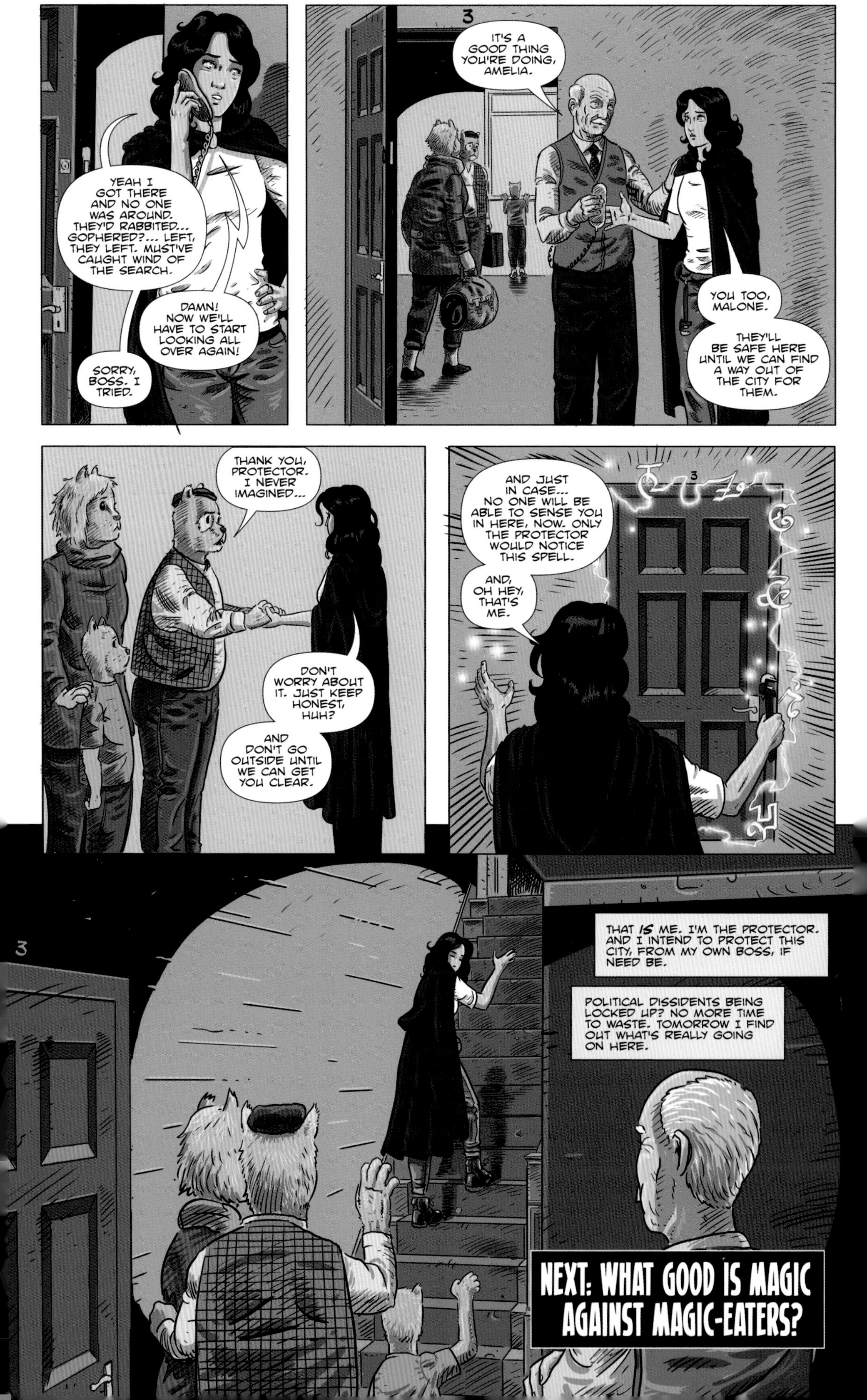
YEAH I GOT THERE AND NO ONE WAS AROUND. THEY'D RABBITED... GOPHERED?... LEFT, THEY LEFT. MUST'VE CAUGHT WIND OF THE SEARCH.
DAMN! NOW WE'LL HAVE TO START LOOKING ALL OVER AGAIN!
SORRY, BOSS. I TRIED.
3
IT'S A GOOD THING YOU'RE DOING, AMELIA.
YOU TOO, MALONE.
THEY'LL BE SAFE HERE UNTIL WE CAN FIND A WAY OUT OF THE CITY FOR THEM.
THANK YOU, PROTECTOR. I NEVER IMAGINED...
DON'T WORRY ABOUT IT. JUST KEEP HONEST, HUH?
AND DON'T GO OUTSIDE UNTIL WE CAN GET YOU CLEAR.
3
AND JUST IN CASE... NO ONE WILL BE ABLE TO SENSE YOU IN HERE, NOW. ONLY THE PROTECTOR WOULD NOTICE THIS SPELL.
AND, OH HEY, THAT'S ME.
3
THAT *IS* ME. I'M THE PROTECTOR. AND I INTEND TO PROTECT THIS CITY, FROM MY OWN BOSS, IF NEED BE.
POLITICAL DISSIDENTS BEING LOCKED UP? NO MORE TIME TO WASTE. TOMORROW I FIND OUT WHAT'S REALLY GOING ON HERE.
NEXT: WHAT GOOD IS MAGIC AGAINST MAGIC-EATERS?

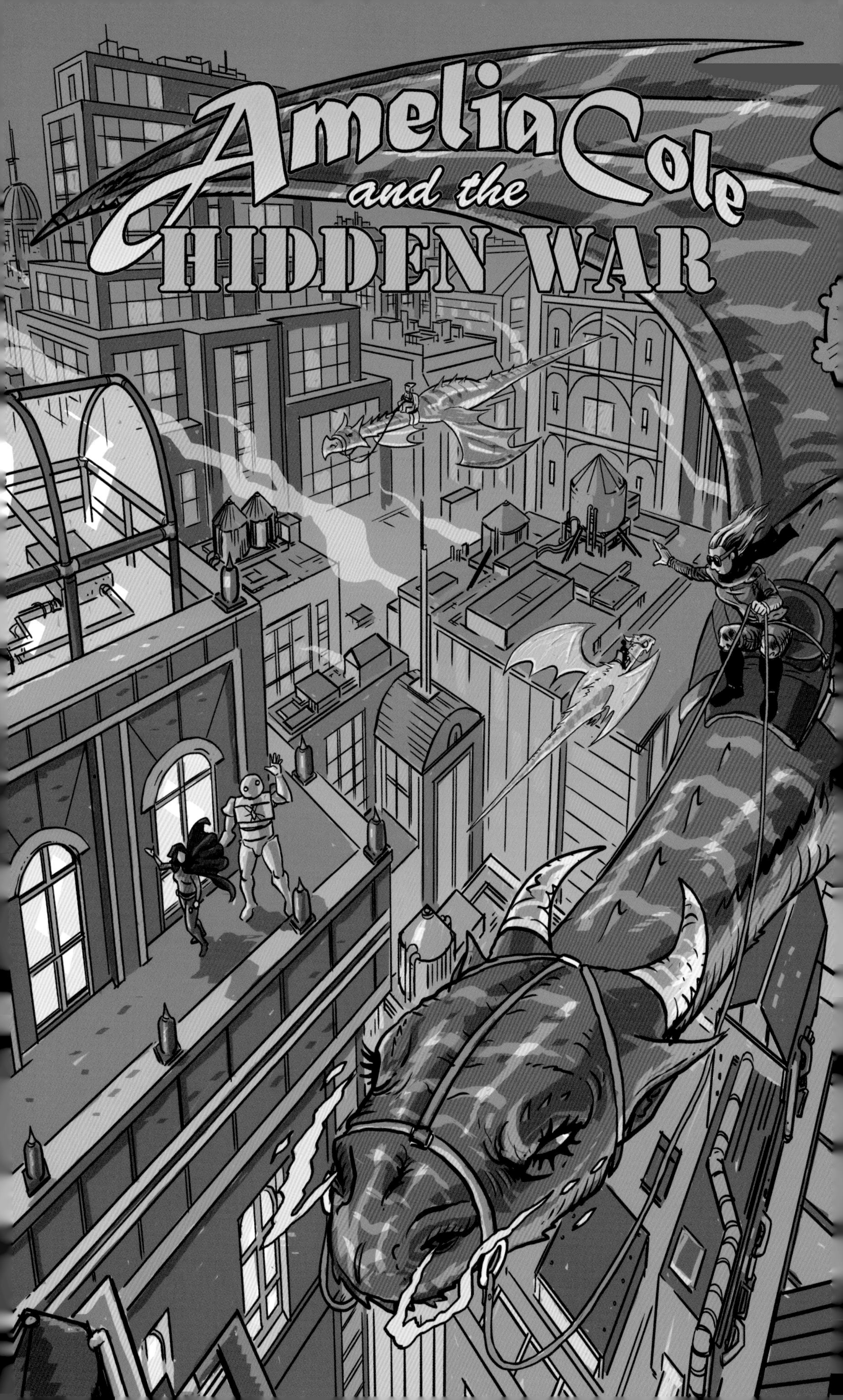
Amelia Cole
and the
HIDDEN WAR

CHAPTER 6

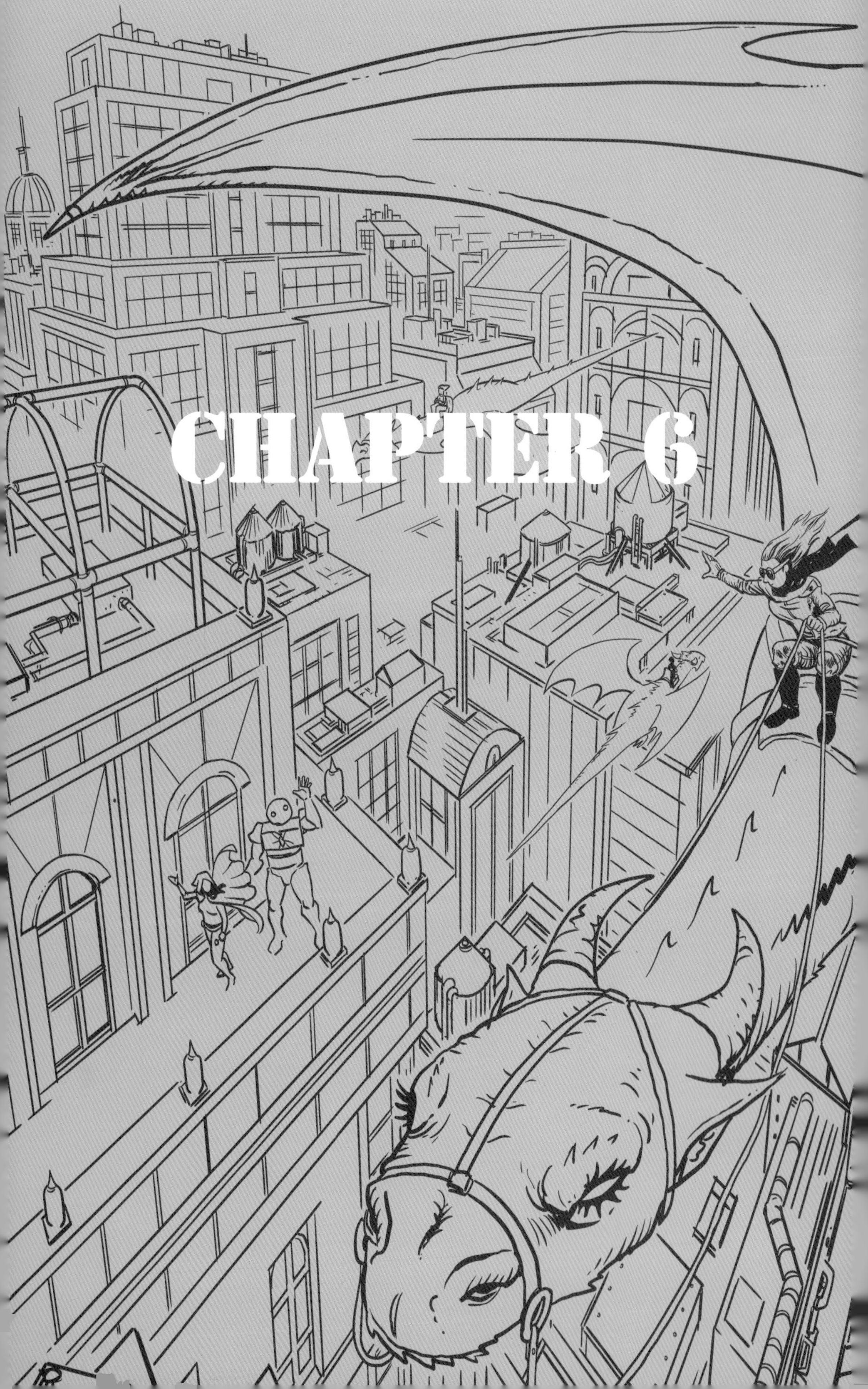

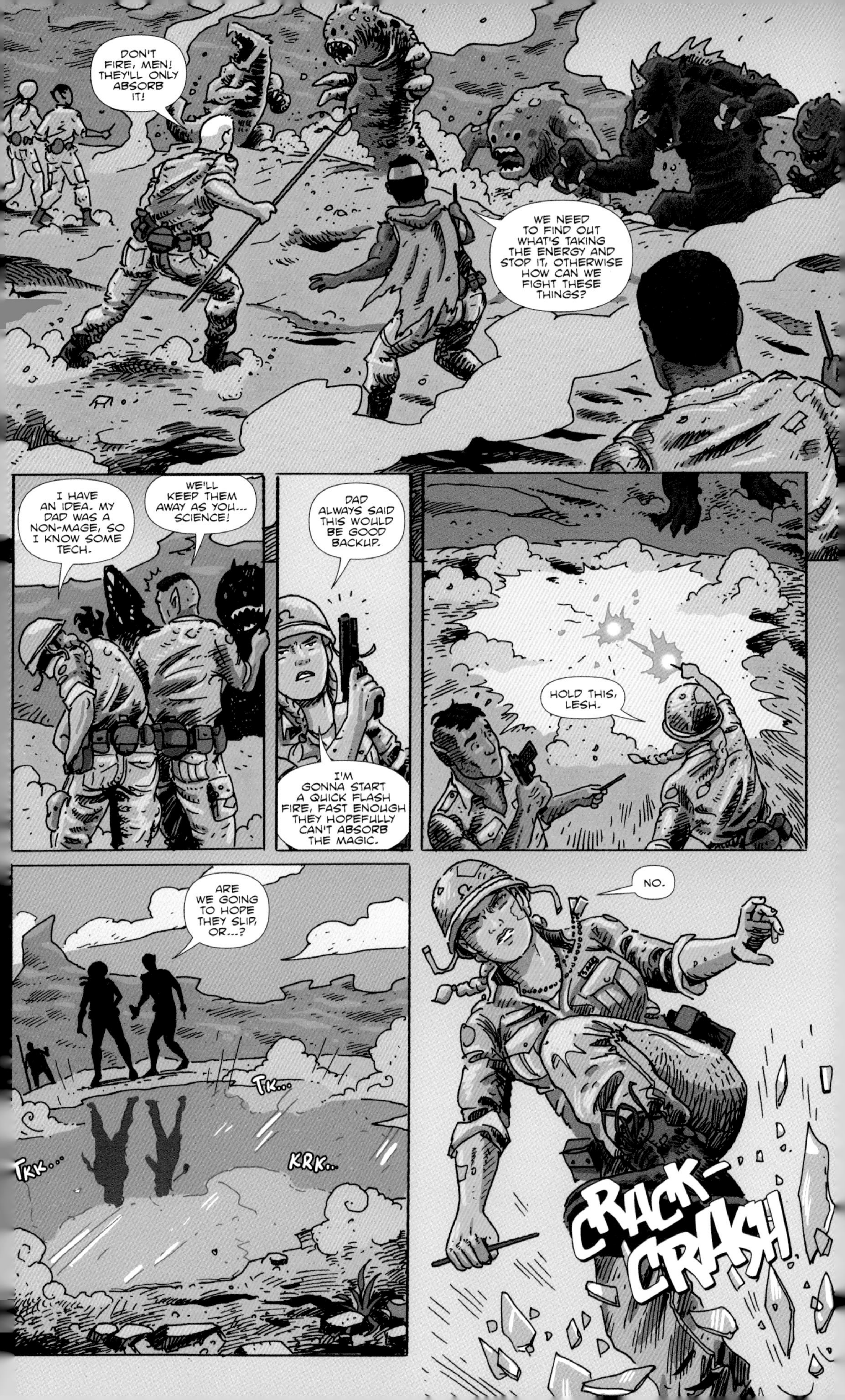
DON'T FIRE, MEN! THEY'LL ONLY ABSORB IT!
WE NEED TO FIND OUT WHAT'S TAKING THE ENERGY AND STOP IT, OTHERWISE HOW CAN WE FIGHT THESE THINGS?
I HAVE AN IDEA. MY DAD WAS A NON-MAGE, SO I KNOW SOME TECH.
WE'LL KEEP THEM AWAY AS YOU... SCIENCE!
DAD ALWAYS SAID THIS WOULD BE GOOD BACKUP.
I'M GONNA START A QUICK FLASH FIRE, FAST ENOUGH THEY HOPEFULLY CAN'T ABSORB THE MAGIC.
HOLD THIS, LESH.
ARE WE GOING TO HOPE THEY SLIP, OR...?
TK...
TKK...
KRK...
NO.
CRACK-CRASH

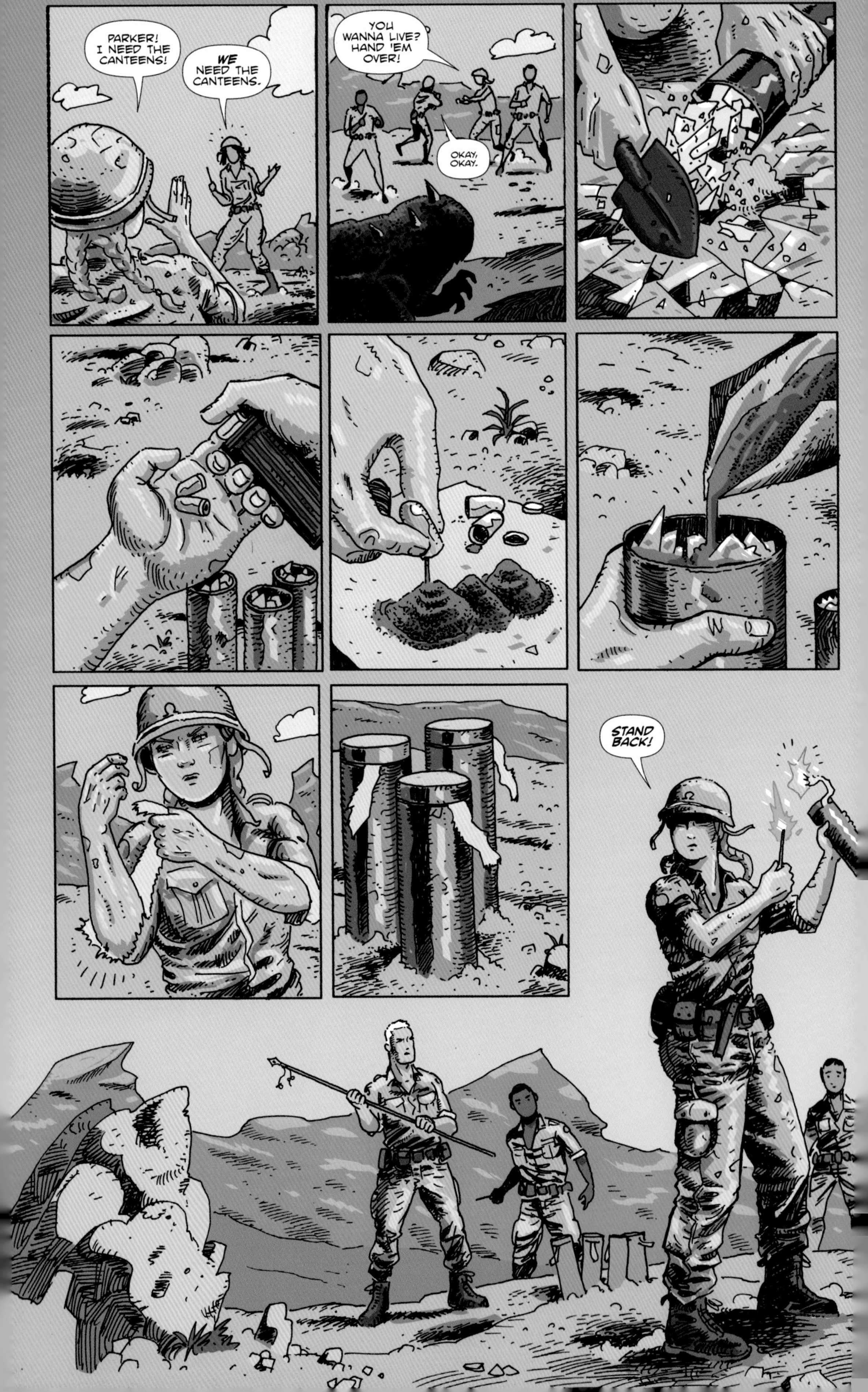
PARKER! I NEED THE CANTEENS!
WE NEED THE CANTEENS.
YOU WANNA LIVE? HAND 'EM OVER!
OKAY, OKAY.
STAND BACK!

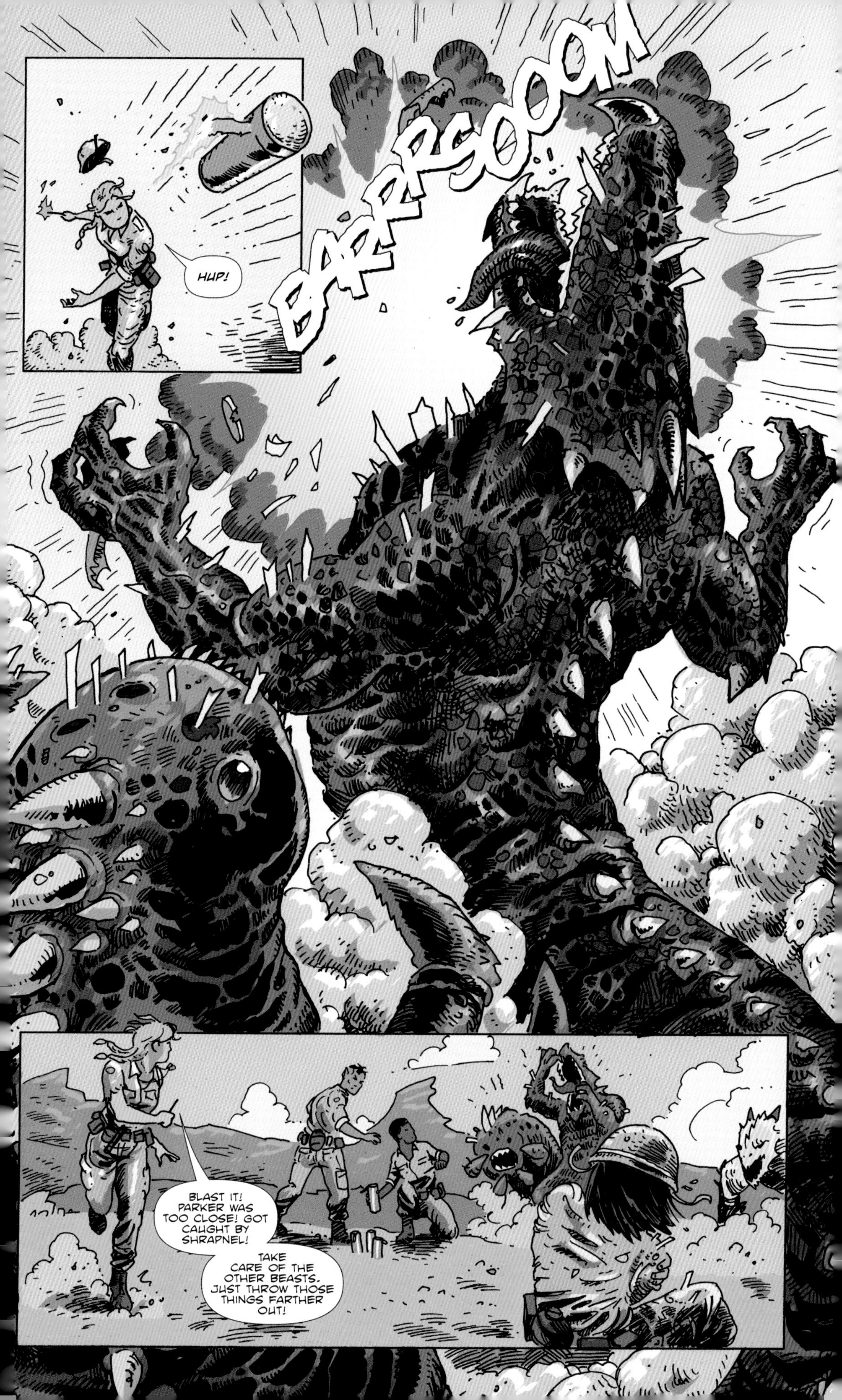
HUP!
BARRRSOOOM
BLAST IT! PARKER WAS TOO CLOSE! GOT CAUGHT BY SHRAPNEL!
TAKE CARE OF THE OTHER BEASTS. JUST THROW THOSE THINGS FARTHER OUT!

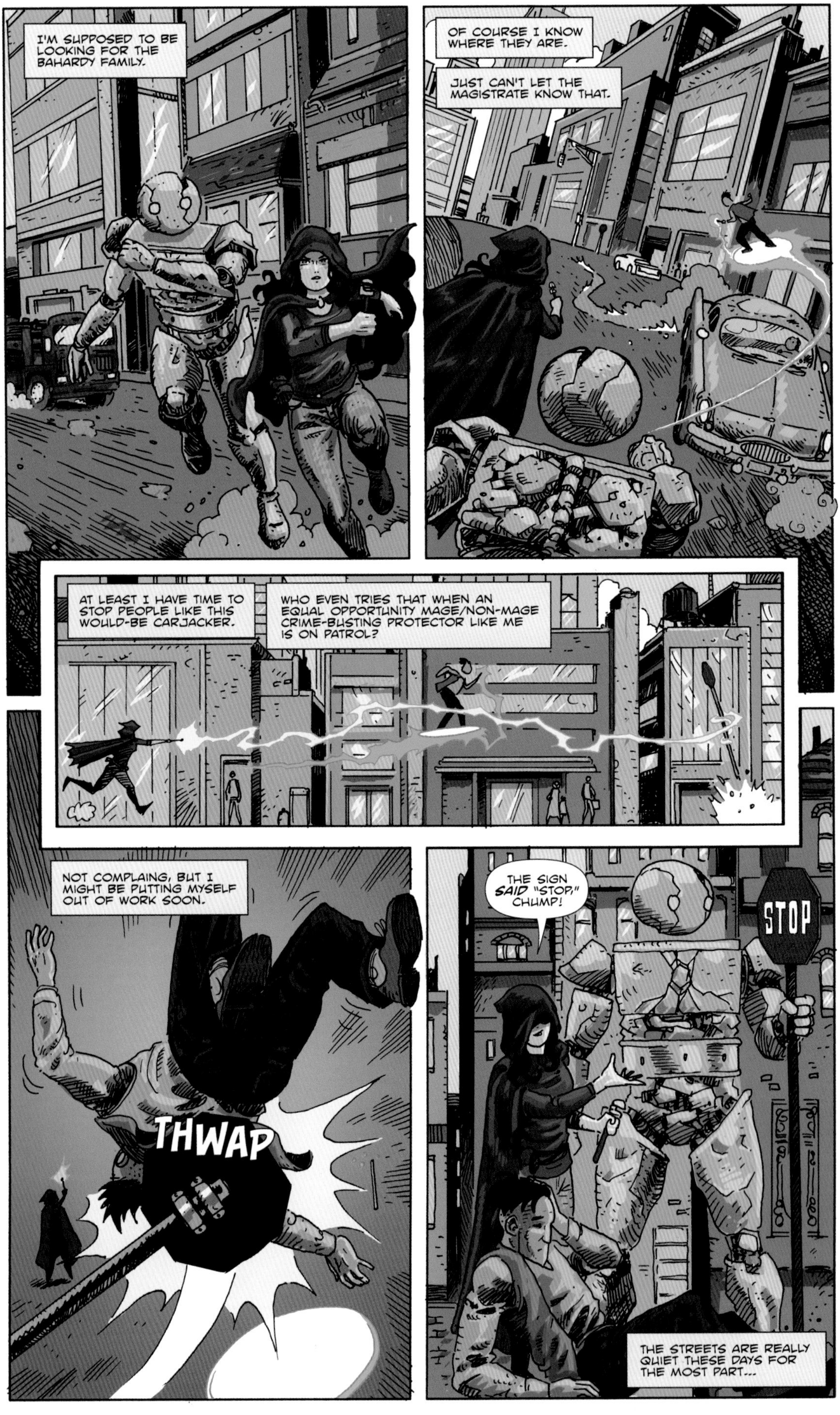
I'M SUPPOSED TO BE LOOKING FOR THE BAHARDY FAMILY.
OF COURSE I KNOW WHERE THEY ARE.
JUST CAN'T LET THE MAGISTRATE KNOW THAT.
AT LEAST I HAVE TIME TO STOP PEOPLE LIKE THIS WOULD-BE CARJACKER.
WHO EVEN TRIES THAT WHEN AN EQUAL OPPORTUNITY MAGE/NON-MAGE CRIME-BUSTING PROTECTOR LIKE ME IS ON PATROL?
NOT COMPLAING, BUT I MIGHT BE PUTTING MYSELF OUT OF WORK SOON.
THWAP
THE SIGN *SAID* "STOP," CHUMP!
STOP
THE STREETS ARE REALLY QUIET THESE DAYS FOR THE MOST PART...

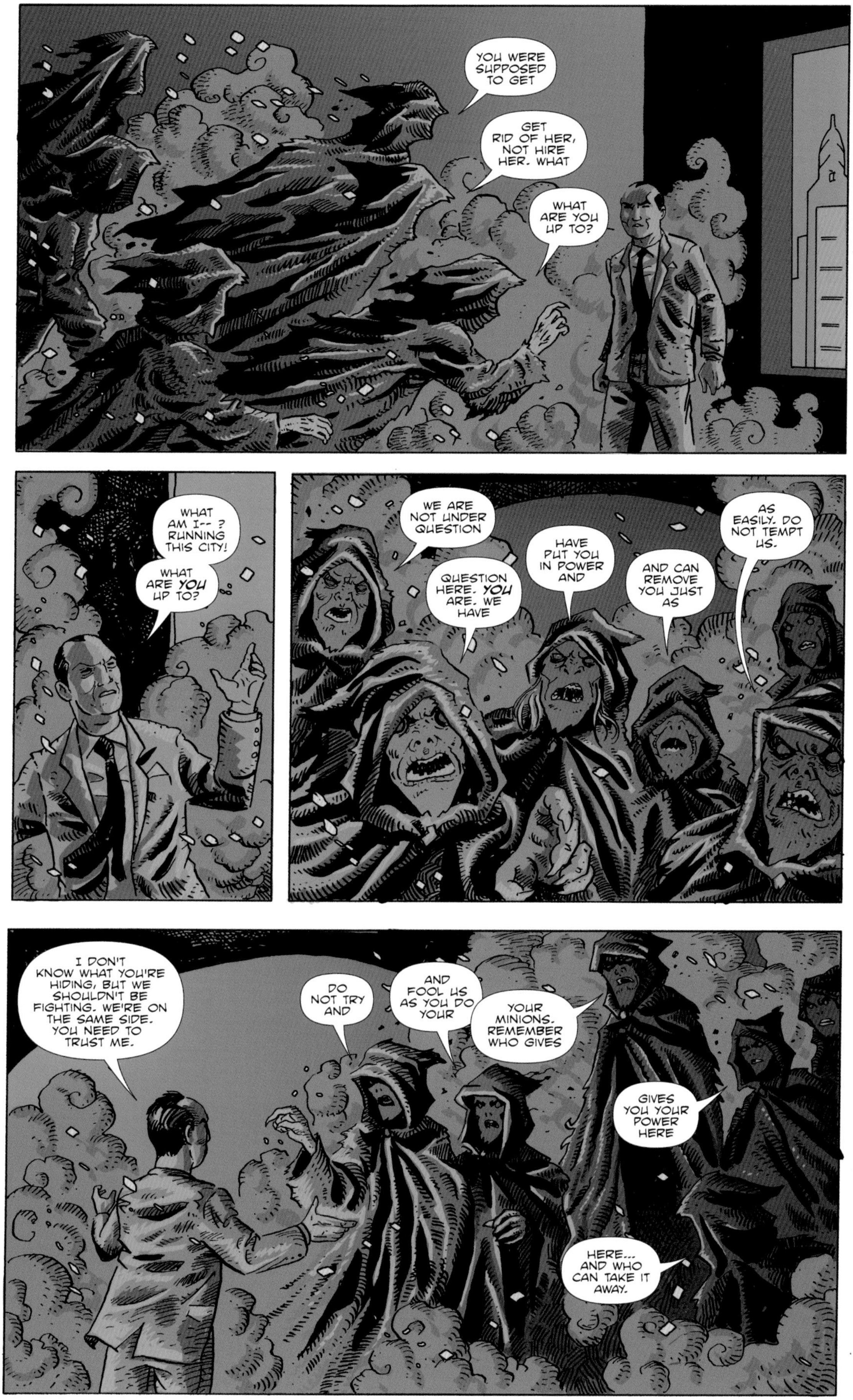
YOU WERE SUPPOSED TO GET
GET RID OF HER, NOT HIRE HER. WHAT
WHAT ARE YOU UP TO?
WHAT AM I-- ? RUNNING THIS CITY!
WHAT ARE *YOU* UP TO?
WE ARE NOT UNDER QUESTION
QUESTION HERE. *YOU* ARE. WE HAVE
HAVE PUT YOU IN POWER AND
AND CAN REMOVE YOU JUST AS
AS EASILY. DO NOT TEMPT US.
I DON'T KNOW WHAT YOU'RE HIDING, BUT WE SHOULDN'T BE FIGHTING. WE'RE ON THE SAME SIDE. YOU NEED TO TRUST ME.
DO NOT TRY AND
AND FOOL US AS YOU DO YOUR
YOUR MINIONS. REMEMBER WHO GIVES
GIVES YOU YOUR POWER HERE
HERE... AND WHO CAN TAKE IT AWAY.

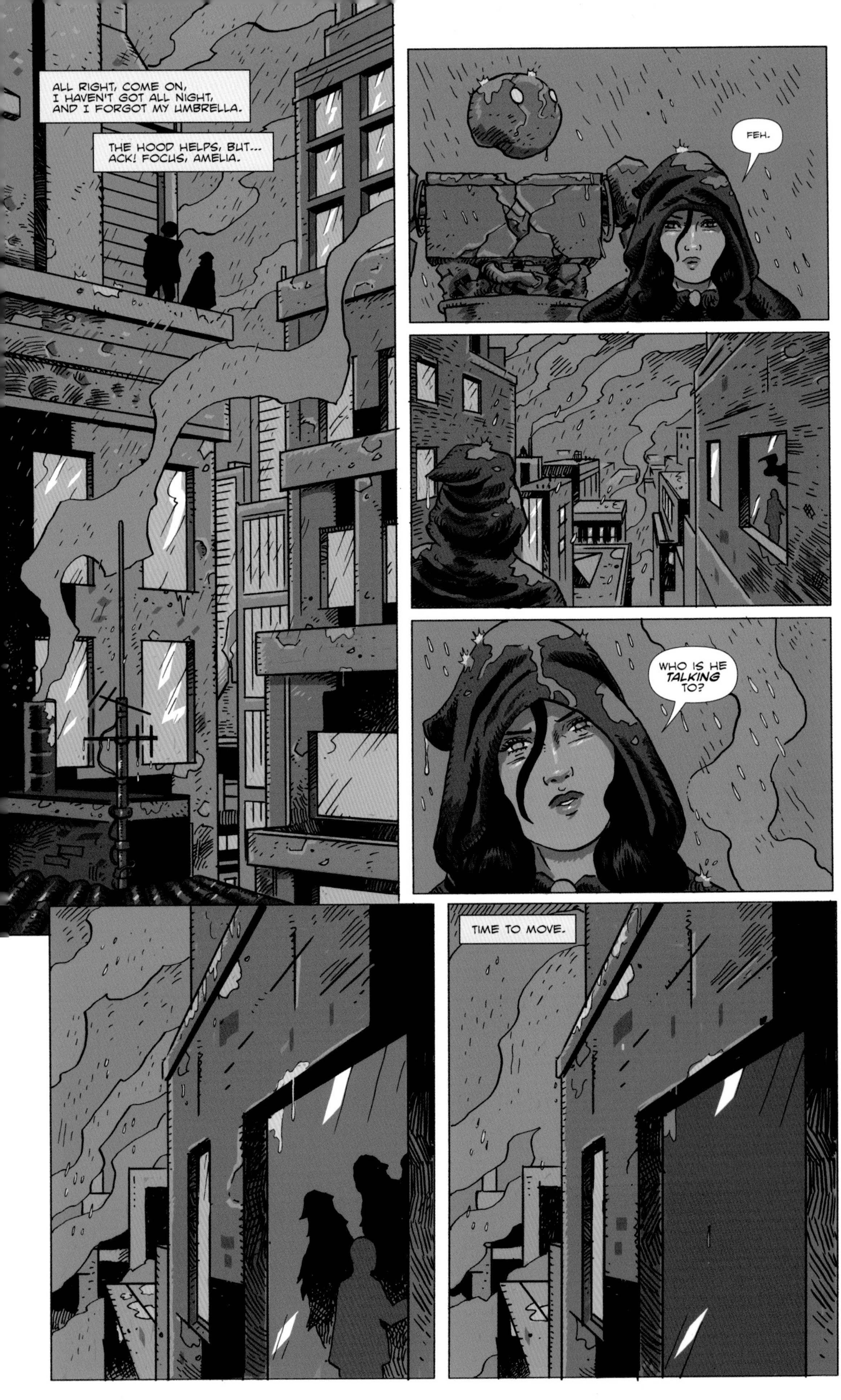
ALL RIGHT, COME ON, I HAVEN'T GOT ALL NIGHT, AND I FORGOT MY UMBRELLA.
THE HOOD HELPS, BUT... ACK! FOCUS, AMELIA.
FEH.
WHO IS HE *TALKING* TO?
TIME TO MOVE.

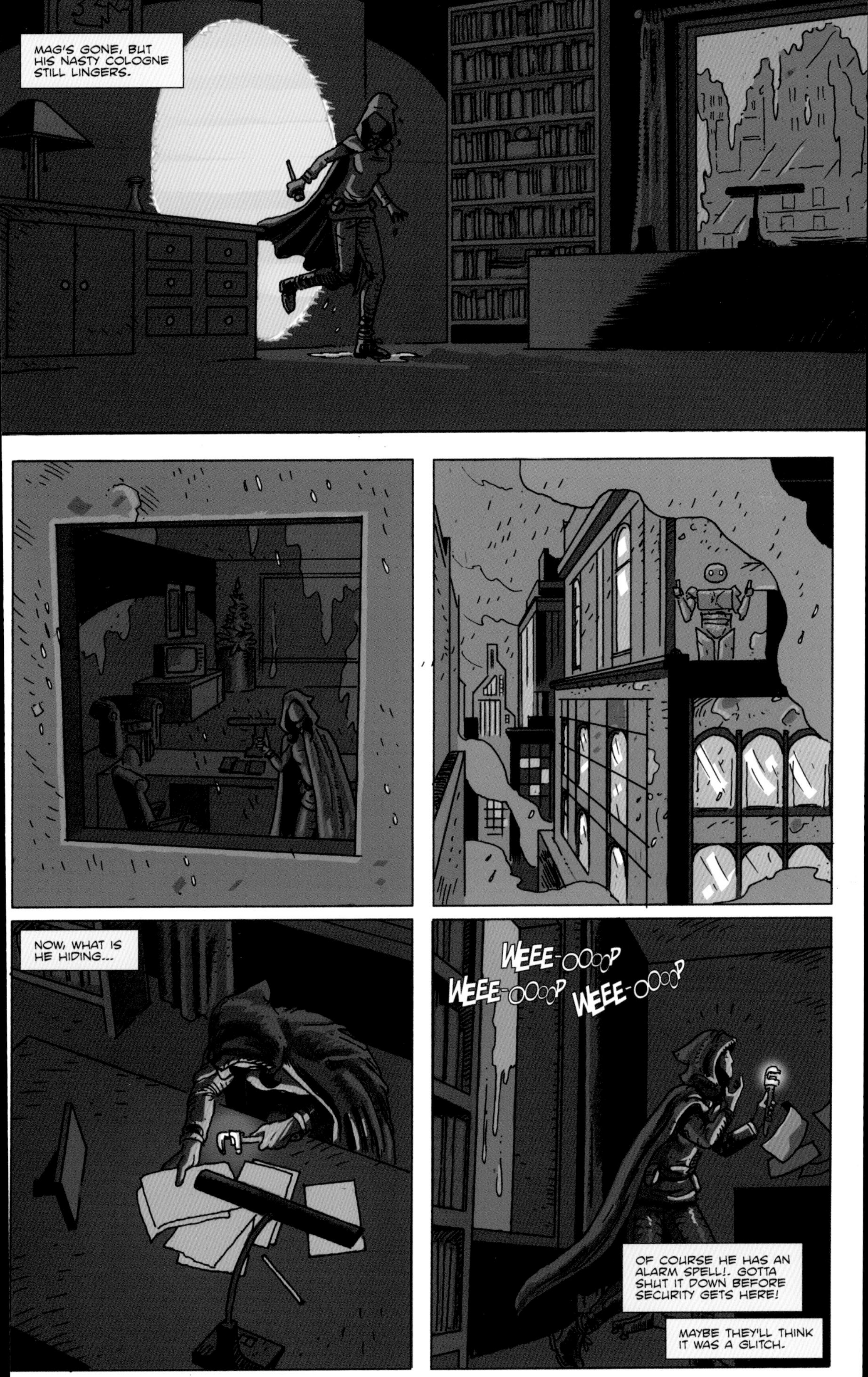
MAG'S GONE, BUT HIS NASTY COLOGNE STILL LINGERS.
NOW, WHAT IS HE HIDING...
WEEE-OOOOP
WEEE-OOOOP WEEE-OOOOP
OF COURSE HE HAS AN ALARM SPELL!. GOTTA SHUT IT DOWN BEFORE SECURITY GETS HERE!
MAYBE THEY'LL THINK IT WAS A GLITCH.

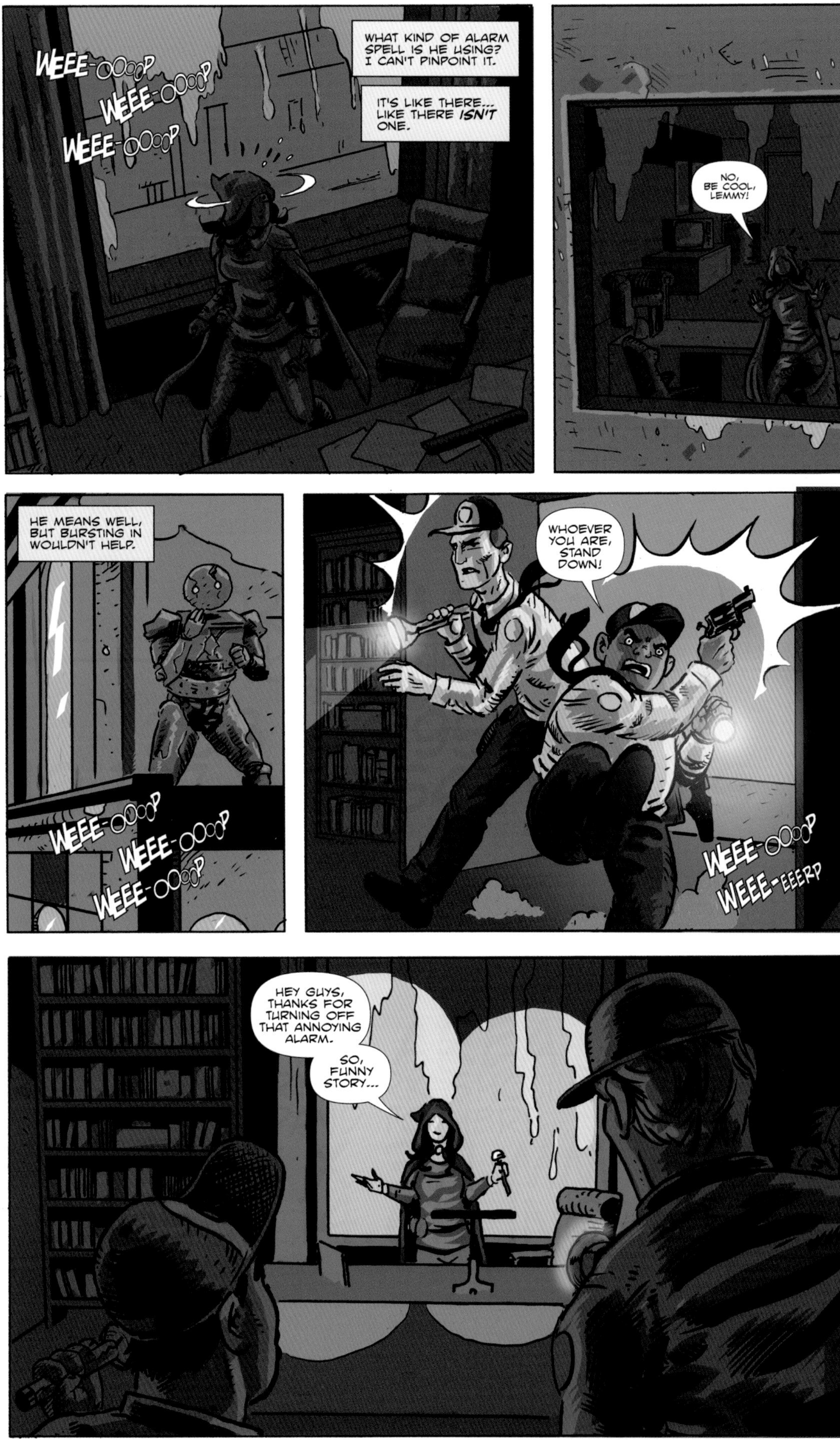
WEEE-OOOOP
WEEE-OOOOP
WEEE-OOOOP
WHAT KIND OF ALARM SPELL IS HE USING? I CAN'T PINPOINT IT.
IT'S LIKE THERE... LIKE THERE *ISN'T* ONE.
NO, BE COOL, LEMMY!
HE MEANS WELL, BUT BURSTING IN WOULDN'T HELP.
WEEE-OOOOP
WEEE-OOOOP
WEEE-OOOOP
WHOEVER YOU ARE, STAND DOWN!
WEEE-OOOOP
WEEE-EEERP
HEY GUYS, THANKS FOR TURNING OFF THAT ANNOYING ALARM.
SO, FUNNY STORY...

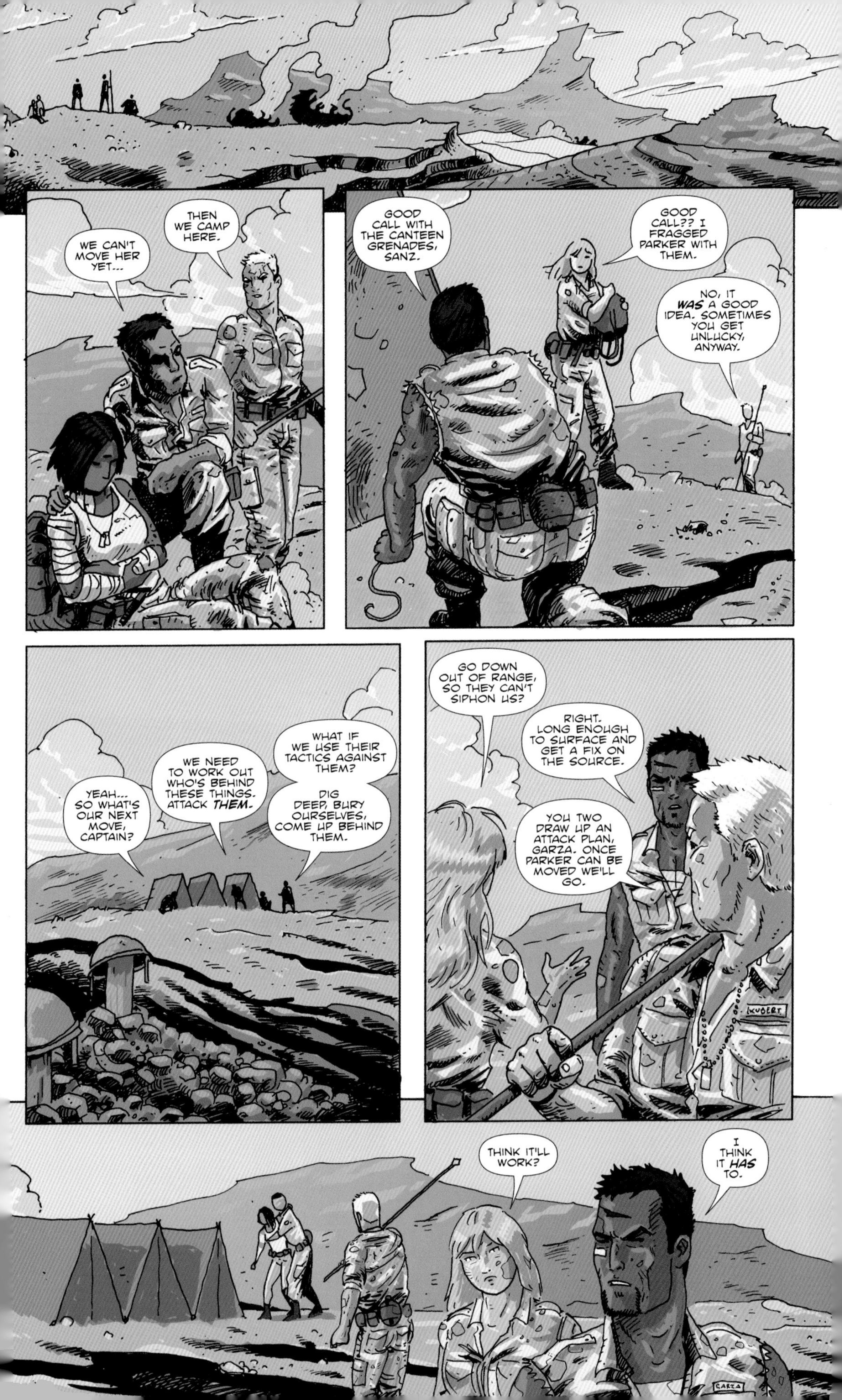
WE CAN'T MOVE HER YET...
THEN WE CAMP HERE.
GOOD CALL WITH THE CANTEEN GRENADES, SANZ.
GOOD CALL?? I FRAGGED PARKER WITH THEM.
NO, IT WAS A GOOD IDEA. SOMETIMES YOU GET UNLUCKY, ANYWAY.
YEAH... SO WHAT'S OUR NEXT MOVE, CAPTAIN?
WE NEED TO WORK OUT WHO'S BEHIND THESE THINGS. ATTACK THEM.
WHAT IF WE USE THEIR TACTICS AGAINST THEM?
DIG DEEP, BURY OURSELVES, COME UP BEHIND THEM.
GO DOWN OUT OF RANGE, SO THEY CAN'T SIPHON US?
RIGHT. LONG ENOUGH TO SURFACE AND GET A FIX ON THE SOURCE.
YOU TWO DRAW UP AN ATTACK PLAN, GARZA. ONCE PARKER CAN BE MOVED WE'LL GO.
KUBERT
THINK IT'LL WORK?
I THINK IT HAS TO.
GARZA

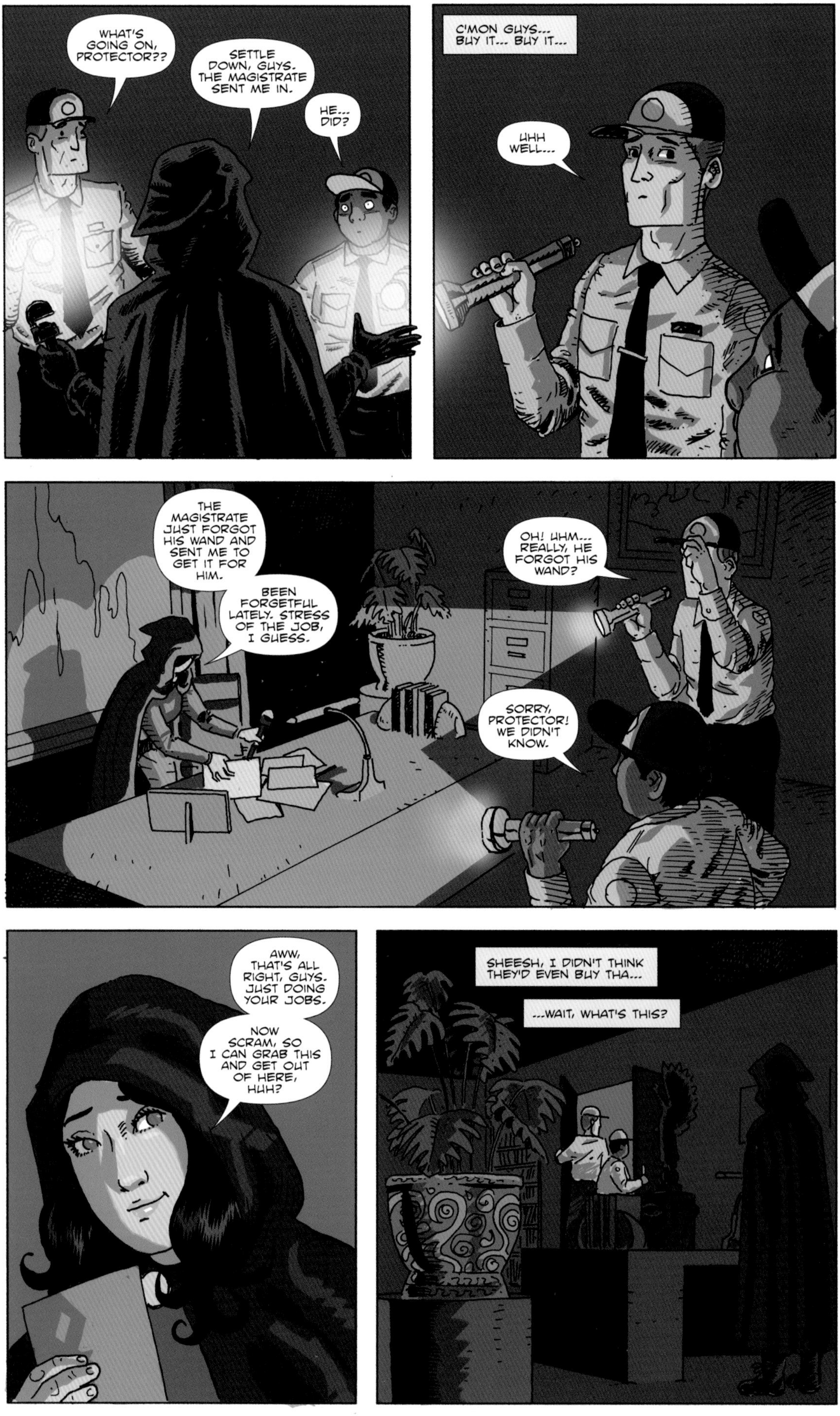
WHAT'S GOING ON, PROTECTOR??
SETTLE DOWN, GUYS. THE MAGISTRATE SENT ME IN.
HE... DID?
C'MON GUYS... BUY IT... BUY IT...
UHH WELL...
THE MAGISTRATE JUST FORGOT HIS WAND AND SENT ME TO GET IT FOR HIM.
BEEN FORGETFUL LATELY. STRESS OF THE JOB, I GUESS.
OH! UHM... REALLY, HE FORGOT HIS WAND?
SORRY, PROTECTOR! WE DIDN'T KNOW.
AWW, THAT'S ALL RIGHT, GUYS. JUST DOING YOUR JOBS.
NOW SCRAM, SO I CAN GRAB THIS AND GET OUT OF HERE, HUH?
SHEESH, I DIDN'T THINK THEY'D EVEN BUY THA...
...WAIT, WHAT'S THIS?

I WAS BLUFFING WHEN I SAID HE LEFT IT BEHIND.

MAGES DON'T GO ANYWHERE WITHOUT A WAND.

FIRST THE PHONE CALL AND NOW THIS... WHAT'S THE DEAL?

WHAT'S A WAND NEED WITH A BUTTON?

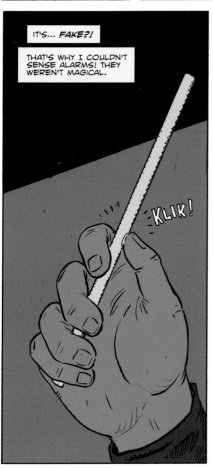

IT'S... FAKE?!

THAT'S WHY I COULDN'T SENSE ALARMS! THEY WEREN'T MAGICAL.

KLIK!

BUT IF IT'S ALL FAKED... IF HE ISN'T A MAGE... HOW DID HE GET ELECTED MAGISTRATE? HOW DID HE FOOL EVERYONE?

LONG LIFE

LONG LIFE

THIS IS ALL KINDS OF NOT RIGHT.

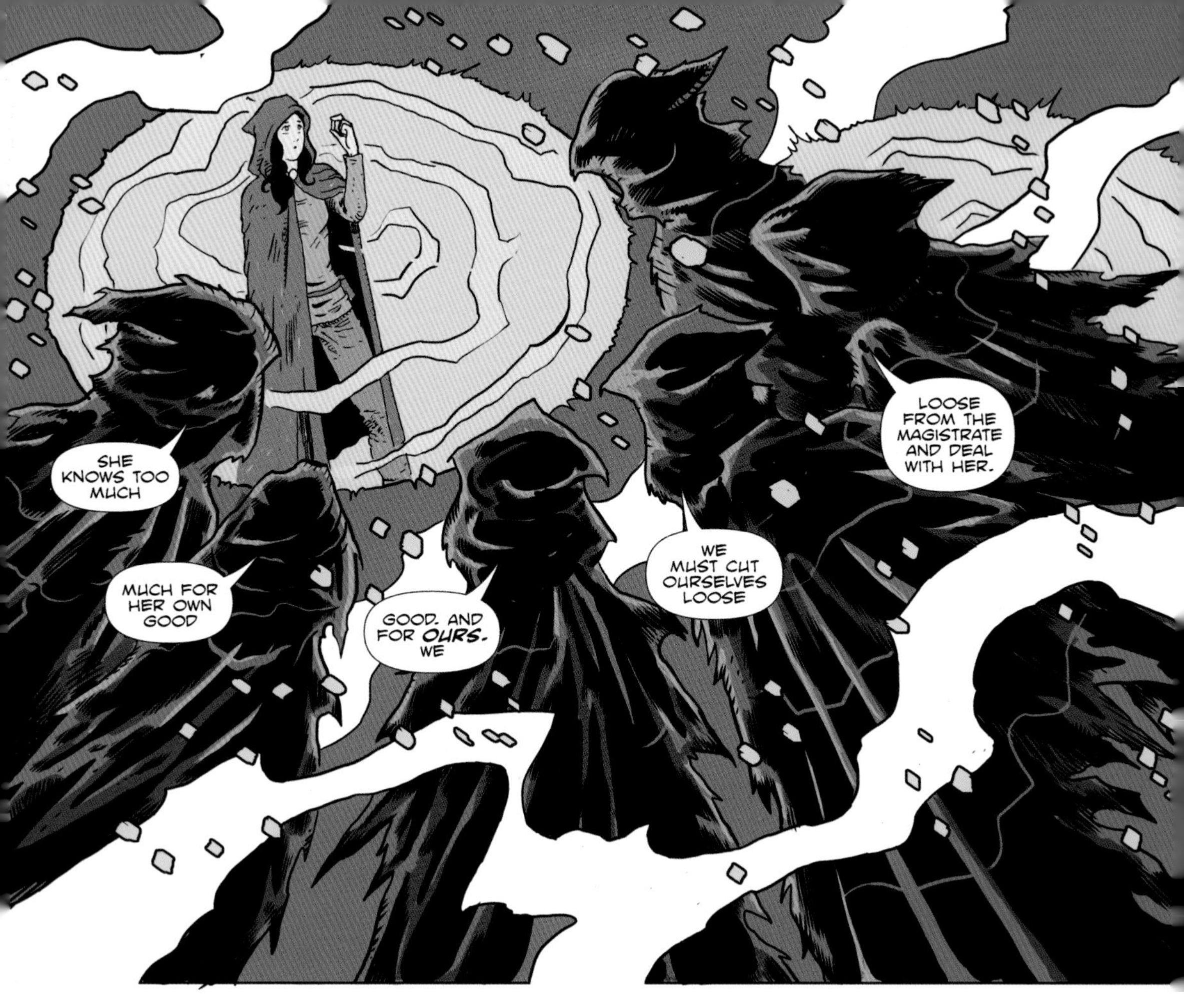
SHE KNOWS TOO MUCH
MUCH FOR HER OWN GOOD
GOOD. AND FOR OURS. WE
WE MUST CUT OURSELVES LOOSE
LOOSE FROM THE MAGISTRATE AND DEAL WITH HER.

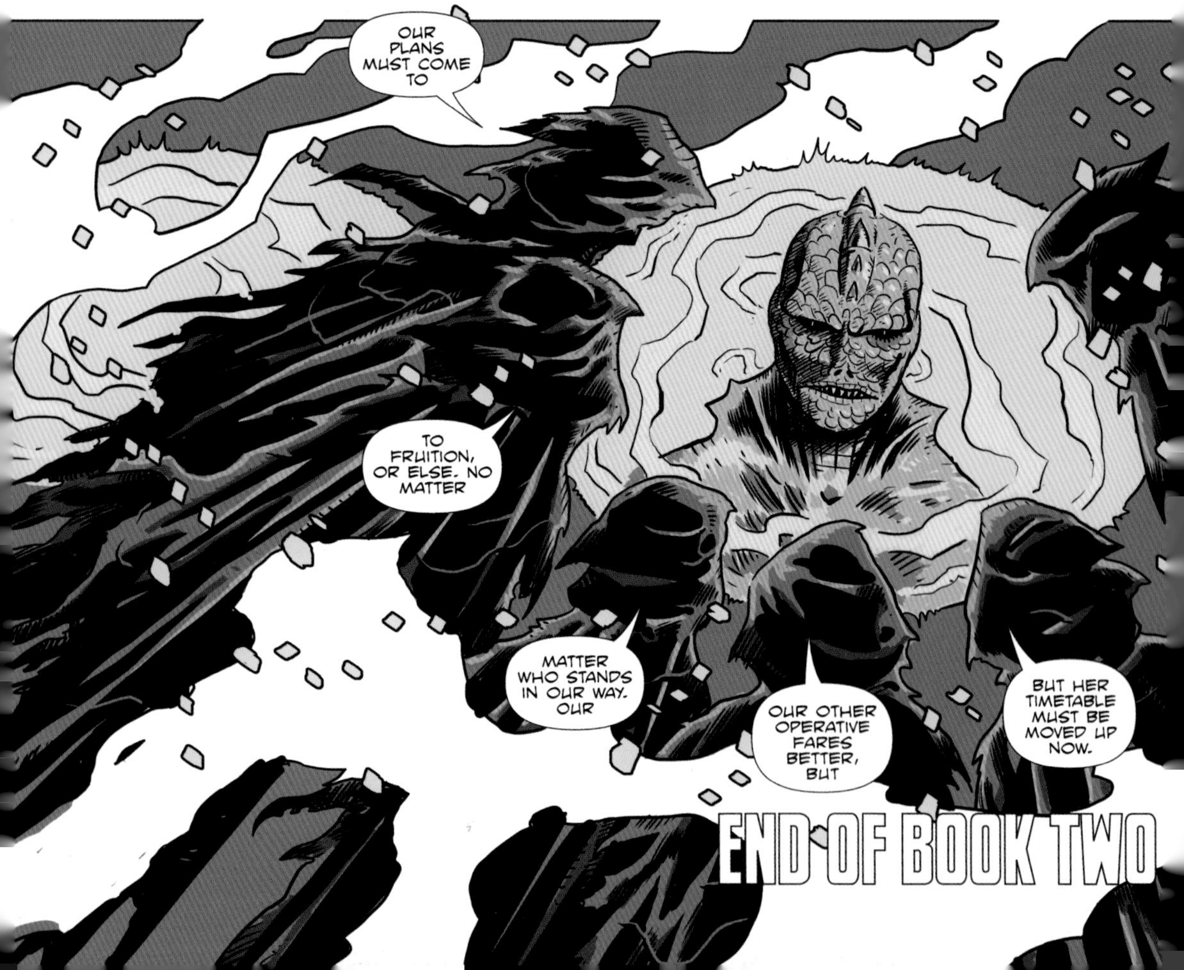
OUR PLANS MUST COME TO
TO FRUITION, OR ELSE. NO MATTER
MATTER WHO STANDS IN OUR WAY. OUR
OUR OTHER OPERATIVE FARES BETTER, BUT
BUT HER TIMETABLE MUST BE MOVED UP NOW.
END OF BOOK TWO

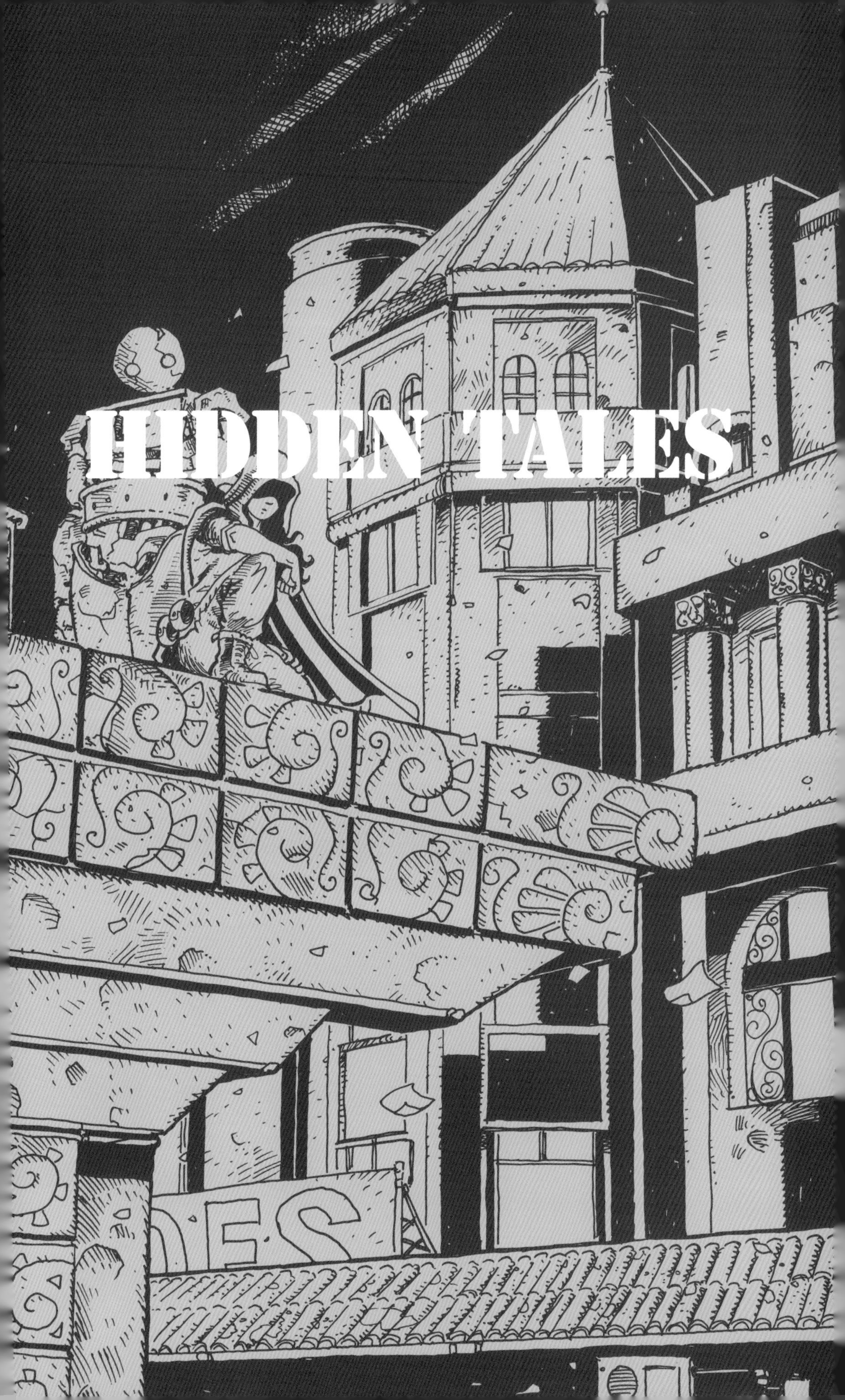
HIDDEN TALES

Nick wanted to show some moments that the main comic just didn't have time to go into. To that end he created, with a couple story ideas from Adam & D.J., the following silent one-pagers. Each comic fills in a bit more about the worlds and events you've been reading about in Volumes 1 and 2!

1. **LEAVING**
2. **PART-TIMER**
3. **BUMP**
4. **CHANGES**
5. **FLYING**

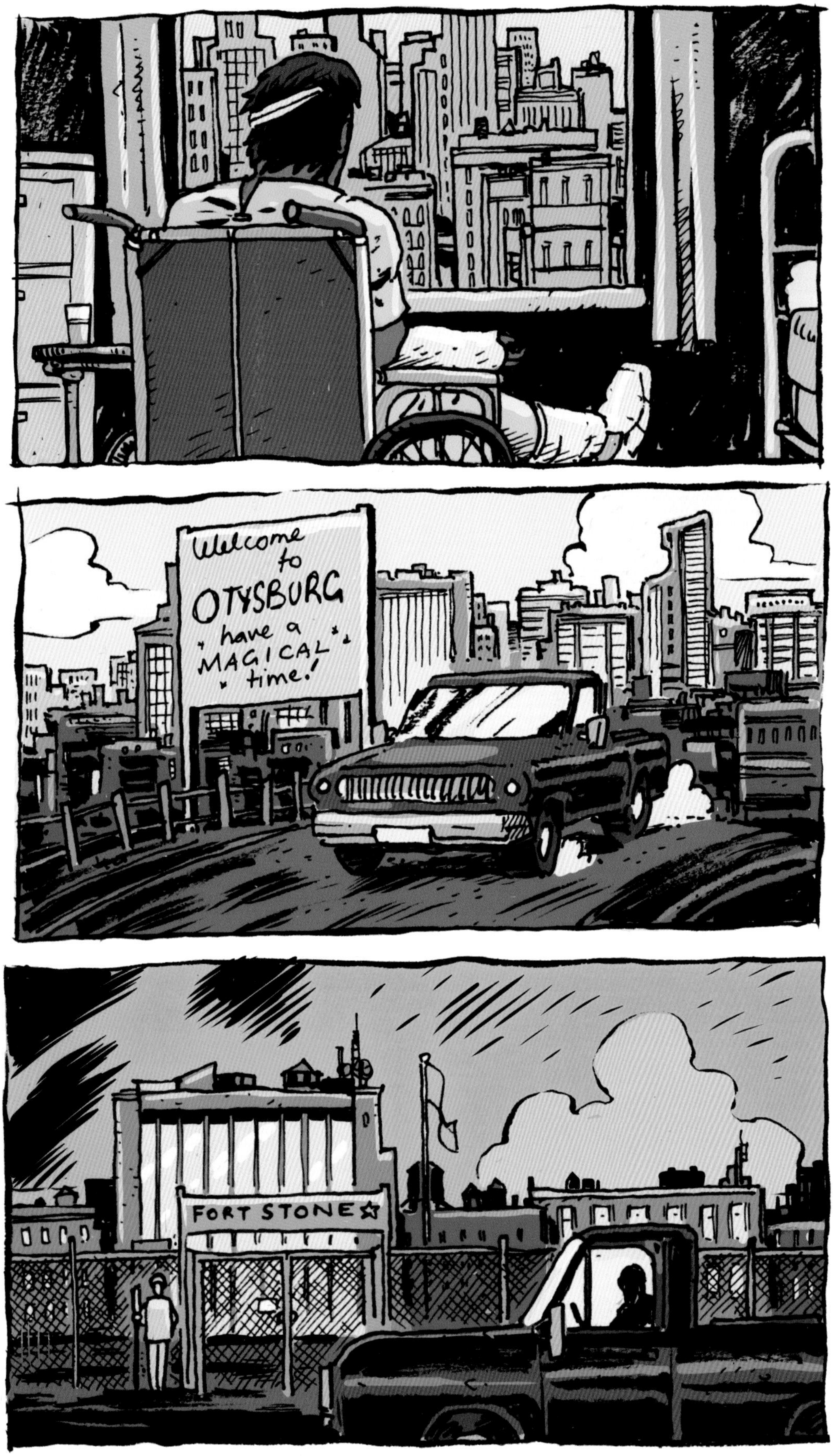
Welcome to OTYSBURG have a MAGICAL time!
FORT STONE

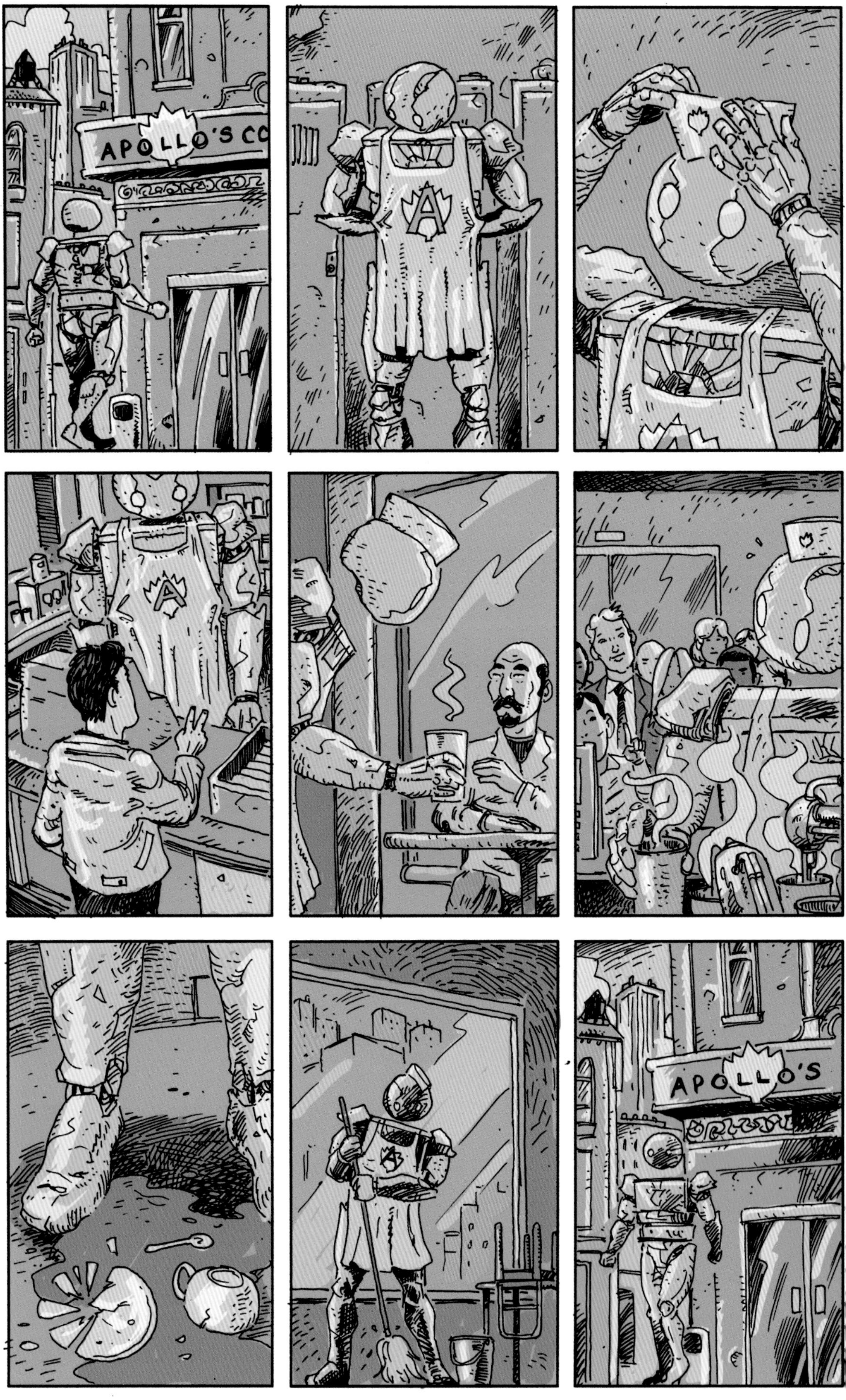
APOLLO'S CO
APOLLO'S

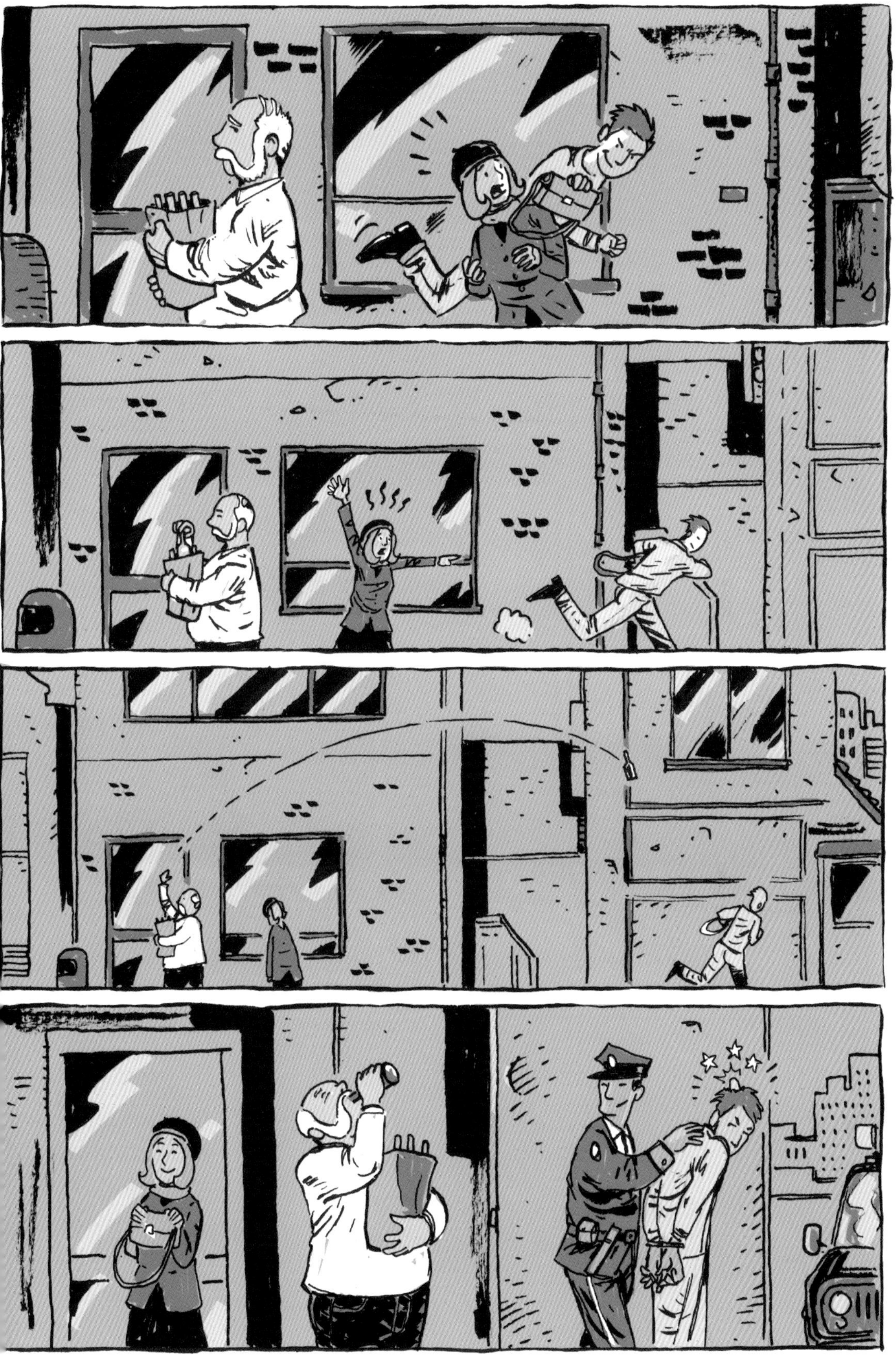

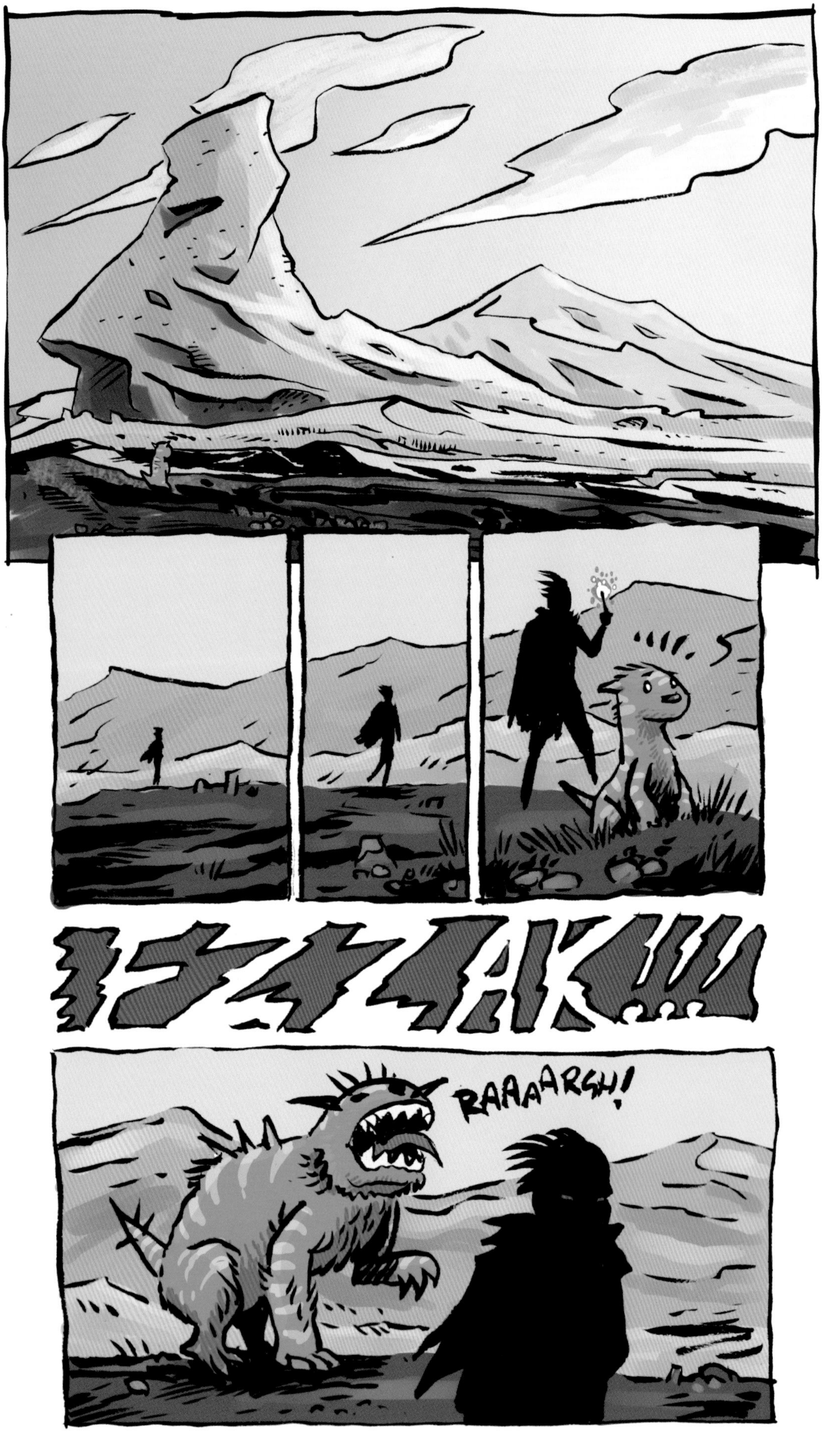
RAAAARGH!

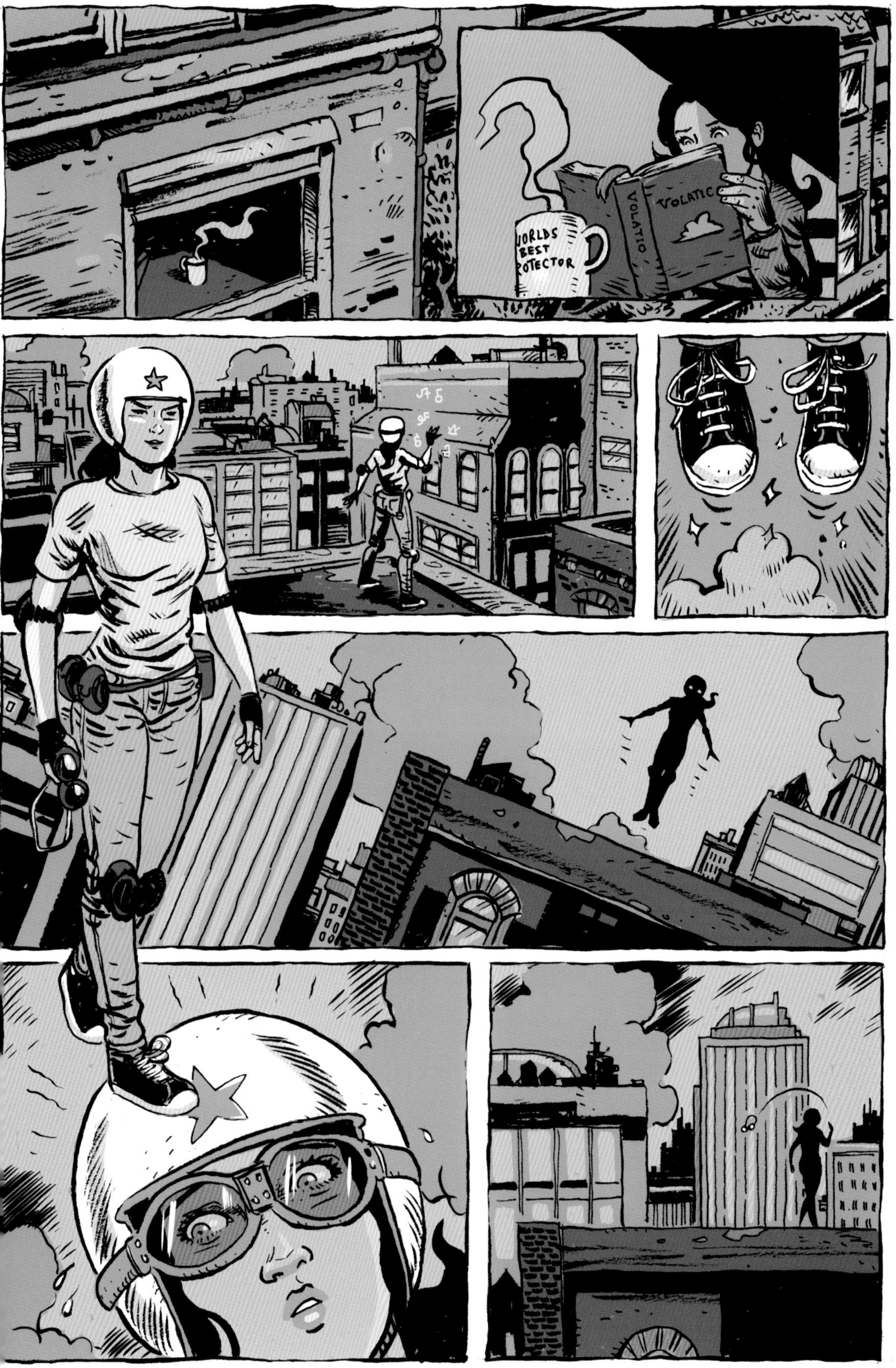
ORLDS
BEST
OTECTOR
VOLATIO
VOLATIC

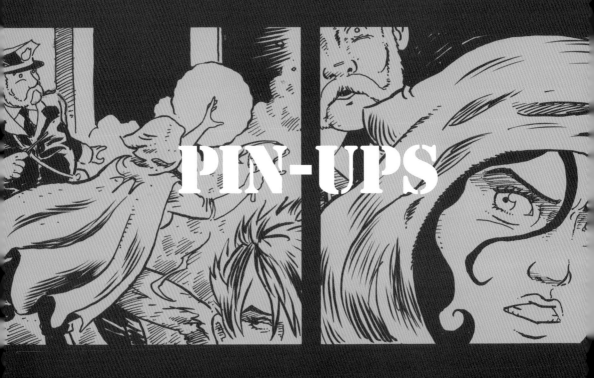

PIN-UPS

ART BY

ED SIOMACCO

JENNIFER MEYER

LAR DESOUZA

ROBERT LOVE

VASSILIS GOGTZILAS

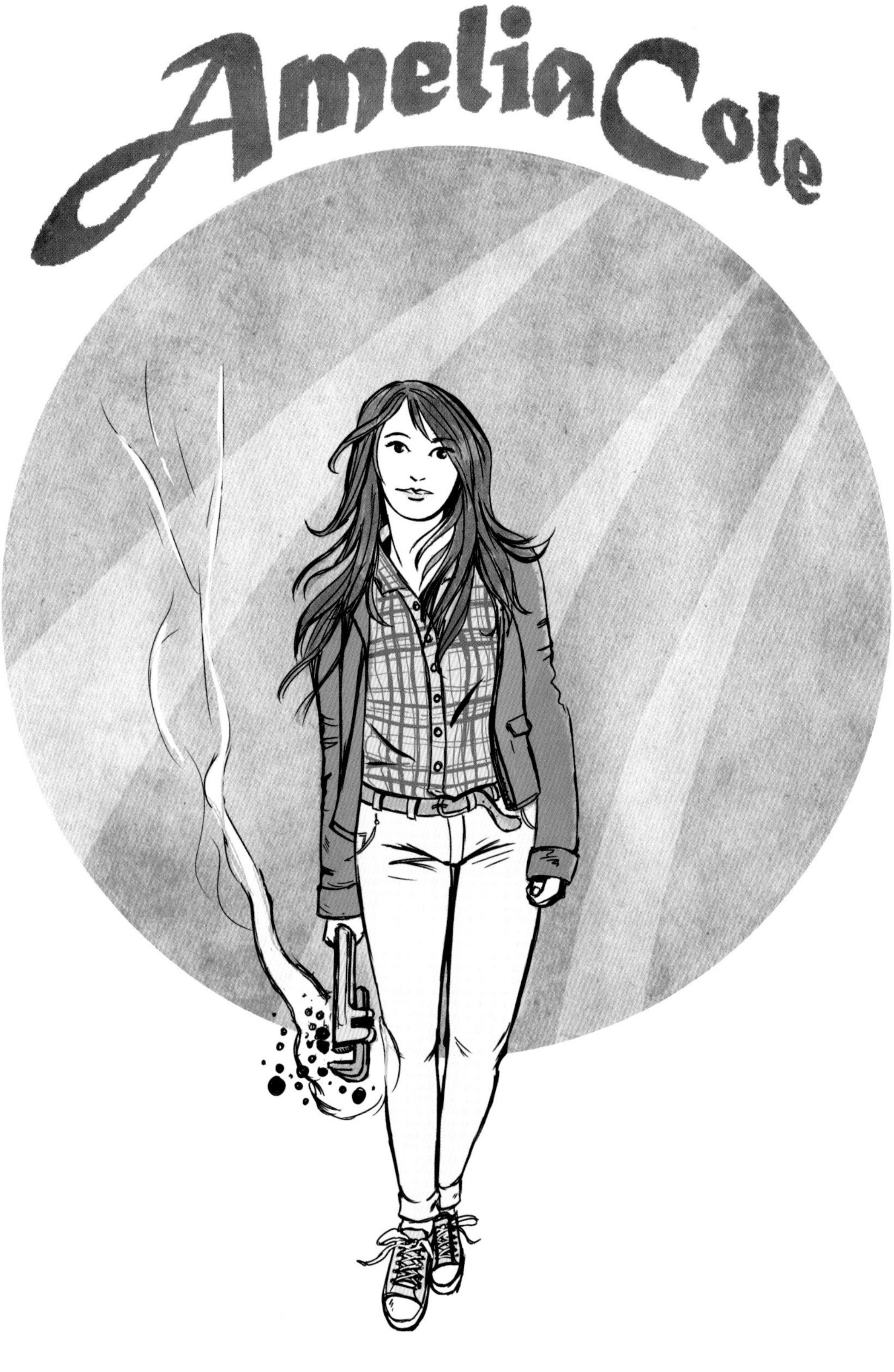
Amelia Cole

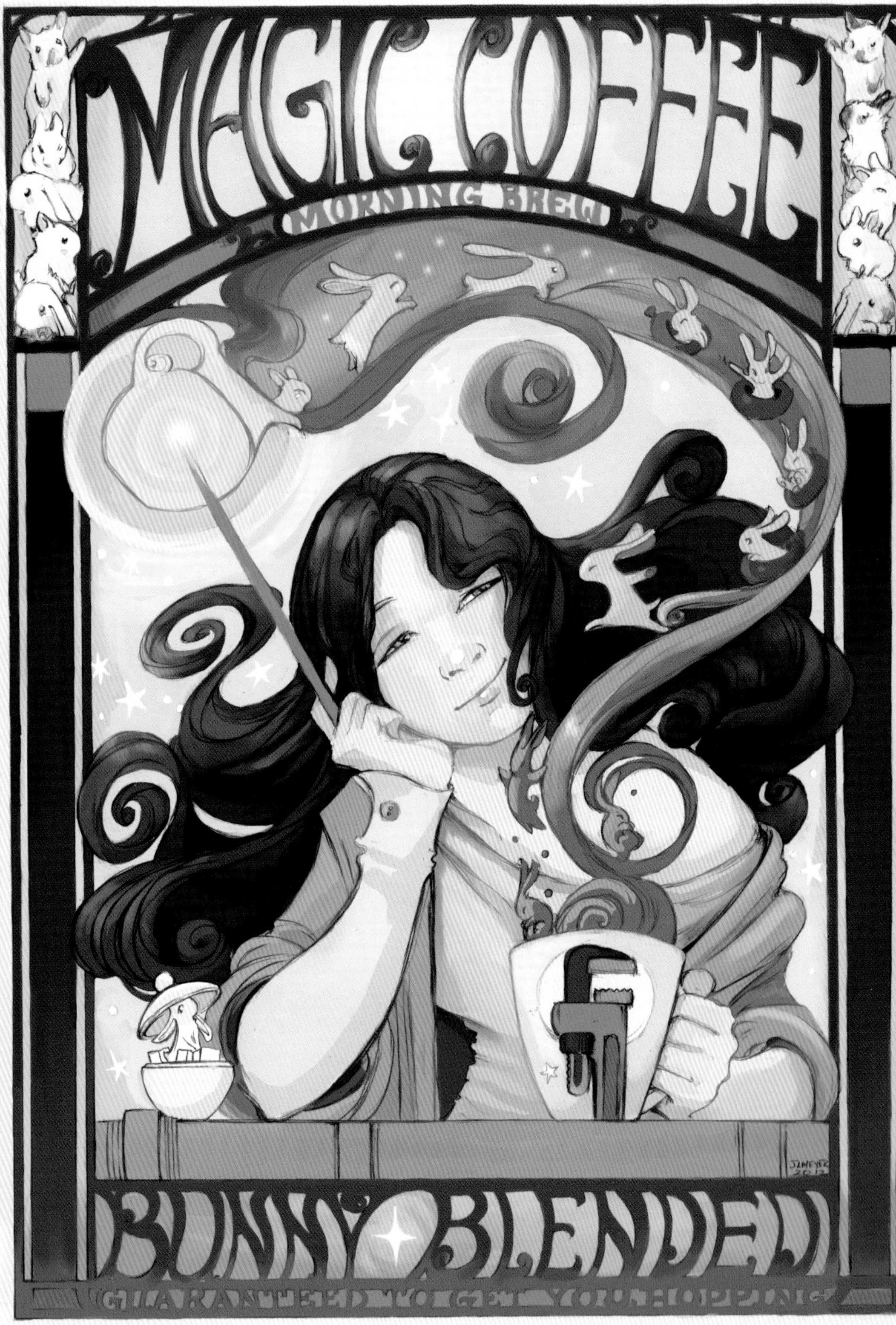
MAGIC COFFEE
MORNING BREW
BUNNY BLENDED
GUARANTEED TO GET YOU HOPPING

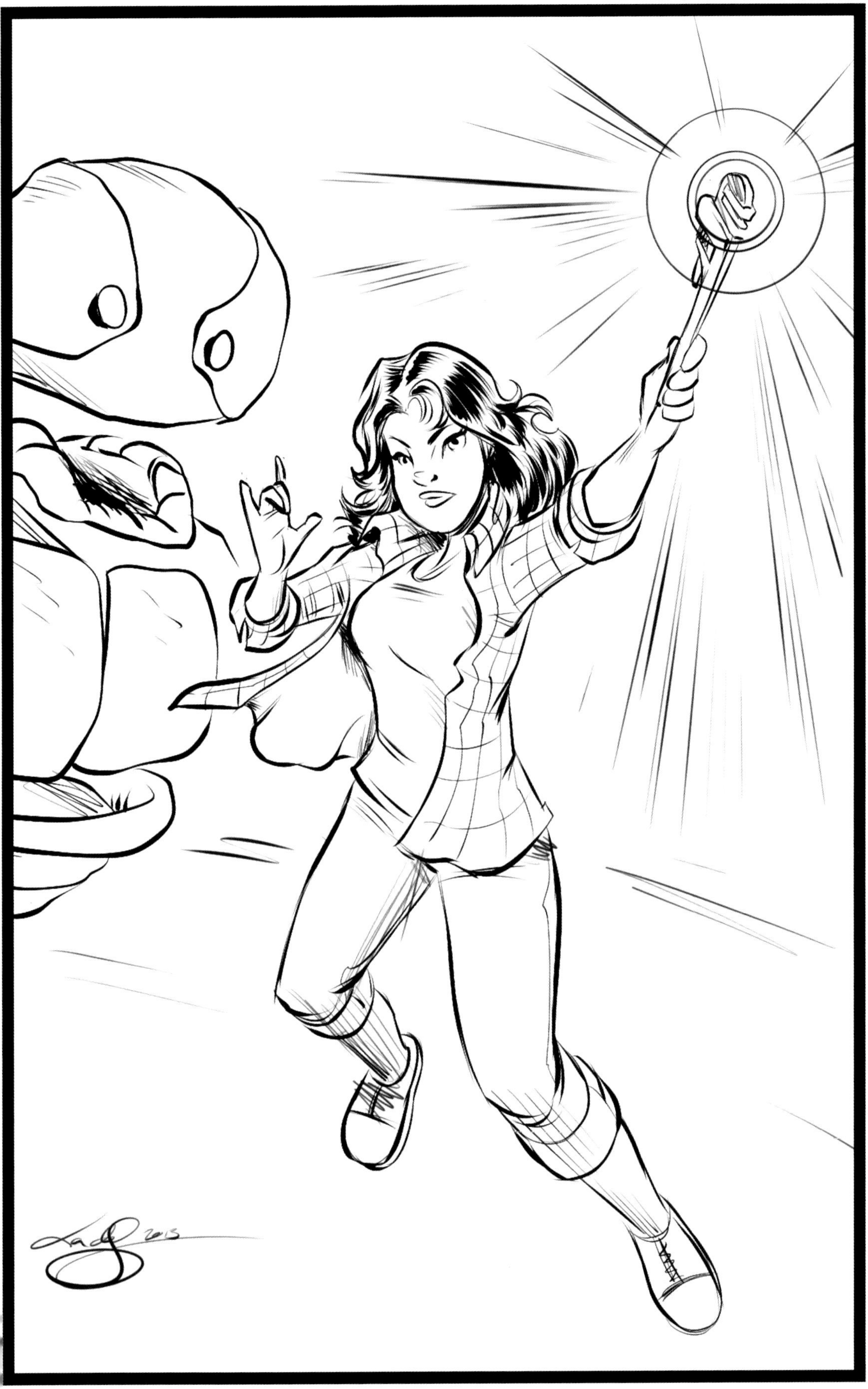
2013

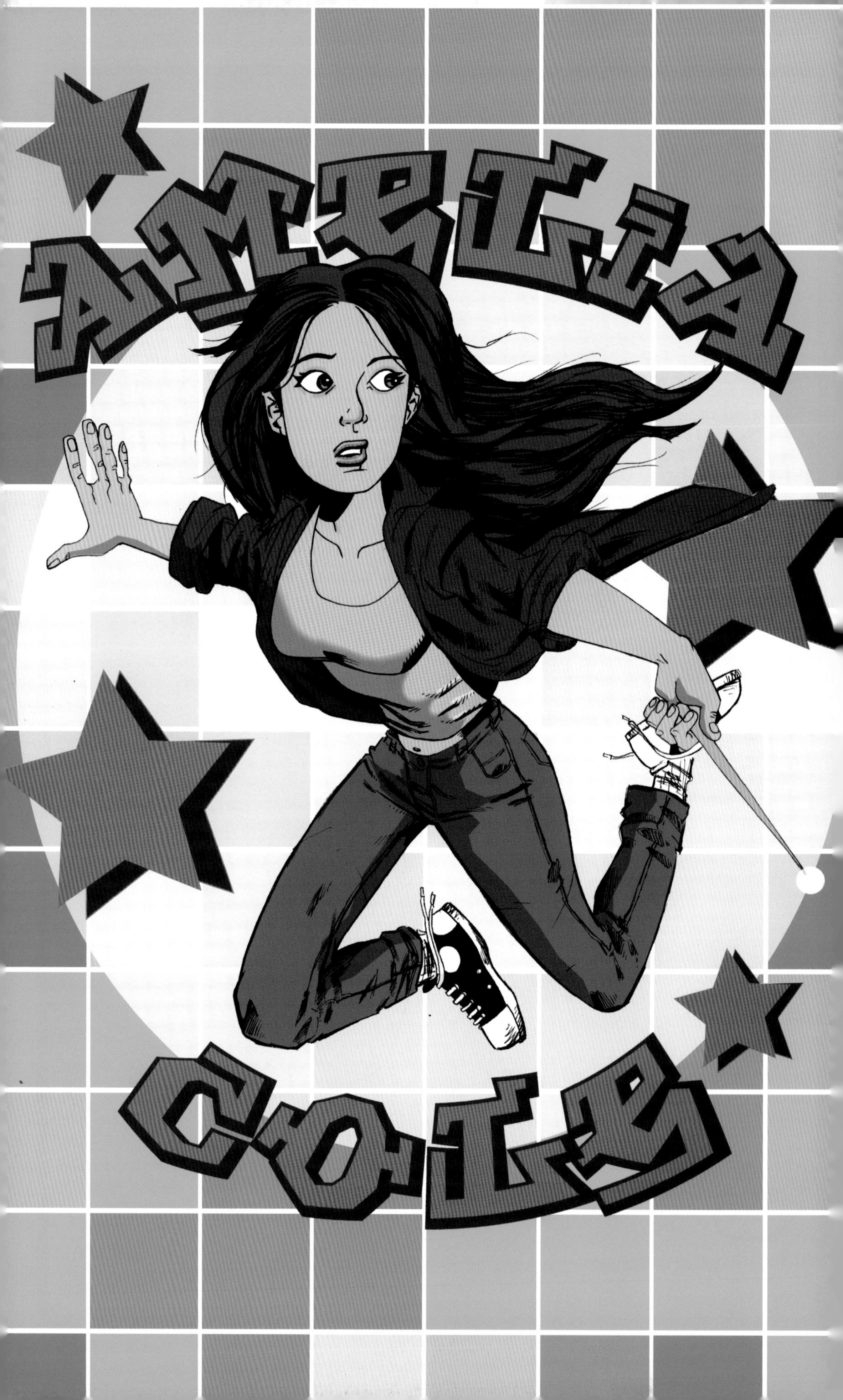
AMELIA
COLE

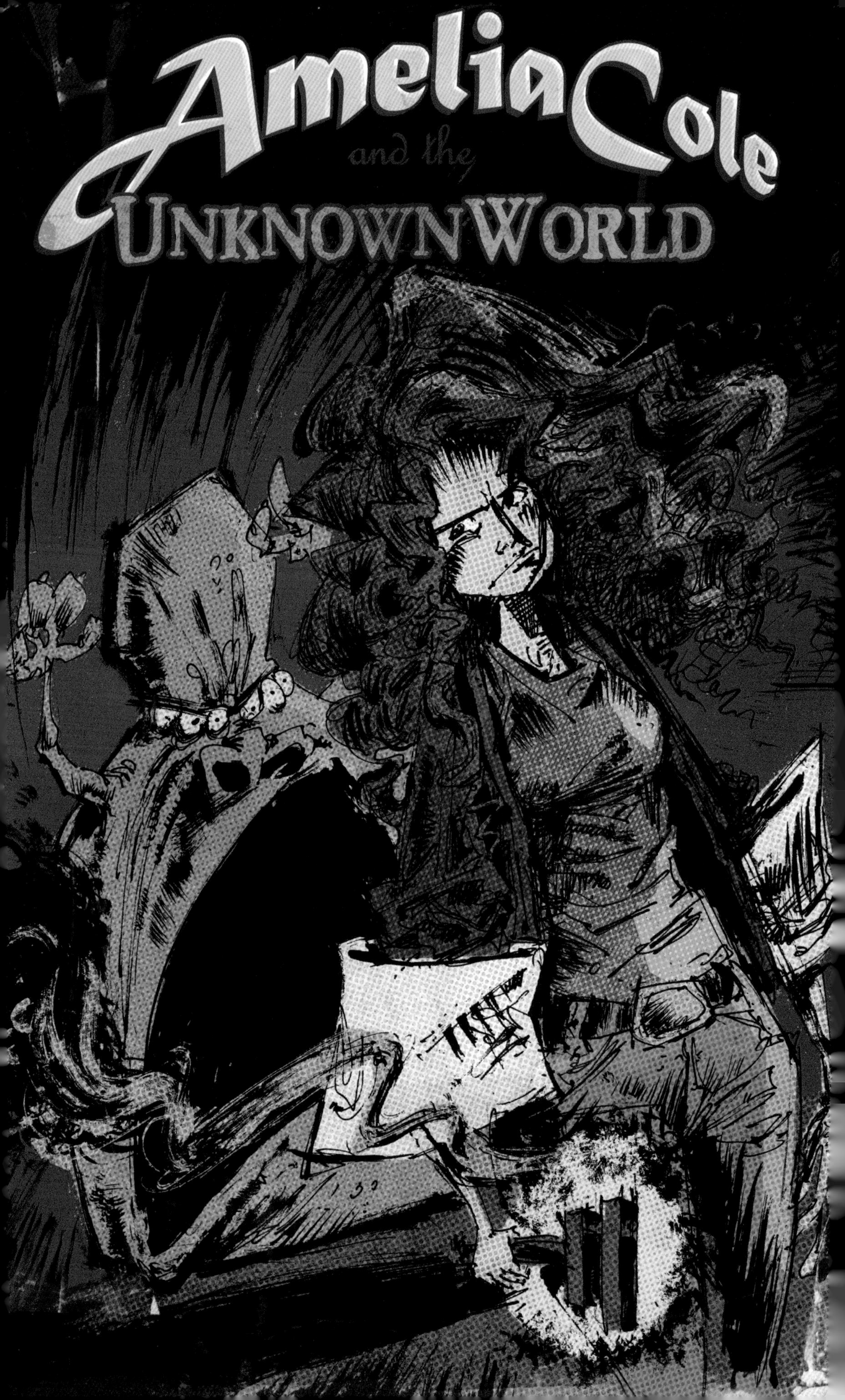
Amelia Cole
and the
UNKNOWN WORLD

SKETCHES & POSTERS

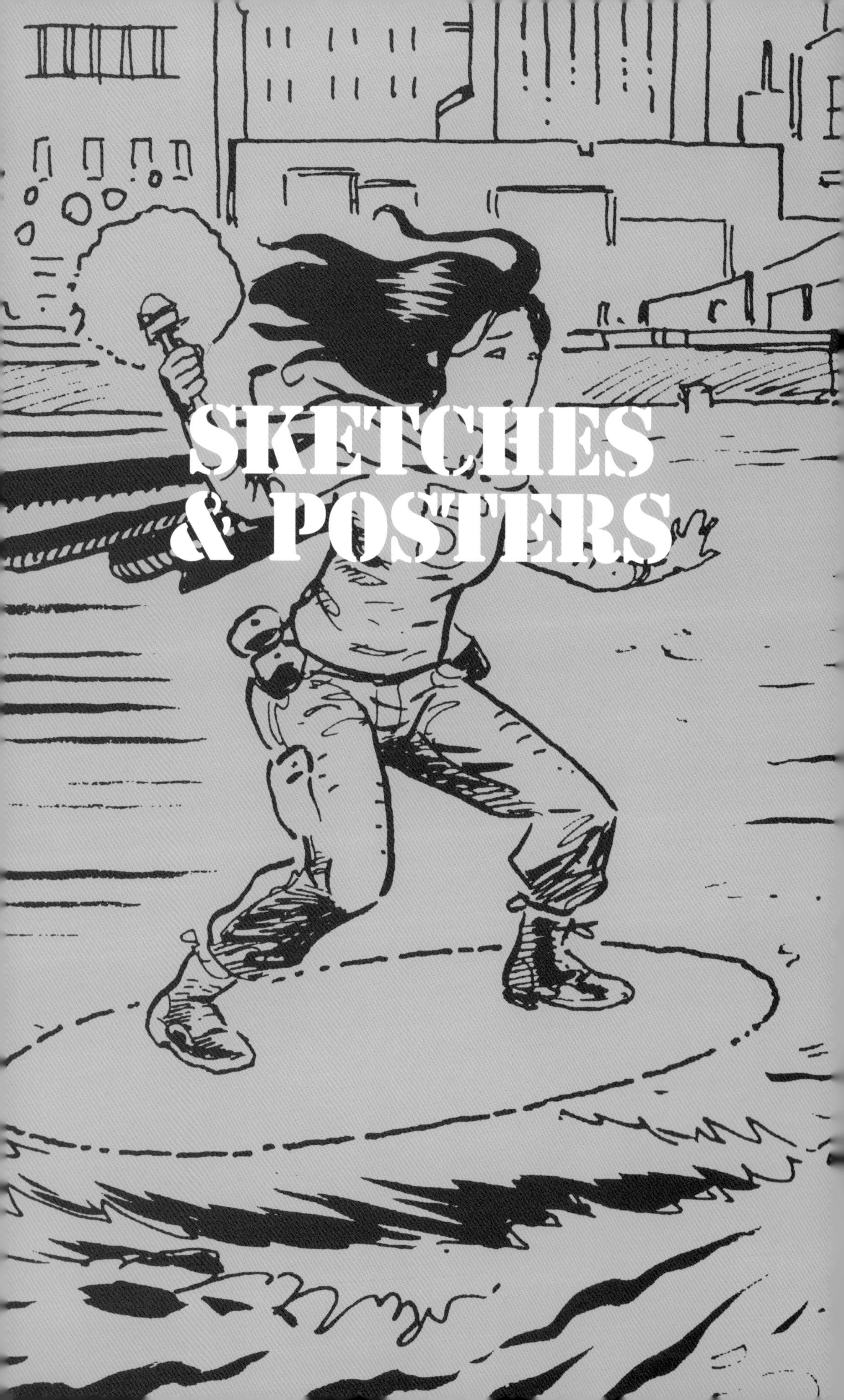

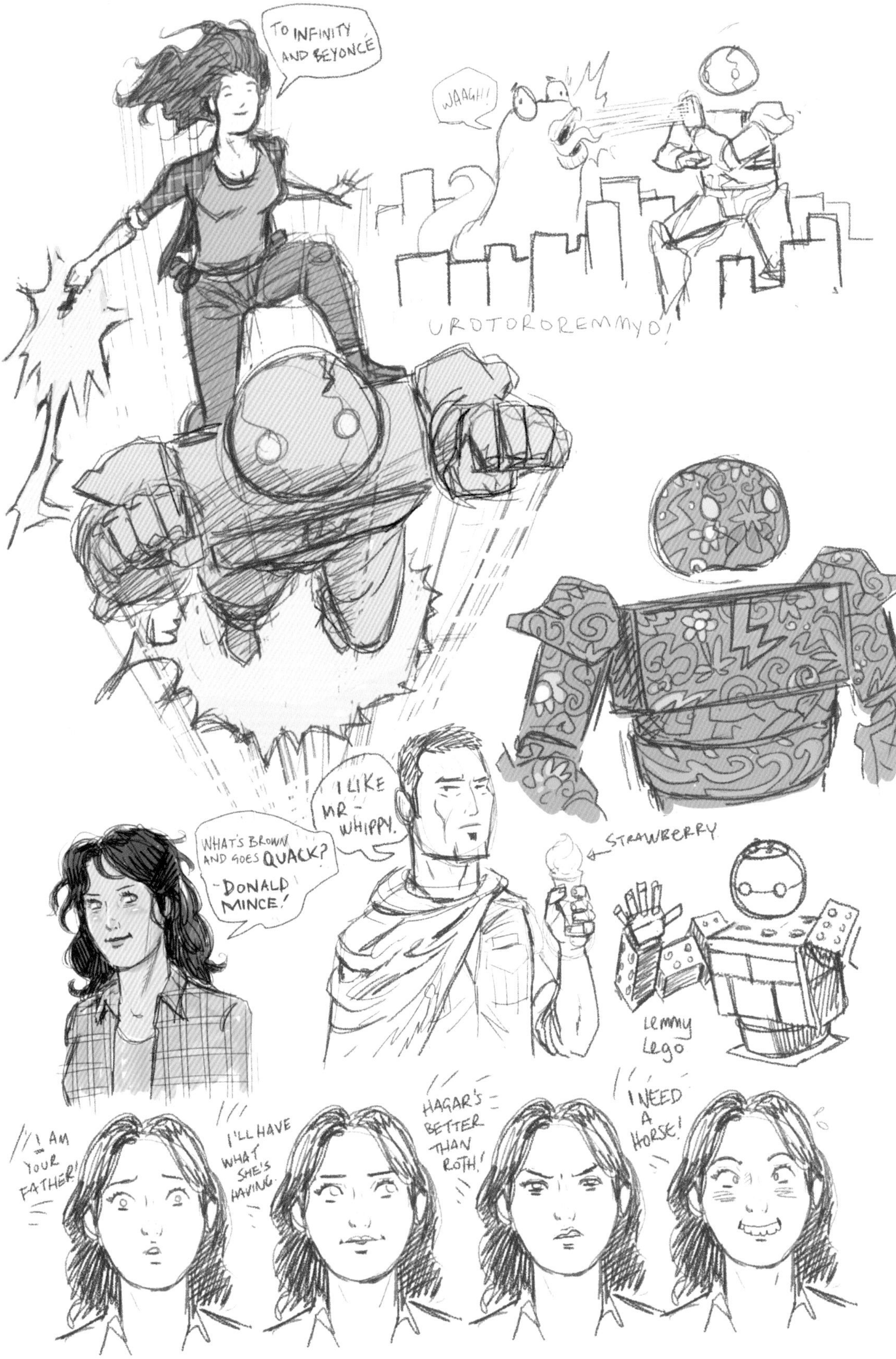
TO INFINITY AND BEYONCÉ
WAAGH!!
URDTOTOROREMMYO!
I LIKE MR-WHIPPY.
WHAT'S BROWN AND GOES QUACK? -DONALD MINCE!
STRAWBERRY
Lemmy Lego
I AM YOUR FATHER!
I'LL HAVE WHAT SHE'S HAVING.
HAGAR'S BETTER THAN ROTH!
I NEED A HORSE!

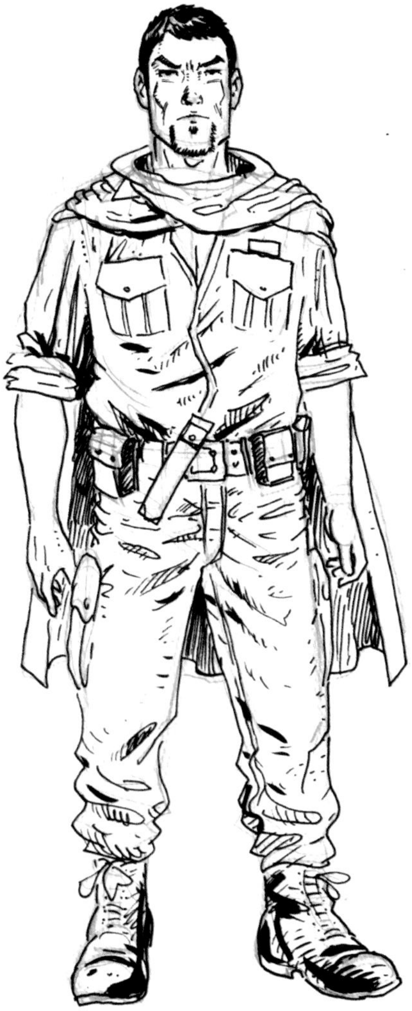

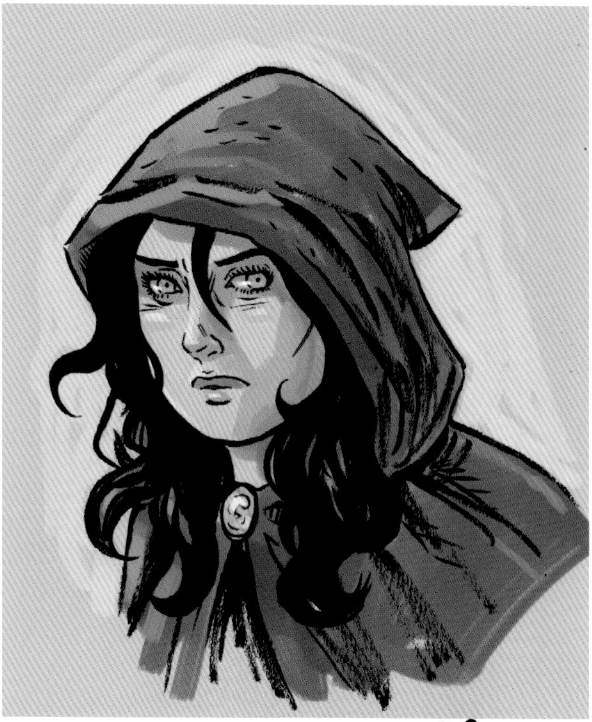

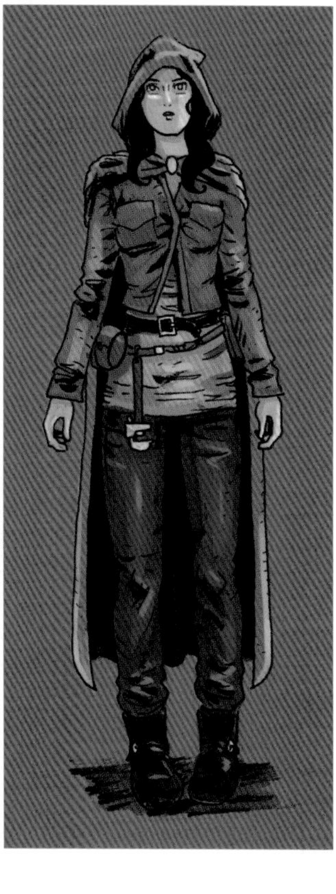

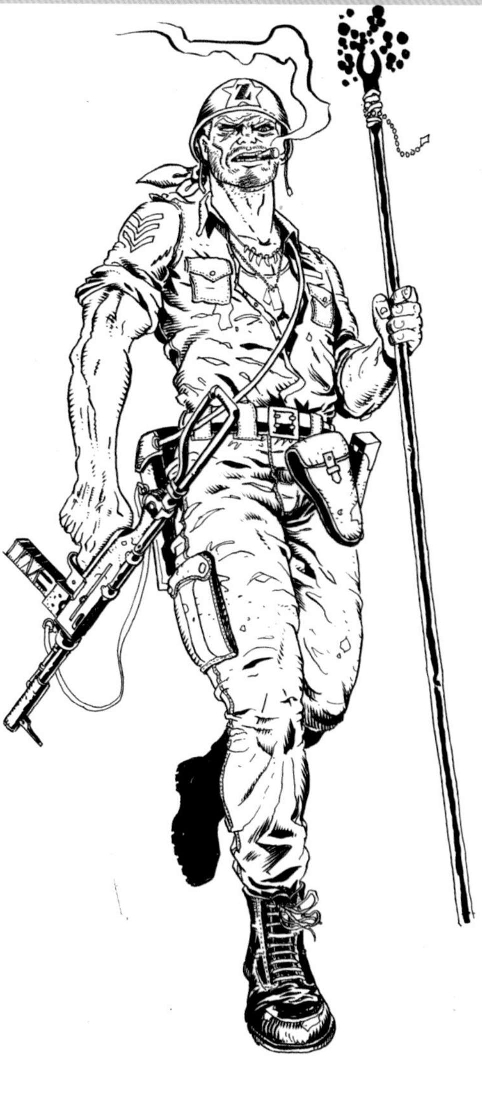

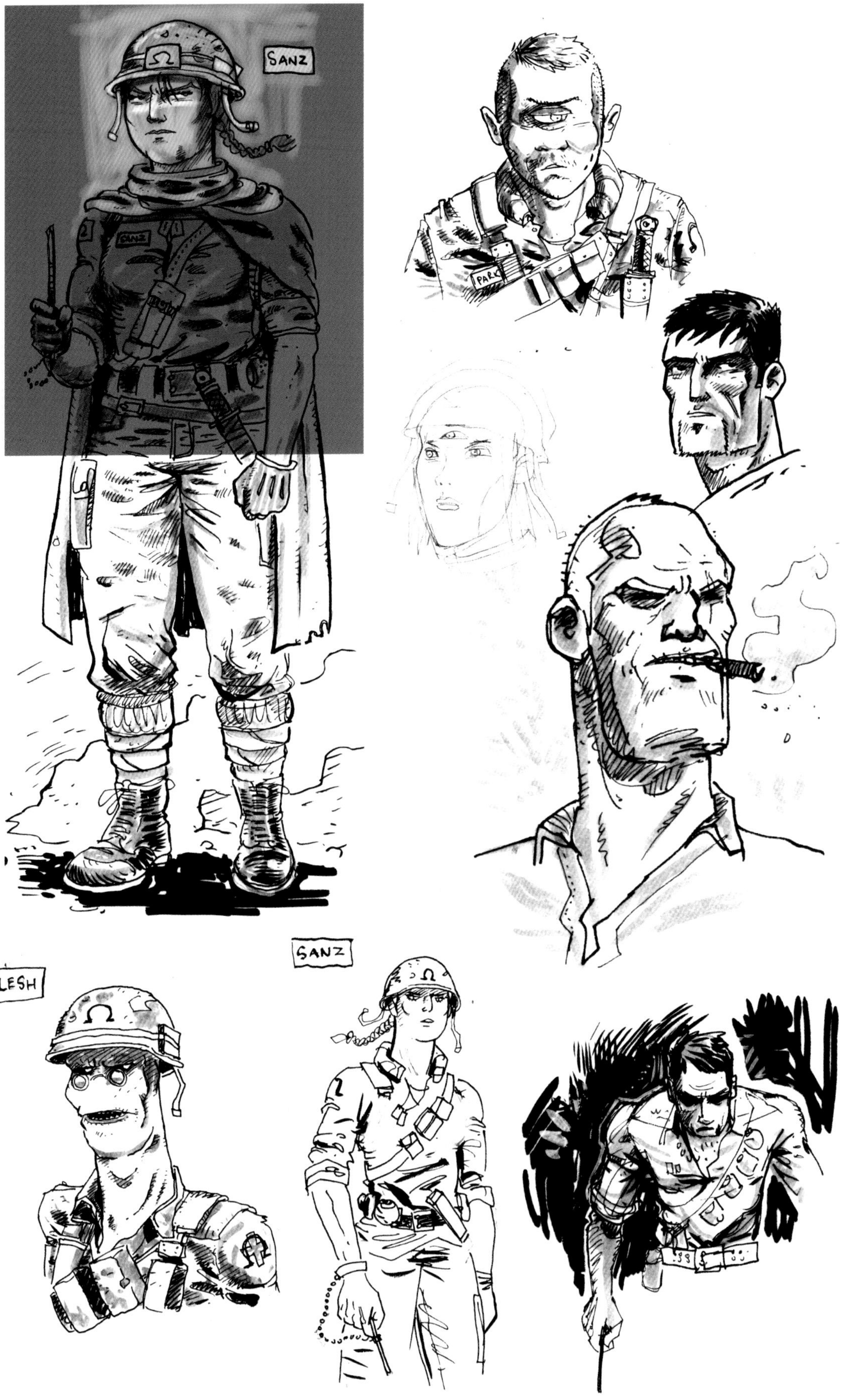
SANZ
SANZ
PARK
LESH
SANZ

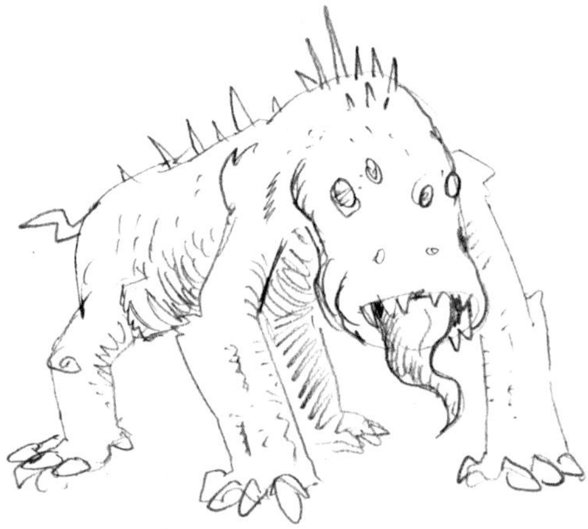

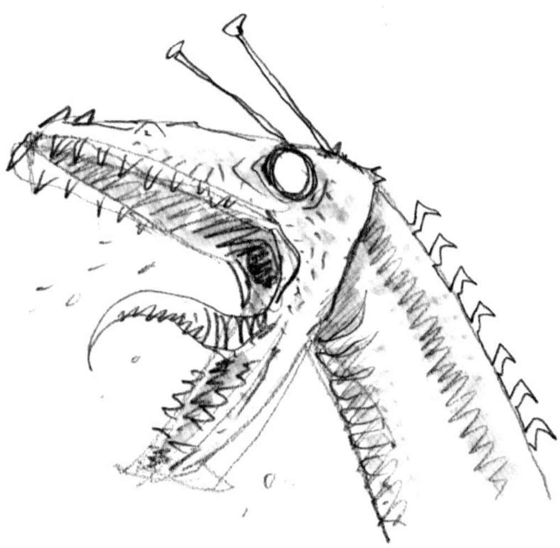

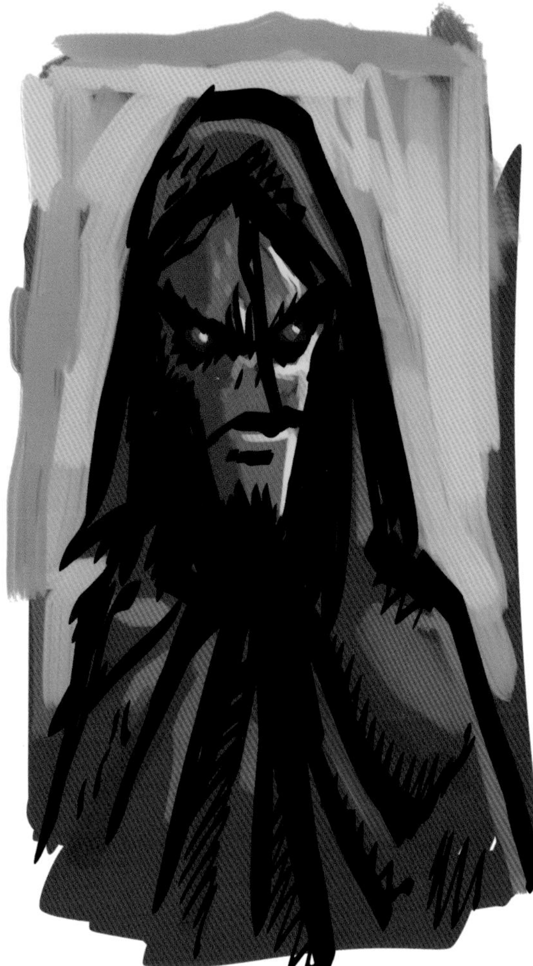

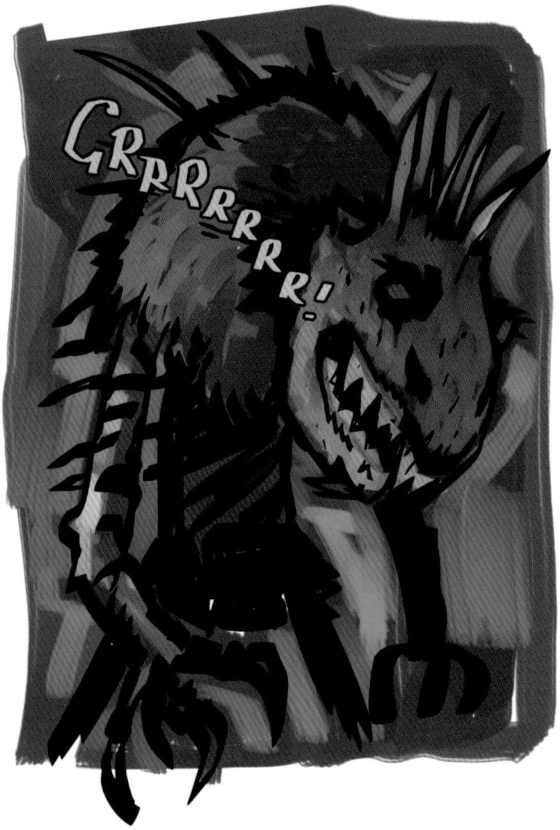
GRRRRRRR!

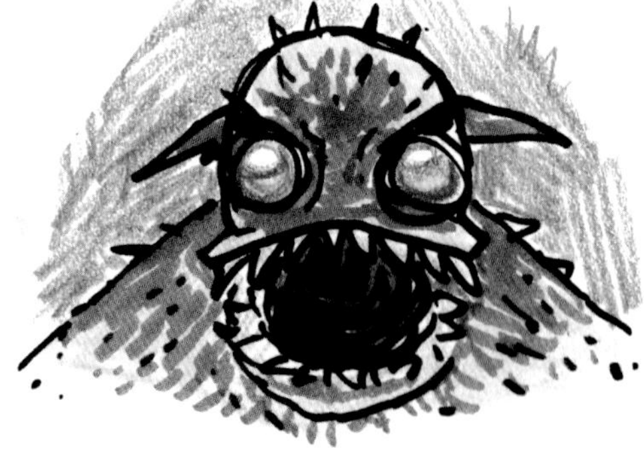

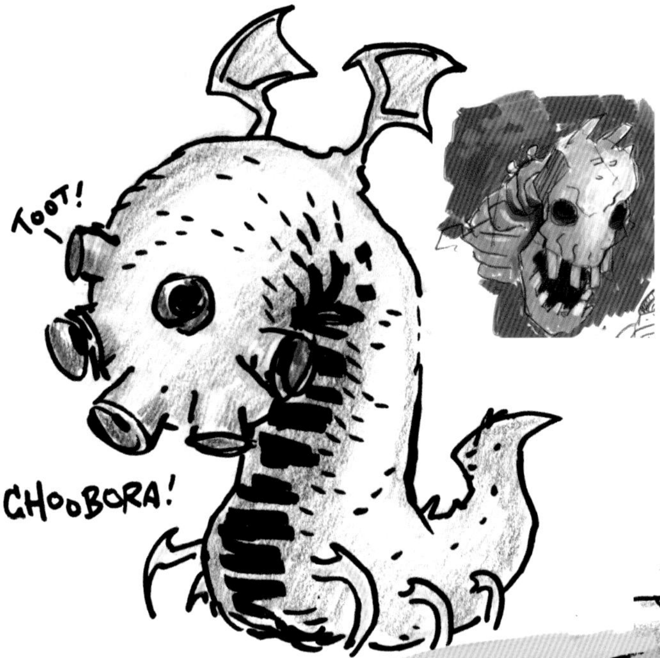
TOOT!
CHOOBORA!

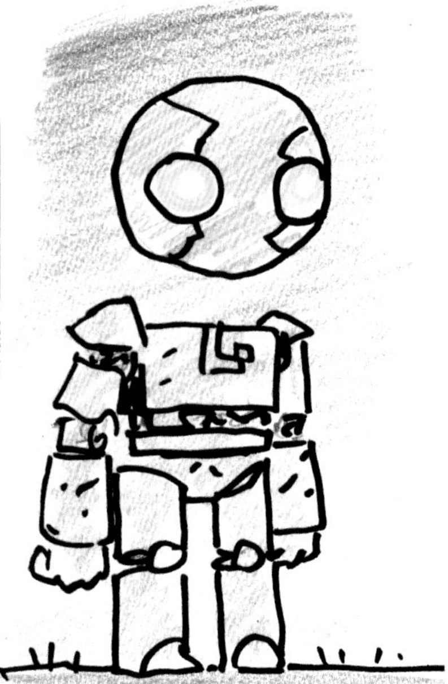

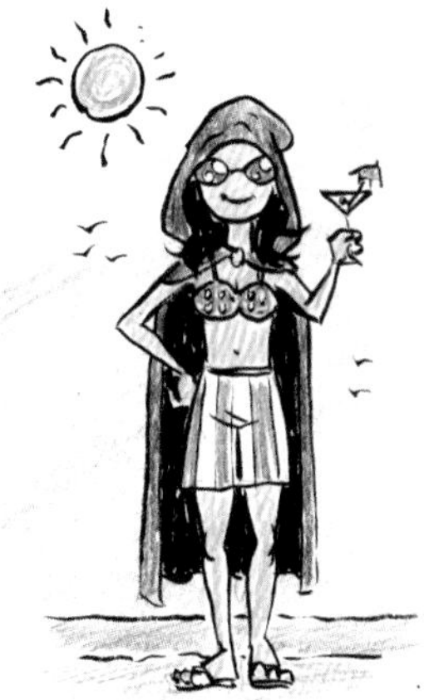

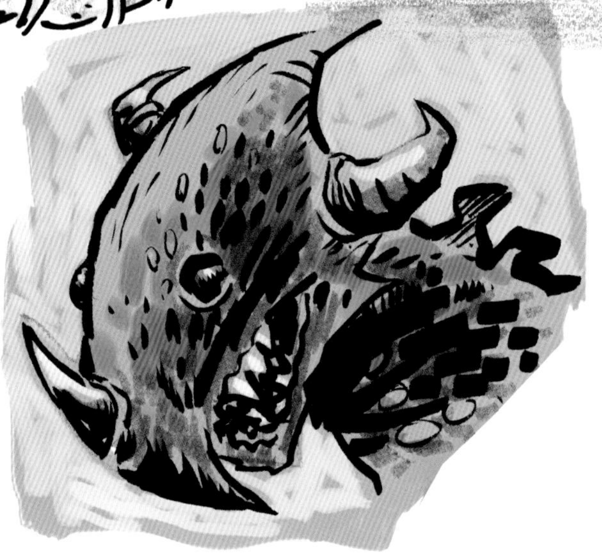

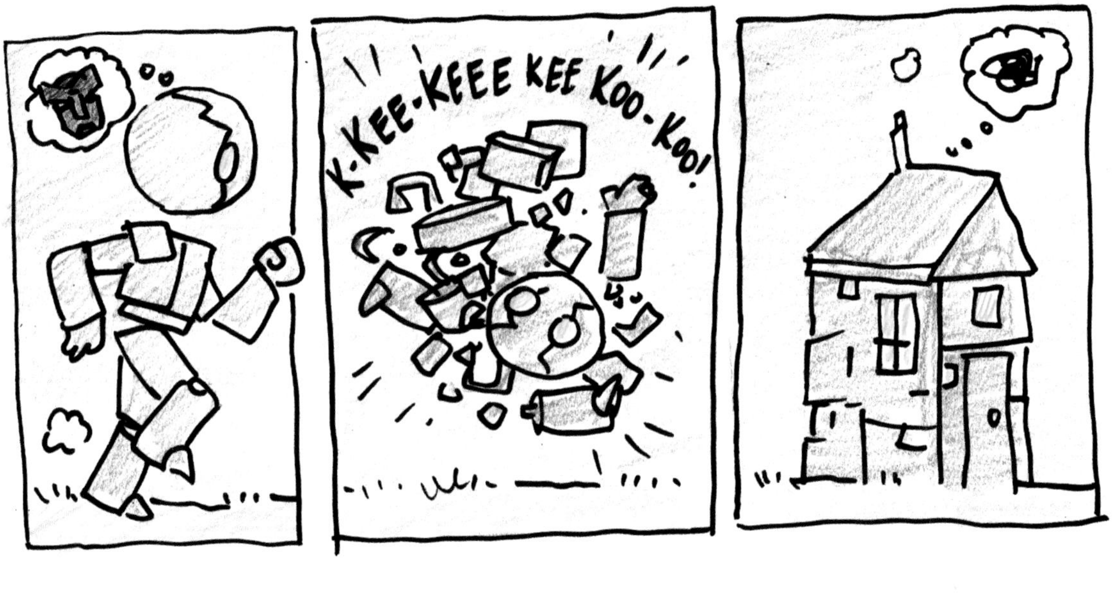
K-KEE-KEEE KEE KOO-KOO!

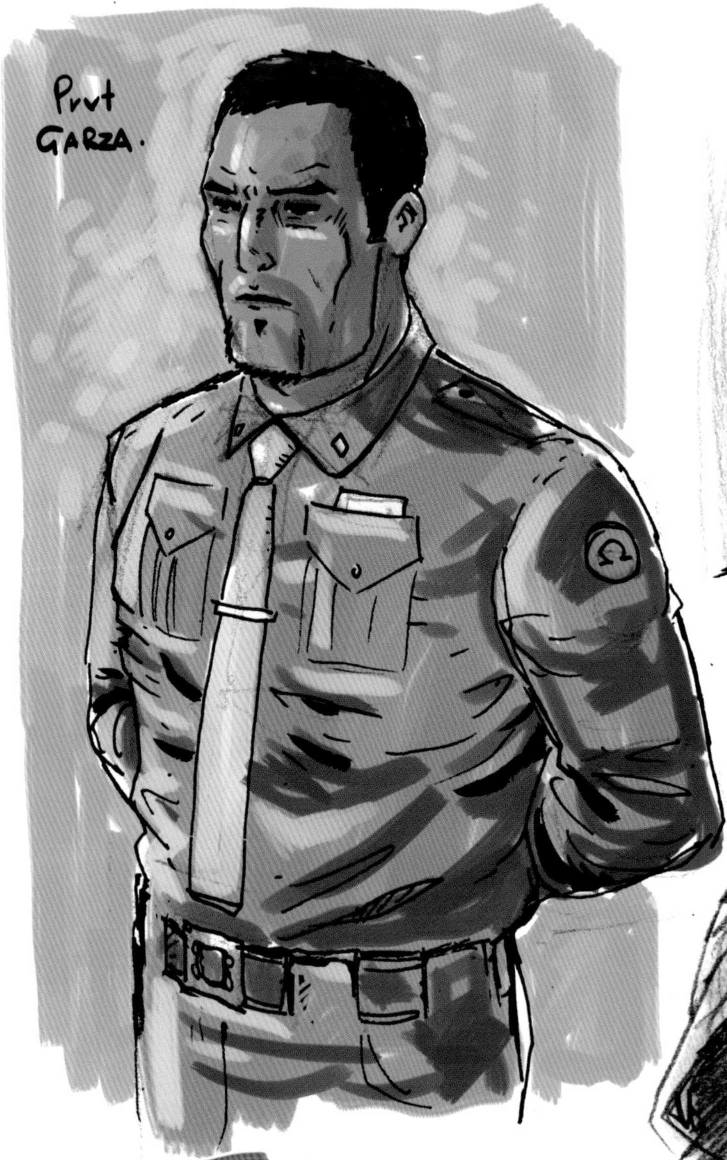
Prvt GARZA.

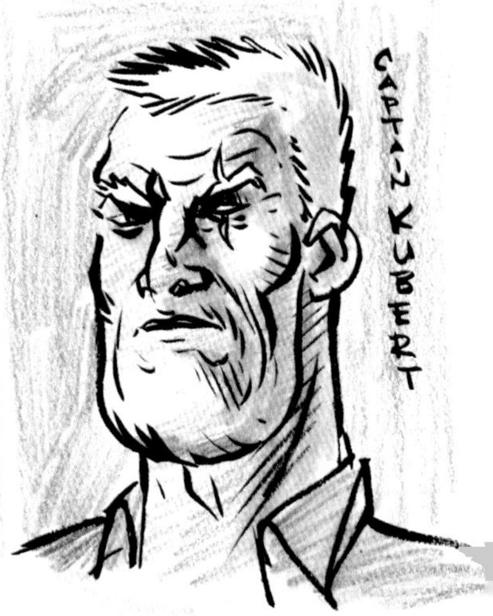
CAPTAIN KUBERT

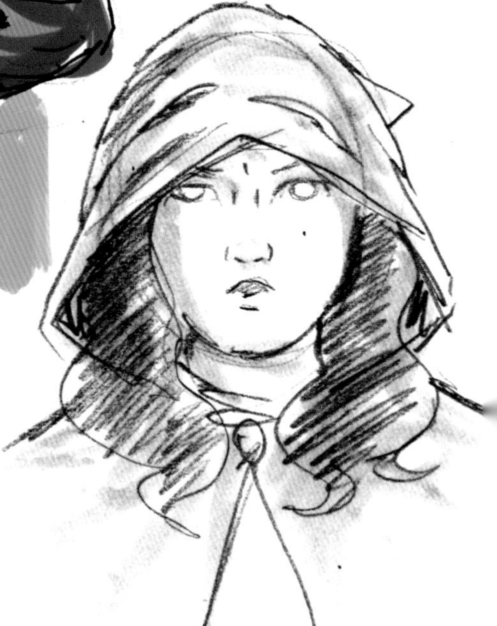

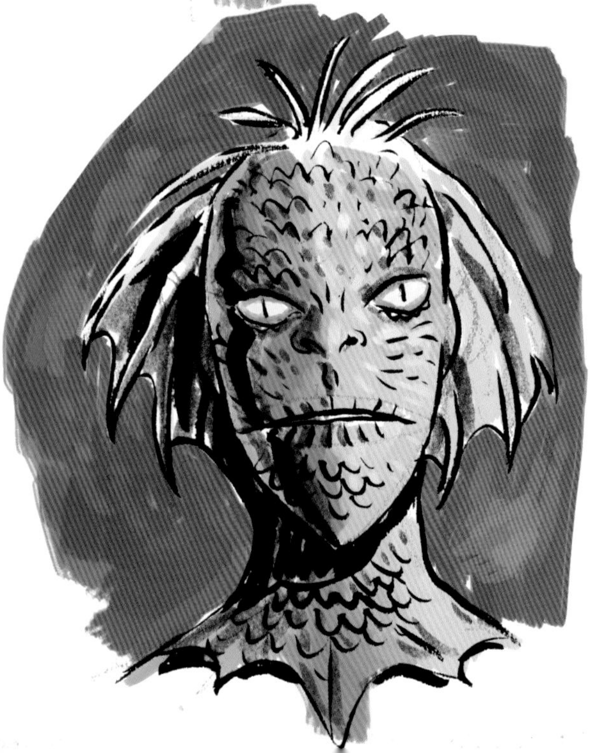

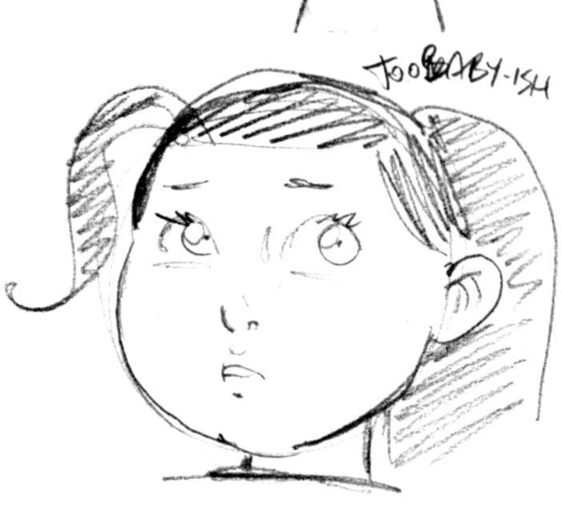
TOO BABY-ISH

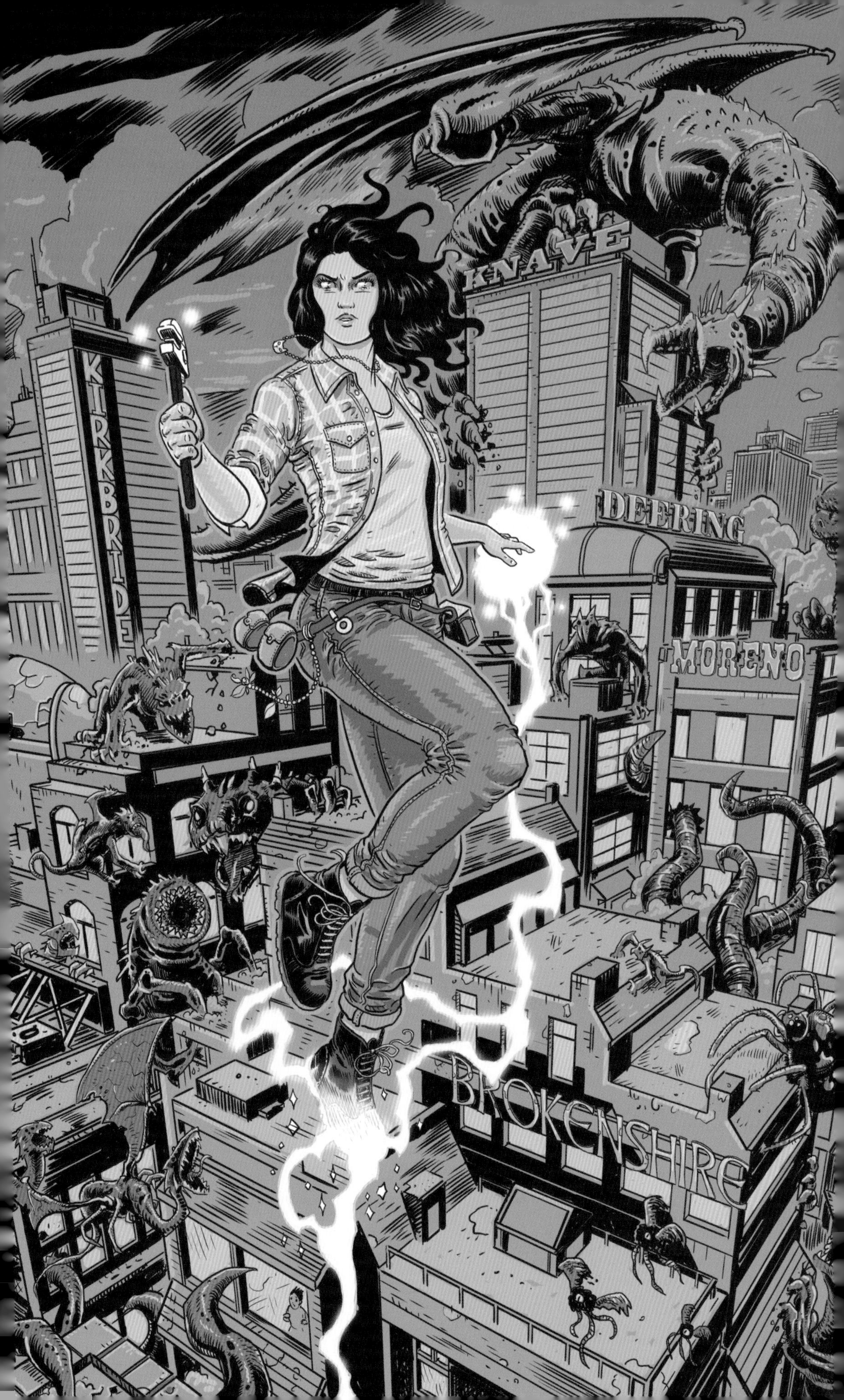
KIRKBRIDE
KNAVE
DEERING
MORENO
BROKENSHIRE

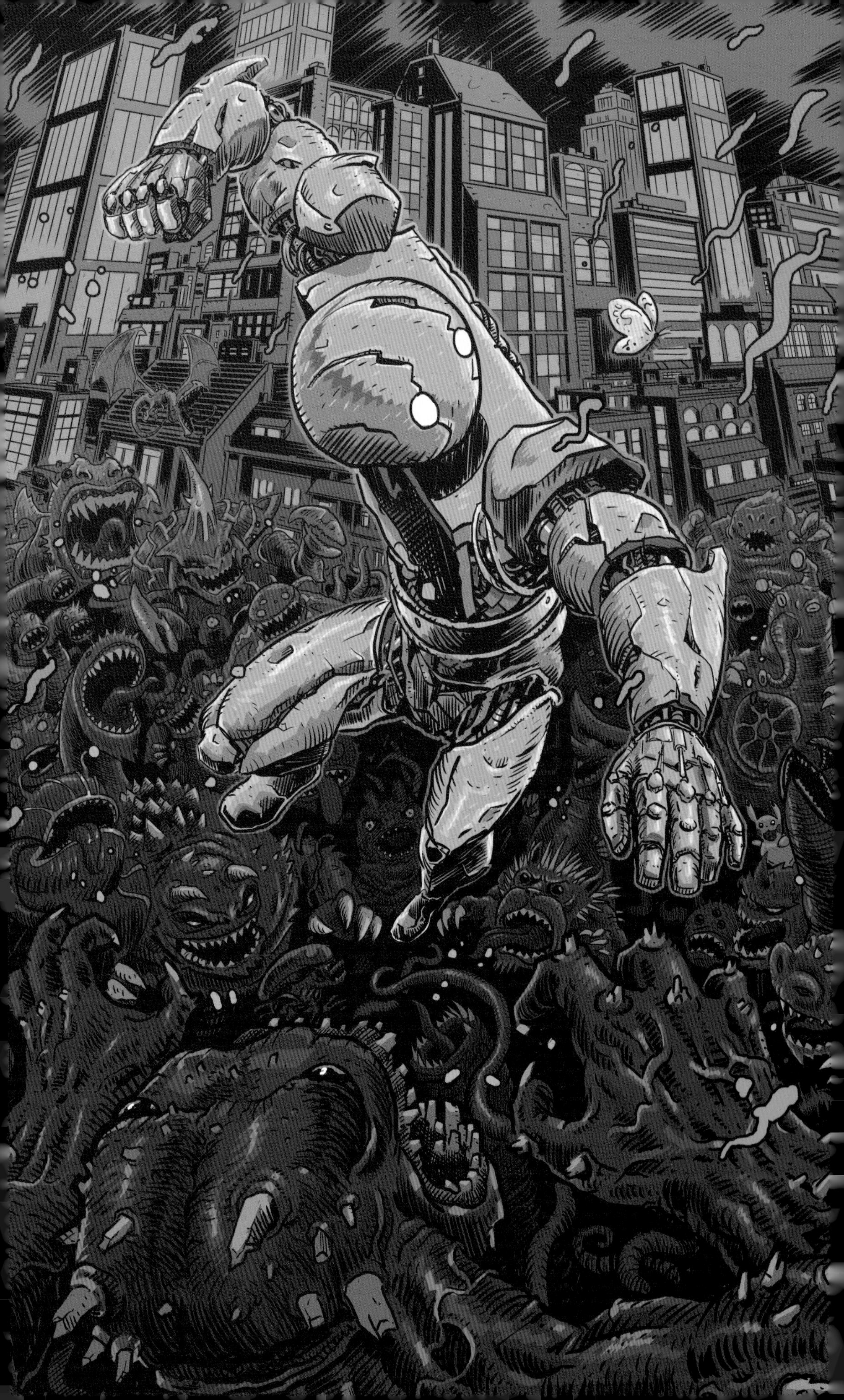

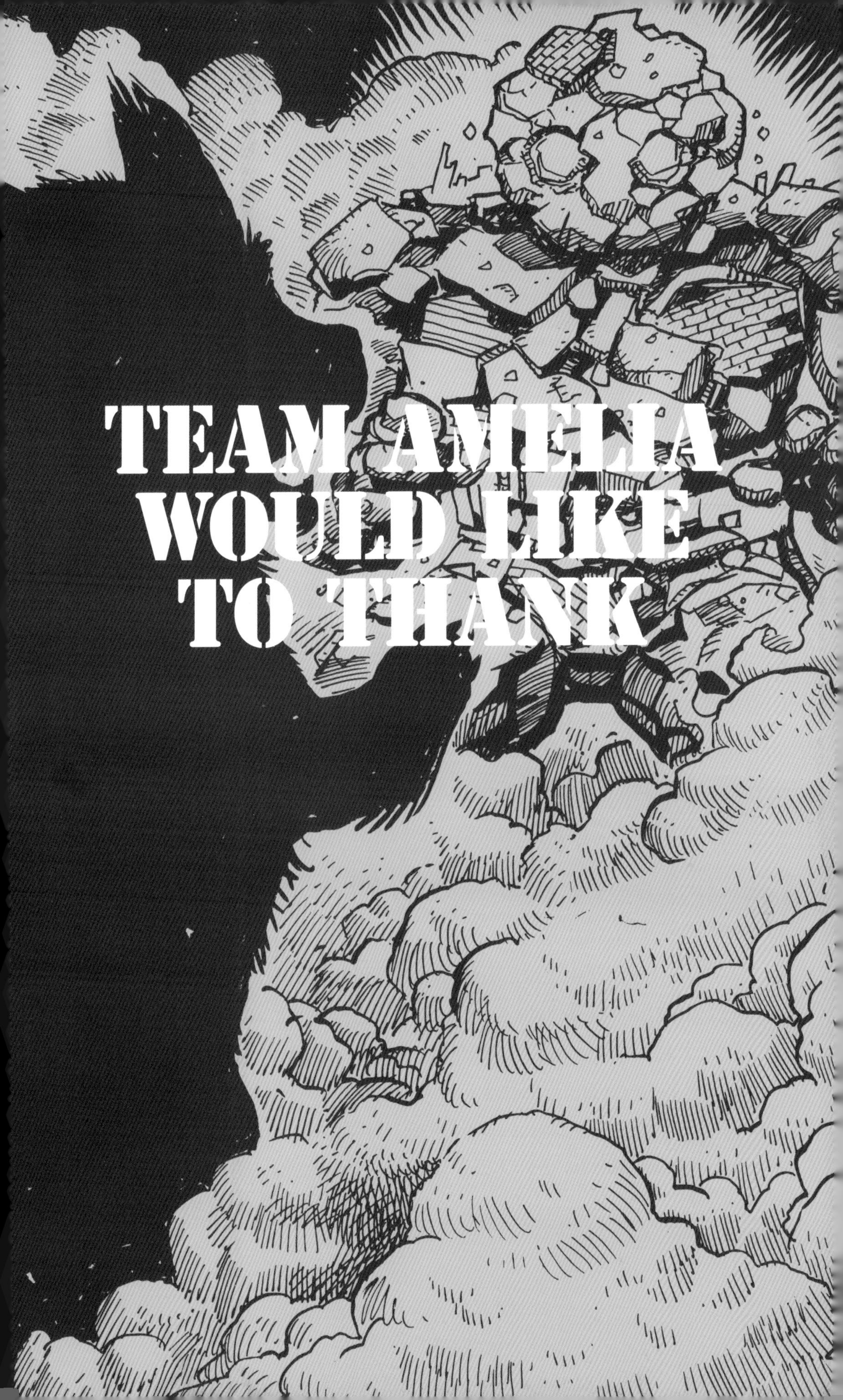
TEAM AMELIA
WOULD LIKE
TO THANK

ADAM

All of our amazing fans, you guys keep us going.
The retailers who took a chance on us, without you
guys no one could even buy the book you're holding!
And, in no order what-so-ever: Verity Lambert,
Christopher Reeve, Glen Cook, Jack Kirby, and
Bill Finger. Plus: David Wolkin, Graeme McMillan,
Esther Kim, Kyle Starks, and Russ Burlingame.

D.J.

You magical *Amelia Cole* readers! I'd also like
to thank Tadd Branum, who used to read comics out
loud with me when we were kids. Now he and his wife,
Rachel, and their kids, Mack and Maura, read comics
I help create, which warms my heart. Also warming
my heart is my lovely fiancée, Jen Lyter, who deserves
more thanks than I can put into words.

NICK

My wonderful wife, Victoria. She makes me believe I can do anything. The Lyth family for being so supportive. Andy, Sham, and Jess for being long suffering pals. Aidan and Matt for knowing that we are what we are and that'll never change. Adam Jones for laughing at my silliness. My new chums Alex and Ellis. Marmite for being delicious. Jack Kirby, Moebius, Robert Crumb, and Jaime Hernandez. Gibson and Fender guitars. Pencils. And of course Adam, D.J., Rachel, and Ruiz. I like you all a fair bit … you know, a decent amount.

RACHEL

Pizza for being the raddest, most delicious, and most filling of all the foods. Heavy metal for being the best music on planet earth. Or any other planet for that matter, because to heck with alien music. Books for not being TV. Warren Publishing for the comics. And finally, Hammer Studios for producing the monster movies that made me who I am today.

RUIZ

I would like to thank my wife, Brittany, and my daughter, Emma, for supporting me in this crazy dream of making comics, and their unconditional love. I'll always be tangled up in you, Brittany! To Adam, D.J., and Nick for being family and believing in me always. To Mom and Dad for making me who I am today. I miss you every day, Mom, and I love you and Dad very much!

TEAM AMELIA

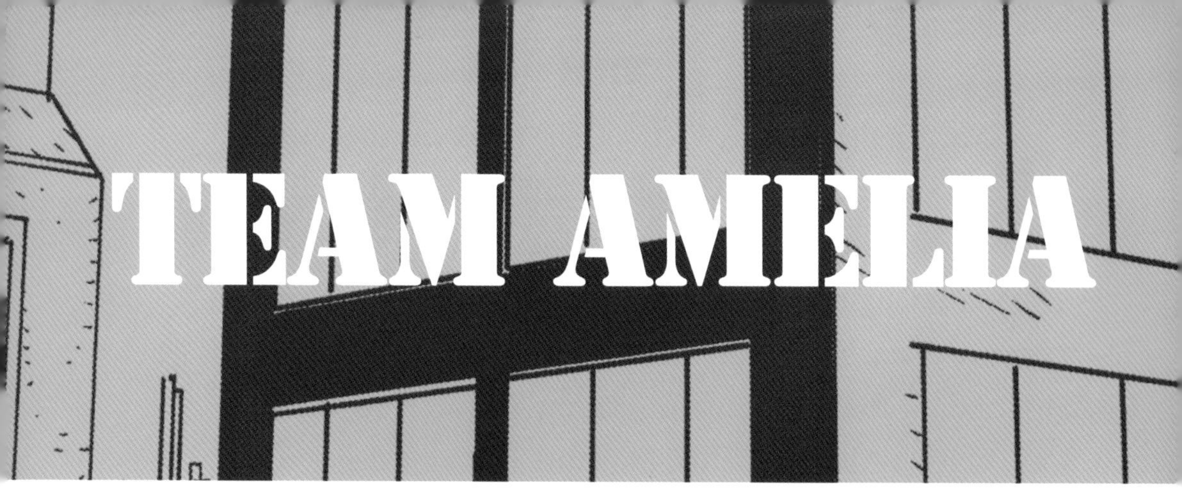

D.J. KIRKBRIDE is the co-writer and co-creator of *Amelia Cole*, an ongoing series published digitally by Monkeybrain Comics and in print by IDW Publishing, as well as the Dark Horse Comics mini-series *Never Ending*. He won an Eisner and a Harvey as an editor and a contributing writer for the *Popgun* anthologies (Image Comics) and has also co-written stories for *Titmouse Mook* volume 2, *Fireside Magazine* issue 1, and *Outlaw Territory* volume 3. In addition to his comics work, D.J. wrote a book of poetry called *Do You Believe In Ninjas?* (Creative Guy Publishing).

Follow him on Twitter **@DJKirkbride**

ADAM P. KNAVE is an Eisner and Harvey award-winning editor and writer who co-writes *Amelia Cole, Artful Daggers* (with Sean E. Williams), and *Never Ending* (with D.J. again, those two, man, inseparable). He edits Jamal Igle's *Molly Danger*, Sam Read's *Exit Generation*, and was one of the editors on Image's *Popgun* anthology series. He also writes prose, short comics, and edits all sorts of things. He recently moved to Portland, Oregon, after spending his first 38 years in NYC.

Follow him on Twitter **@AdamPKnave**

NICK BROKENSHIRE is a freelance artist who grew up in Scotland but now lives just outside of Manchester in England with his wife, Victoria. Nick's work can be seen in the 11 O'clock Comics anthologies *Low Concept 1 & 2*, and he is working on his own story *Rag & Bone Girl*, which he hopes to share with everyone soon. Nick also creates posters for music concerts and festivals such as Kendal Calling. He draws inspiration from Kirby, Ditko, Moebius, Crumb, Hernandez Bros, and Frank Zappa. Nick plays music of his own in Los Vencidos (rock and roll stuff) and Blues Harvest (a *Star Wars*-themed blues band). He wants to make comics that everyone can enjoy.

Follow him on Twitter **@NickBrokenshire** and "like" *Nick Brokenshire Comics & Illustration* on Facebook.

RACHEL DEERING is a freelance writer, editor, and letterer for comics. Her past works include IDW's *Womanthology,* and her creator-owned horror series *Anathema.* She lives in Columbus, Ohio, with her wife and their tiny Chihuahua, Hazel, and spends way too much time watching old horror movies.

Follow her on Twitter **@RachelDeering**

RUIZ MORENO lives somewhere in Texas. He has three loves in his life: his wife, Brittany, and their daughter, Emma, are his first two. They are his everything. They are awesome. His third love is comics. He has consumed comics since day one. He loves the comics. He wants to keep making the comics. Give me cookie you got cookie.

Follow him on Twitter **@Ruiz_Moreno**

DYLAN TODD was raised in the neon wasteland of Las Vegas and its mixture of glitz and kitsch, class and crass has tainted him forever. When he's not designing or thinking about designing, he can be found rocking, rolling, reading, or relaxing with his family. If he likes you, he'll make you a mix tape. You can find him at *bigredrobot.net.*

Follow him on Twitter **@BigRedRobot**

COMING SOON

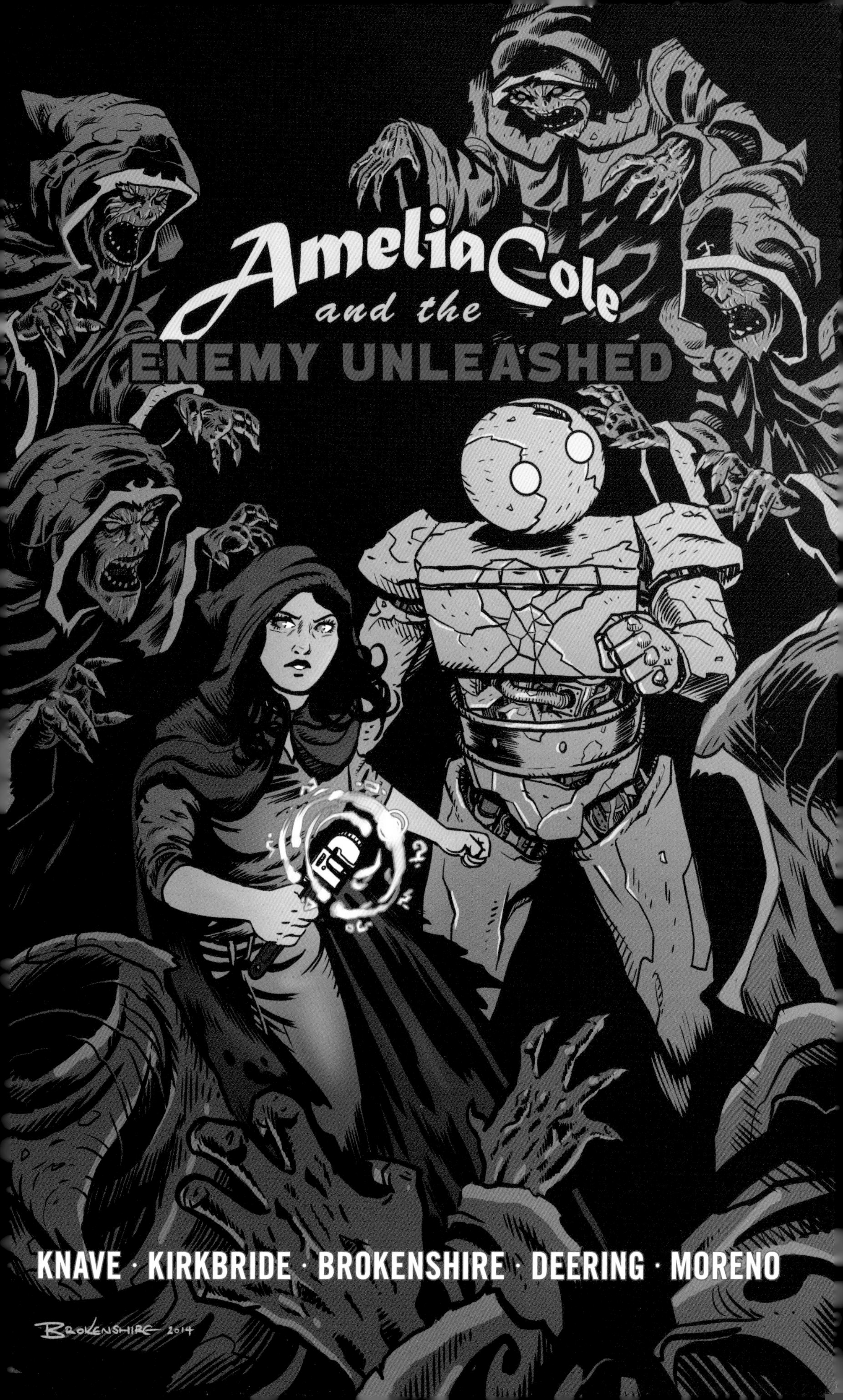
Amelia Cole
and the
ENEMY UNLEASHED
KNAVE · KIRKBRIDE · BROKENSHIRE · DEERING · MORENO
BROKENSHIRE 2014

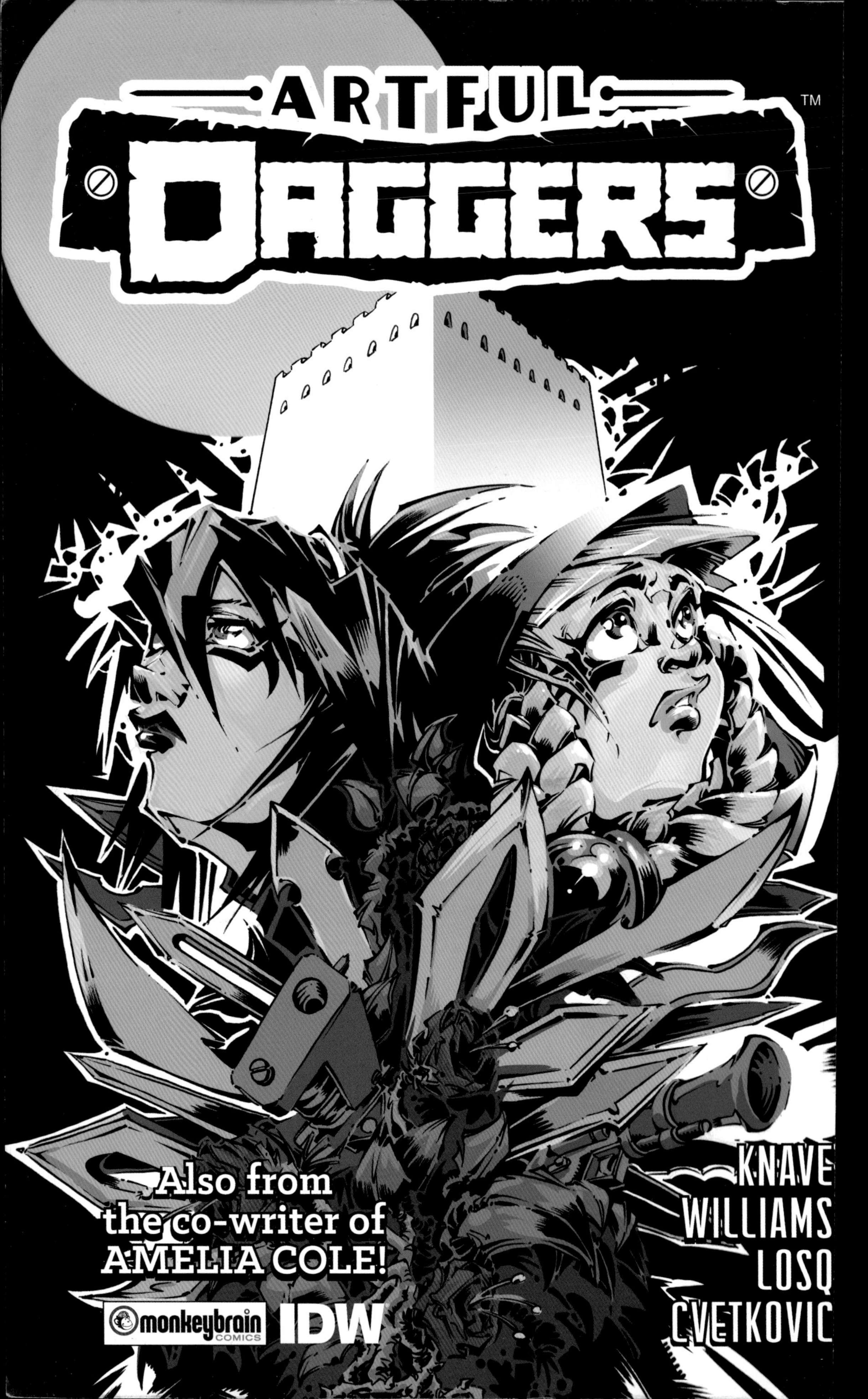
ARTFUL DAGGERS
TM
Also from the co-writer of AMELIA COLE!
KNAVE
WILLIAMS
LOSQ
CVETKOVIC
monkeybrain COMICS
IDW